Skeeter Hill Rascals

SKEETER HILL RASCALS

Rounding Third Trilogy

By
James O. Jenkins

JamesJenkinsWritersMagicPen.Org

CONSIDERATIONS

This book is not authorized, endorsed, sponsored, approved, or licensed by Little League Baseball, Incorporated. "Little League" and "Little League Baseball" are the registered trademarks and service marks exclusively of Little League Baseball, Incorporated. The book titled Skeeter Hill Rascals *is a fictional accounting of a summer baseball story played out between two boys on opposing teams in the fictional town of Skeeter Hill. Liberties concerning the rules have been adopted for the sake of dramatization. These are not necessarily the rules adopted or in practice by "Little League" and "Little League Baseball" or the trademarks thereof.*

﹩﹩﹩

DARE AMERICA shall not have authority to share in or use the story *Skeeter Hill Rascals* for any expressed purpose; the use of any reference dialogue; any illustration(s); conceptual reference or to be an educational tool for DARE AMERICA; and shall not allow DARE AMERICA to utilize any portion of the story contained herein without permission of the Author, James O. Jenkins. DARE AMERICA must have in writing said permission to exercise authority to use any portion of the literary work.

﹩﹩﹩

Appreciation and gratitude is extended to the Bishop Machebeuf Catholic High School, Denver, Colorado 80230, for the privilege and permission to photograph the baseball announcer's box at the high school baseball field as a model for the story.

﹩﹩﹩

Gratitude is extended to the Major Baseball League for the advice, guidelines and legal considerations concerning the MLB, and the counsel granted referencing the MLB pertaining to the writing of the story.

﹩﹩﹩

FMS Digital, Denver, Colorado 80222, deserves appreciation for re-mastering and digitalizing many of the images used to illustrate the action transpiring in the story.

v

꙳꙳꙳

Gratitude and appreciation is extended to editornancy with Fiverr.com for her guidance and direction to help make this writing a reality.

꙳꙳꙳

Gratitude and appreciation to Ben Claybrook with Fiverr.com for his Photoshop genius touch to help with the graphics to enhance the pictures and caricature used to illustrate the story.

DEDICATION

This book is dedicated to my son, Jereod Owen Jenkins, because his humor helps to make me laugh. This is dedicated to my son for his love reflected in his diligent care and concern when I needed it the most; this is dedicated to my son for his smile that helped let me know that everything would somehow turn out okay; this is dedicated to my son who I love with all my heart and soul. In life, son, hit one for me.

INTRODUCTION

Baseball has been given the moniker, *America's pastime.* Since the late 1800s, baseball has held a fascination with players and spectators alike. In *The Boy's Own Book,* the game of Rounders is described as being played with a bat-and-ball and with base-running on what later became known as *a diamond.* In the mid-1830s, the game became known as "base or goal ball." When becoming involved in the game of baseball as a coach or a player, we are indirectly linked to the past and share in the wonderful heritage of baseball.

As a coach, winning is important because it validates a coach and makes him feel like he is doing a good job. But for youth baseball, winning is not the only thing that matters. Looking back, a coach may have some regrets for not playing some of the players more and instead favoring the more skilled players. In reflection, there is more to the game than demonstrating skills at a position on the field or hitting for the fences when at bat. Typically, coaches must help players develop discipline and respect for the rules of the game, advocate the ideals of sportsmanship, build character, cultivate player honesty, help players set goals, most importantly help players learn to work together as a team by caring for self and others, and owning up to their individual responsibility. These intangible concepts are no less important than the skill of hitting or fielding a baseball.

Every coach has the rare opportunity to observe and nurture young boys and girls to not only understand the fundamentals, the offensive and defensive rules but to develop in many of the intangible concepts to be incorporated later in life off the field. This happens when a coach communicates in a positive manner.

As a coach, I regret not doing a better job. I should have paid as much attention to the player(s) resigned to sitting on the end of the bench as I did to the stand-out players. A coach's vision must extend to every member on the team. A coach must see the player not for who they are but for who they can be. It is vital as a coach to help each player understand that he/she is a contributing factor to the success (or failure) of the team.

"All coaching is, is taking a player where he can't take himself." Bill McCartney, NCAA football coach at the University of Colorado.

TABLE OF CONTENTS

BUY ME SOME CRACKER JACK

Skipping backward between the crosswalk's solid white lines, Willie Wince keeps a watchful eye on his father trudging along toward the next corner. Pivoting, Willie dances through the chaos of fans to reach the next curb on his journey to Gunslinger Stadium.

Darting in and out, he slips through the plethora of people, anxiously racing to the next corner. Excited beyond his wildest dreams, he reverses to search for his father and then gestures by flicking his finger back and forth to beckon his father to pick up the pace and join him.

As his father plods along to catch up, Willie thinks about how this August 11, 1994, game between the Gunslingers and the Portland Oregon Lumberjacks might be the last game of the regular season unless the United Federation of Baseball Players Association and owners come to an agreement on labor issues. The looming possibility of a strike creates a sense of urgency for the fans. In other words, the game purports to be the last hoorah for the baseball season, but the first ever professional baseball game seen in person by Willie. He can hardly contain his exuberance.

"Come on, Dad. It's just over there. You can rest inside," Willie coaxes, knowing his father must be getting tired. Finally, his father meets him at the curb. The steady pace tires his father because his daily exercise usually consists of walking from his desk to the copy machine. His father welcomes the opportunity to rest for a moment to recover while shielded from the drove of fans by the lamp post.

The two keep pace with other fans en route to the Colorado Gunslingers' Baseball Stadium. Year after year his father would promise Willie they would attend a Gunslinger baseball game. Unfortunately, last-minute business meetings, his mother's gallbladder surgery, or Willie's grandfather's passing (the reason why they missed last year's scheduled game) kept them from attending. His father insisted the baseball game must be a game close to Willie's birthday because he wanted it to be more memorable and have special significance. Unfortunately, everything seems to happen around Willie's birthday. This year, however, on his eleventh birthday, there have not been any circumstances to prevent them from attending a game.

Gunslinger Stadium Wall

In the distance, Willie catches a glimpse of the top perimeter of the brick stadium wall extending skyward. Unable to maintain the snail's pace with his father, he races on ahead. It has to be the most magnificent building he ever laid his eyes on. He thought to himself, *What must it look like inside?*

Willie stops at the curb to survey the pedestrian traffic and allow his father to catch his breath. In the distance, he lays his eyes on a cowboy, the Gunslinger's meet and greet mascot, wearing an oversized black Stetson hat, a western duster coat, and a waxed handlebar mustache, holding a Winchester in one hand and brandishing a Colt revolver in the other. He periodically demonstrates the not-so famous quick-draw from a sagging holster on his hip. The Gunslinger mascot waves his handgun greeting fans as they approach on their appointed journey to the stadium.

The "walk" light illuminates. Progressing through the crosswalk, Willie glimpses more of the stadium standing at the curb.

Fans travel across the street toward the cobblestone courtyard before dispersing toward their designated gate entrance.

Gunslinger Stadium Entrance

When he steps up on the curb to the courtyard, Willie sees peanut vendors patrolling in front of approaching fans. Willie stands speechless at the spectacle of grandeur. He cannot believe his eyes. He recalls the story about "the house that Ruth built." Willie's memory carries him back to what he read about the 1920 season when the disgruntled New York Giants Ball Club became upset over the arrangement with the New York Yankees at the Polo Grounds. The New York Giants' management having a say decided to serve notice to their rival team, called the Yankees, to move out. The reason prompted by the New York Yankees to decide to capitalize on the slugging sensation by the name of Babe Ruth and erect a colossal stadium pinning their hopes on him. The New York Yankee baseball games in a new stadium became synonymous with "the house that Ruth built." His celebrated home run hitting adopted him the publicized name as the "King of Swat" and brought in fans.

Willie would spend hours at the local card shop, Wassermann's Baseball Cards and Collectibles, learning all about baseball. Fascinated by the story, it stuck in his mind. Willie marveled at Babe Ruth's achievement at the plate. His home run record withstood challenges by Johnny Mize, Willie Malory, Mickey Mantle, and Jack Hargrave. Mr. Wasserman told him Baseball story after story when he visited Wasserman Cards and Collectibles. A short distance in front of his he lays his eye on a vision of grandeur in his time, Gunslinger Stadium.

His father did not understand how important baseball was in Willie's life. Yes, he understood collecting baseball cards like every other boy is age. But little did he know Willie's knowledge extended to all baseball cards from Topps, Fleer, Ultra, and Upper Deck. His fascination with baseball did not begin at the age of collecting baseball cards like other boys his age. In kindergarten during naptime, Willie curled up with his baseball glove instead of a cuddly, soft, plush toy. Cartoons did not interest him on Saturday morning or after his afternoon nap. Instead, baseball games played the day before suited him. His interests never wavered. Collecting bugs, flying kites, or any childhood fun and games took a back seat to baseball. His father's workaholic ethic kept him from understanding his son and how much baseball meant to him.

Standing on the cobblestone courtyard, Willie feels like he is part of something bigger than life itself. In his mind he has reached the Promised Land at eleven years old. With all the commotion, reading the cobblestones proves to be a nearly impossible task he should save for another time. Mr. Wasserman said the inscriptions on the bricks varied from fan support to memorials. Regardless, Willie wants to read as many as he can, not today.

"Hey, Willie!" calls his father. "Can you step it up a little? In case you forgot, we've got a game to go to." Souvenir carts decorate the landscape with pennants, hats, bandannas, and toy Winchester shot guns.

Straight ahead, Willie observes the lines leading to the turnstiles positioned between the arches in front of the stadium entrance. Above the ticket window, he admires an unusual clock. Crafted into the brick wall on a smooth cement slab he casts his eyes on a hand sculptured logo revealing the two Colt six gun pistols crossed with a baseball resting between the gun barrels. Ornate

Roman numerals decorate the outside of the face on the clock. The stadium resembles baseball's version of a cathedral—the difference being the structure harbors a playing field to play the game of baseball, an entirely different kind of worship. Mesmerized by the colossal structure in front of him, Willie takes baby steps in the direction of the ticket window line.

Swallowed up by the congestion of fans, Willie and his father make very little progress. Placing his hands on Willie's shoulders to avoid being separated, Willie's dad inches along behind his son. Willie becomes amused by the antics of the peanut peddlers mingling through the sea of fans, yelling, "Get your peanuts, fresh Gunslinger peanuts, get 'em right here." At the same time, Willie hears the program vendors waving a program, yelling, "Programs, get your official Gunslinger programs. Know the names of players. Get in game with your very own program."

"Come on, son. Let's get a move on. The line is over there. We need to move a much faster." His father motions with a tug on Willie's shoulder to change directions. The pair move at a snail's pace through the plethora of fans.

Willie catches a glimpse of the large white iron tiara artistry and the precious word, TICKETS, mounted in large letters above the teller window a short distance in front of him. Finally they differentiate the line from the fans migrating to the turnstiles underneath the arches. While they wait at the end of the line, Willie counts the number of people in front of them in order to make sure the line is really moving. At first, he counts fourteen people. Moments later, there are only eight people. His excitement escalates in direct proportion to the line becoming shorter. The small service light above the window suddenly is extinguished. The line disbands. There is a vacant space between him and the ticket window as the fans disperse. He can see the ticket window bars. Emerging from the darkness behind the teller bars, Willie sees an attendant's hand place a desktop sign on the shelf behind the wrought iron bars, TODAY'S GAME SOLD OUT. Next, the hand pulls down a shade with the word CLOSED printed on the side facing outward.

Immediately, Willie releases his father's hand and drops his baseball glove. Without a word of explanation, he runs through the rush of the crowd. Dodging in and out, he races up to the ticket window. In the blink of an eye he pulls himself up to see through the wrought iron bars. Holding on to the wrought iron bars as tight as he can, Willie cries out, "Open up! Open up!" The mixed emotions stir him to cry relentlessly.

A hot stifling wave of remorse sweeps over Willie's father. There are no words to say, no words to utter; he is speechless. He bends down and picks up Willie's baseball glove and hurries over to the window. Forlorn over the turn of events, he gives Willie a big hug with all the love that God set blooming in his heart. Apologetically, he stares into Willie's eyes and says, "I'm sorry, son. We'll make it another day. Maybe not this year, but we'll make it another day. I promise."

"Stop it, Dad. Nothing you can say will make me feel any better," Willie says, admonishing his father. "You said..." Tears well up in his eyes and trickle down Willie's cheeks like a river flooding over its banks. His thoughts are disrupted by the steady stream of tears rolling down his cheeks and the disappointments over the years welling up inside. More than anything he wants to forget this moment. He closes his eyes to shut out the vision of the people and of the cobblestone courtyard. He wrestles with the realization that the tickets are sold out. He witnesses another disappointment for his birthday, undoubtedly it will be memorable.

"I know, son," says his father, groping for words to comfort. "Son, I'm sorry. Sometimes things don't work out the way we planned." Not knowing what else to say, his father goes down on one knee in front of Willie and draws him closer. Willie rests his chin on his father's shoulder. He realizes nothing will change his disappointment.

Willie's father desperately tries to offer an explanation, "I'm sorry, but I couldn't afford to buy tickets until yesterday. I have bills to pay. I've said maybe next year too many times. I will change that to 'I promise next year.' I'll save up the money like you do for your baseball cards."

It's time to leave. His father stands up and holds out his hand for Willie's hand as an unspoken gesture of forgiveness.

"Hey, pal, for you and the kid," a voice says. A man has been observing the two struggle with the unsettling circumstances. Mr. Wince comes to his feet. "Gotcha some choice seats," the scalper assures with a suspicious grin on his face. Willie uses the sleeve of his Gunslinger jacket to wipe away the tears. He senses a glimmer of hope as he fixes his eyes on the tickets in the man's hand.

His father takes his wallet out from his back pocket with a very solemn expression on his face. "How much you asking?" requests Mr. Wince, riffling through the back part of his wallet where he keeps the higher denomination bills.

"I can let these beauties go for $80. What ya say, ol' man? Gonna make the kid's dream come true?" he says, showing the tickets to Willie to taunt him.

"...for two?" Mr. Wince asks with surprise written all over his face.

"Naw. I'm a nice guy but not that nice. Get real, old man!" The stranger's business style changes. He talks gruff. The folksy good-natured stranger has disappeared. "This is gonna be the last game of the season. With the strike talk and all, it'll be historic. These tickets are like gold today. I can let them go for $80 each. That's my going price," the Scalper replies.

Replacing his wallet in his back pocket, Mr. Wince responds, "I want my son to enjoy a game, not own the seat he's sitting in!" He refrains from saying what's really on his mind. "Good as gold you say. Fool's gold, maybe. Come on, Willie, we can catch the game on TV." He steps away from the ticket scalper tugging on Willie's hand. Reluctant, Willie balks and stands his ground, pulling his hand back.

"You're not one to disappoint the dear child, now are ya?" the man challenges Mr. Wince, flashing the tickets back and forth in front of Willie to tease him. Afraid of another embarrassing moment, Willie buries his face in his baseball glove and presses it against his face with his other hand. Curious he sneaks a peek through the openings between the fingers of his glove.

The man holds the tickets out then pulls his hand back when Willie tries to snatch them away from out of his hand. At that moment, a police officer strolls up to the two men. He directs his eyes toward the tickets. "Is there a problem here?" the officer questions as he alternates his stare between the scalper and Willie.

"Not if scalping isn't a crime," Mr. Wince declares out loud in a critical disapproving tone. The scalper casually conceals the tickets and exhibit a very sneaky move to shove his hand into his pocket. In a coy manner, he sneaks away, disappearing into the crowd. "Thank you, officer." Mr. Wince extends his regards. "He tried to lure us into buying those tickets for an exorbitant price."

7

"Good day, sir," the officer replies as he resumes his patrol of the courtyard. Willie remembers the sign in the ticket window and wonders how the man can have tickets to sell if the tickets are sold out.

"Come on, Willie. Let's get a program since we can't go to the game," suggests his father, trying to lighten the mood, "How about a bag of peanuts?" He glances down to see Willie pouting. "They're Gunslinger peanuts!"

"Dad, I don't know if I want a program since we can't go to the game. Ya know, this being the last game of the season if they go on strike, that program will only will remind me of how I feel," objects Willie with sad eyes and shoulders sagging.

"Hear me out, son. You'll be glad you got this program. Maybe not today, but some day you'll look back and say, 'I got a historic game day program.' You can even say, 'I was there.' You don't have to say you didn't go to the game. It'll be a memory you can add to your collectables. But, it's the best I can do."

A man wearing an expensive leather Colorado Gunslingers' team jacket and matching baseball cap shadows Mr. Wince and Willie to the souvenir stand. As Mr. Wince retrieves his wallet from his back pocket to purchase a program, the man introduces himself.

"I couldn't help over hearing your conversation..." He pauses for a moment as he removes a pair of Gunslinger tickets from his inside coat pocket. Tension mounts as Mr. Wince prepares to do battle with the imposing stranger.

"Just leave me alone. I don't want your tickets for $50.00 or for $40.00, not even $10.00. Ya hear me! I'm not going to be part of any scam. I know how you guys work in pairs," Mr. Wince angrily barks back scowling at the man offering the tickets.

The man holds the tickets out for Willie to accept from him, then says, "I beg your pardon! You've got me all wrong." The stranger seeks reconsideration. "I can wait until next season. Take the tickets and enjoy the game with your boy."

"What's in it for you?" Mr. Wince questions the Gunslinger fan still suspicious.

The stranger crouches down and peers into Willie's eyes. A little afraid of the stranger Willie side steps to get closer to his father's side. The man extends his hand with the tickets. "Take them, son. No trick, I promise. Just hold out your baseball glove. I can wait until next year. Be my guest." The Gunslinger fan glances over his shoulder casting his eyes on the stadium for a moment. He returns his gaze to the tickets in his hand.

For a moment, Willie suspects the stranger might be reconsidering and change his mind.

The Gunslinger fan continues, "What's in it for me, you ask? Those are corporate tickets. I'm out nothing. I never got the opportunity to enjoy a baseball game with my father." He pauses choking back a tear. "I'd given anything to have gone to a Gunslinger or any professional baseball game with my dad. We hardly did anything together because he was a workaholic. Nothing will make me happier than for the two of you to see the game together. My wife won't mind. I'll treat her to a fancy mid-afternoon lunch at the Brown Palace instead of watching the game. Take them, son. Box seats, behind first base; there's not a better seat in the house."

Without any more ceremony, the stranger drops the tickets into the open baseball glove. Willie reverently claims the tickets from his baseball glove.

The Gunslinger fan winks at Willie and says, "Whatcha say, slugger? Catch a foul ball for me, okay?" He then casually saunters away merging into the crowd, becoming swallowed up by the sea of fans.

Willie hold them out and stares at the tickets with visions of Cracker Jacks and cotton candy dancing in his head. His father retrieves the tickets from Willie's hand to examine them for authenticity. He studies each ticket carefully making funny grunting sounds. He finally concurs, "Okay. Let me put it this way—I have two things to say."

"Two things?" Willie repeats, somewhat confused and dumbfounded.

"Thank you, Lord!" Wilfred Wince says looking heavenward. His hand shaking, he holds out a ticket to Willie with a grin from ear to ear. "...and, take me out to the ball game!"

"Take me out to the crowd!" Willie chimes in with a robust smile as he quickly snatches the ticket from his father.

The two hustle toward the line waiting for the turnstiles darting in and out of fans. Willie stares at the brick wall knowing in a few minutes he will have the opportunity to explore the other side. Since the moment he stepped onto the bricks of the courtyard, he yearned to know what might be in store inside the stadium. It felt like Christmas morning. The stadium was Willie's one big Christmas package. Now he could hardly wait to know what was inside. The ticket was his way of unwrapping the oversized present. He had an idea but not exactly.

Leaving the turnstile, they walk double time into the confines under the stadium. Voices and sounds carry a dull echo inside the stadium cement corridor. The two meander through the corridor toward the portal for their seats. Willie marvels at the bright flashing neon lights around the concessions. A plethora of posters and banners decorate the walls. He sees souvenir kiosks that line the center of the corridor. The souvenir shops are impressive with jerseys, jackets, and Stetson hats. He marvels over the selection of pennants, sunglasses, six-gun pistols, an array of drinking cups and mugs, and balloons of every shape and size. On the way to their box seats, they stroll through some of the shops and scan the souvenirs in the kiosks. He hesitates at the batting cage.

Willie cannot believe the six-gun toy pistols. His eye catches a demonstration of a more realistic pistol that actually fires blanks. The pistols are so real! Never in his wildest dreams could he have imagined all this merchandise. On the way his father stops to purchase a game day program for Willie as a keepsake. Willie keeps his eye on the cage with the radar gun to track the speed of a pitch. He watches to see how many miles an hour the ball is thrown by each eager participant.

Finally, they reach the number of the portal printed on the tickets. They trudge up the incline to find the box seats. At the landing on the top of the incline, Willie stops. He is in awe! Transfixed he stands poised with his line of sight directed toward the baseball outfield. It is an immaculate piece of acreage with the grass cut in a checkerboard pattern.

Gunslinger Baseball Field

The Skeeter Hill Baseball Field resembles a cow pasture in comparison. The gigantic scoreboard is a vision, unbelievable by any measure of the word. "Hey, Willie! Catch up!" summons his father, leading the way to the box seats.

Willie quickly catches up and trails close behind. Within minutes of being seated, the announcer asks everyone to stand for the singing of the national anthem. During the final words of the "Star Spangled Banner," the Thunderbirds fly in formation overhead. Willie covers his ears thinking the Thunderbird squadron will break the sound barrier. On the scoreboard, which looks is bigger than his house, Willie reads ARE YOU READY FOR GUNSLINGER BASEBALL? scrolling across the screen.

"Play ball!" the announcer proclaims over the public address system.

Willie sits down and scoots back on the seat with his feet dangling a few inches from the cement flooring. The scoreboard screen is the biggest television screen he has seen in his entire life.

The Gunslingers take the field for the last pre-game warm-up exercises. Willie watches the field mascot frolicking with the players by the dugout.

Gunslinger Team Mascot

Before the game starts, two cowboys have an Old West re-enactment of a shootout between the pitcher's mound and home plate. Willie and his father find the reenactment comical. A solemn atmosphere settles in as the first batter approaches the batter's box. The words PLAY BALL appear on the scoreboard screen in vibrant colors and flashes back and forth in different sizes. The fans erupt with cat whistles and cheers. The batter taps each shoe to remove the caked on dirt from his cleats. The pitcher holds the ball in his right hand and rests his hand on his back as he bends over to read the signals from the catcher.

"Heybattabattabatta! Heybatta…" Willie yells out with his hands cupped around his mouth to help project his voice. All of a sudden, he realizes he's the only person yelling. Embarrassed, he slides back in his seat. Humiliated by his spontaneous chant he wishes he could hide under his seat. He realizes he is not in Skeeter Hill. Nevertheless he watches the pitcher go into his stretch, Willie's heart races faster and faster. The batter raises his right elbow and proceeds to step into his swing. The batter holds up on the swing.

The umpire shouts, "Strike!"

The pitcher delivers the second pitch. The batter does not flinch. The umpire declares strike. On the third pitch, the umpire yells, "Strike three. You're out!"

A fan sitting behind Willie yells at the top of his voice. "What's the matter, ref? Ya blind? That was as far outside as the moon."

Darrel Driskell bats next for the Lumberjacks. He has the highest batting average in the league. The pitcher throws a fastball low and outside. Darrel swings *Crack!* The sound of the bat hitting the ball reverberates throughout the ball park.

Fans jump to their feet. Willie jumps up on his seat to watch over the adults in front of him. Instinctively, Willie surveys the sky for the baseball. The center fielder races back toward the warning track.

"Willie, looks like its a goner," comments his father.

The high pop-up appears to be a home run. Keeping his eye on the ball, the outfielder waits until the baseball's descent. The fans become extremely quiet in anticipation as the tension mounts. At the last moment outfielder raises his glove and nonchalantly makes the catch.

Willie keeps a close eye on the game while chit-chatting with his father, all the time quoting facts and figures pertaining to the players on both teams. In the same inning, Willie witnesses his first United Federation of Baseball double play with a throw from shortstop to second then to first to make the force outs. The organ music swells over the public address. The oversized scoreboard displays OUT. Willie jumps up and down with his arms flailing back and forth, "What a game! What a game!" he shouts as loud as he can. Excited for the first completed three outs he longer has a concern about being embarrassed.

The Gunslinger players leave the field and travel to the dugout. Willie uses the time to read his Gunslinger game day program. He sees Jovan Neske in the lineup and takes out his special card case. With his index finger, he sorts through the cards until he comes to Jovan Neske's rookie card. Placing his fingers on the opposing sides of the rookie card, he holds it up carefully not to touch the face of the card and soil it. He draws his father's attention to the card.

"He's the Gunslinger's lead-off batter. Has a .335 batting average. Not too good at running the bases," Willie explains while holding up the card for his father to get a look.

"We'll see what he can do today." His father returns his eyes to home plate.

Jovan Neske steps up to the plate from the on-deck circle. After a few practice swings, the players are ready to play the bottom half of the first inning. The umpire stations himself behind the catcher. The Lumberjack's pitcher starts his unorthodox delivery with a high leg kick during the pitching motion. Jovan raises his elbow in preparation for his power swing. With the release of the ball instantly, he drives the bat toward the speeding sphere. The bat slams into the ball, driving it in the direction of left field. The left fielder scissor-steps across the outfield in order to get underneath the high pop-fly ball. Unfortunately, he misgauges the baseball's descent. The baseball plummets toward the ground out of reach. Jovan Neske charges down the first base line. The first base coach instructs him to take second. He peddles as fast as he can to get a stand-up double.

"Hey, Dad, did you see that?" Willie enthusiastically asks.

"Sure did!" answers his father. "Just as advertised..."

"This is better than TV—*way* better," comments Willie, feeling overwhelmed by the experience of seeing the game in person.

Jose Jimenez strolls up to the plate to bat next. He taps his bat on the plate and takes a few practice swings. Tapping the plate helps him determine how close to stand to the plate. He swings one more time and directs the barrel of the bat toward third base with an extra shake pointing at third when he trails off his swing. Jovan sees the signal from the batter and removes his base running hat, slicks back his hair with is hand, and replaces it back on his head. This signals back to the batter that he understands Jose will swing at the first pitch to allow sufficient time for him to try to steal third base. The Gunslinger players have created a set of signals for the batter to communicate with runners on base. Jovan takes a long lead off second base. The batting stance epitomizes a contortionist. The bat hovers above his head instead of being cocked to his side by his shoulder. Willie scoots up and sits on the edge of his seat, eyes wide open.

The catcher juggles the pitch. Jovan decides to make a furious dash to third base. He safely reaches third before the catcher can throw to the third baseman. The next pitch, Jose taps a line drive over the pitcher's head into center field. Jovan races down the third base line to home plate. The Gunslingers score the first run for the afternoon. The game goes back and forth through the seventh inning stretch. The Gunslingers hold a three-run lead going into the eighth inning.

All of the excitement exhausts Willie. An empty popcorn box, wrappers from two hot dogs, and the cardboard cone he gripped while eating the cotton candy lie by his feet. Tired, his eyes droop. He wraps his jacket around his baseball glove for a pillow and curls up in the stadium seat and drifts off to sleep.

As the game continues, the fans become rowdier. Going into the ninth inning, his father tries to wake Willie with a nudge. Startled, Willie wakes up, "Wha-what did I miss?" Half asleep, he sits up dazed. "Is it over? Who won?"

"Come on, son. It's time for us to go." His father coaxes him to gather up his belongings for the journey to the car. Not quite awake Willie slowly puts on his jacket, picks up the game day program, and situates his trusty baseball glove on his hand. Still sleepy he trudges behind his father to the portal ramp. Before scampering down the ramp, he stares back over his shoulder at the field for one last look. Suddenly, commotion erupts in the right field by the warning track. The outfielders race toward the infield.

"Look, Dad! What's that smoke coming from the outfield," Willie announces, seeing a plume of smoke rise from left right side of center field and fans free-falling onto the field. Riotous action consumes deep right field. Security personnel run toward the outfield. Players in the outfield run toward the infield. Panic stricken the infielders race toward the dugout.

Immediately his father grabs his hand and pulls him along. "Willie, we gotta go! Now!" Willie senses panic in his father's voice." We can't wait here! Come on, run! We hafta leave now!" They run down the ramp to the corridor. Willie glances over his shoulder to see a crowd of fans crowd into the corridor hysterical. His father yanks on his hand to urge Willie to pick up the pace. They exit the stadium and race across the cobblestone courtyard to the street corner. Immediately, the crowd ushers up a cheer in unison. "What ya think happened, Dad? Can it be fireworks?" Willie asks while watching the smoke billows above the stadium.

"Have no idea. It's too early for the fireworks. Could be an uproar over the players strike. We'll find out when we get home. We can watch the sports on TV."

"Are they really going on strike or is it just talk?" Willie expresses his concern about the pending players' strike.

"Well, son, I think it's gotten to the point that there will be a strike," answers his father plodding across the street to the next corner.

"When I become a professional baseball player, I'm not gonna disappoint no one by not playing ball. You can bet on me, Dad."

"It's a promise you can make to yourself. When the time comes, maybe you may have to persuade others," suggests his father with a chuckle in his voice. *The folly of being a young boy with big dreams,* his father thinks to himself.

Baseball, crowned as America's favorite pastime, reigns supreme in Willie's mind. The strike possibly will threaten the conference play offs and the Federation World Title. Repeatedly, he tries to come to terms with the fact that the future of professional baseball hangs in the balance.

At home, his father escorts the sleepy-eyed lad into the house and follows him as he trudges up to his room. In his bedroom he catches sight of his bed and plunges straight ahead before he wraps up in the pillow. His father pulls the game day program out of his dead man's grip and lays it on the foot of the bed. Still wearing the Gunslinger's baseball jersey, Willie's mother tucks him in for the night. Oblivious to the world, he will not know until morning the score at the end of the game, the reason for the commotion that erupted, or if the United Federation of Baseball Teams across the country decide to go on strike at midnight.

TOUGH BREAK KID

Everything shiny or with a glossy metal finish in Willie's bedroom reflects the early the morning sunlight and glistens. Baseball cards in protective cases, posters, framed pictures, and pennants decorated with team buttons shimmer from the sunlight. His bedroom is decorated with an array of baseball collectables and memorabilia. Reproduction portraits of Babe Ruth, Jackie Robinson, Hank Lund, Mickey Mantle, Jack Hargrave, and Billy Munson decorate the wall. Framed baseball cards of Orlando Martinez, Brent Williams, and Jevon Neske form a collage. Around the room there are numerous collages with other cards depicting an organized confusion and Willie's own mystical sense of baseball balance on his wall. Over time, Willie managed to collect a number of team posters of the Renegades, Rustlers, White Sox, Lumberjacks, Red Sox, and Gunslingers. Magazines are arranged in neat piles in every nook and cranny of his room. Special articles and player's photos clipped from magazines are kept in the under drawers of his bed. His bedroom has been converted into Willie Wince's 'locker room of fame'. Friends call it the Willie Wince Baseball Shrine.

The incessant barking of South Paw, Willies back yard dog, arouses Willie from his slumber. Trying to drift back to sleep, he hears a strange sound. Something lands on the roof and slowly tumbles down. *Maybe it's a branch?* But a branch would not continue to roll over and over. Moments later, he hears it again. Then the sound abruptly stops. He swings his feet over the side of the bed and sits up. He slides out of bed; still sleepy-eyed, he weaves his way to the window. Again, the puzzling sound repeats as he pulls back the curtains in time to catch sight of a pinecone rolling off the shallow gable of the roof to the abyss below and disappear. He directs his line of sight to the front yard. Wee Bones and Izzie stand in the front yard gazing up at his bedroom window, both holding a handful of pine cones.

Willie has a special sign he made that hangs in his window. On one side, the sign says "in" and on the other it says "out." Reaching through the curtain, Willie points to the "out" sign and hopes his friends will leave him to sleep away the morning. Instead, Izzie and Wee Bones think he is telling them that he will be "out" to meet them soon, and so they decide to wait on the porch. Through the curtain he sees his friends make tracks to the porch to wait for him.

Willie, grumbles and then swaps his new jersey for an older Gunslinger jersey. He jumps into a pair of everyday jeans with deep side pockets his mother sewed on special for him. After tying his shoes, he snatches up the Gunslingers' game day program from the foot of his bed. In the blink of an eye, he bounds down the stairs and explodes out the front door.

On the porch, Willie squats down on the top step. Izzie and Wee Bones join him sitting on each side. He opens the program like it's a precious document and thumbs through the pages to find the overhead picture of the stadium. Before explaining the major points of interest in the overhead picture, he glances up to catch sight of Gooch and Punzak strolling across the yard. *Ugh, more company.* Always one to realize the reality of a situation, Willie decides to make the most of his company and says, "The heck with it!" and skips down the porch steps to the sidewalk below. "Beat ya to the clubhouse!" Rolling up the game day program, Willie starts running. Izzie has the longest legs and overtakes Willie. Wee Bones trails behind as usual because his legs are the shortest. Being a shorter person, he struggles at most everything athletic. Kids at school call him Pee Wee and Short Stuff. Coach Waterford is the one who gave him the nickname Wee Bones. His best friends adopted it and in no time, Wee Bones became the most popular name at school.

Gooch, on the other hand, was a tall lanky Japanese-Black American. His father served in the military. While in Japan, Papa Gooch met a female Japanese USO program director. She and his father became exceptionally good friends. After his discharge from the military, he returned to Japan to bring her home to the United States to be his bride.

Punzak did not have any particular interests or background to share with his friends. His father works for Remcore Technologies. Izzie took Punzak under his wing, especially since the guys needed another player for a sandlot game. Before long, Punzak became friends with everyone in the group.

Izzie became friends with Willie in when they played T-Ball. Then they joined Cub Scouts and attended in Mrs. Schackleford's Den. They worked together to obtain their Tiger, Wolf and Bear. They enjoyed building the pinewood derby cars. Izzie's father helped them with tools from his shop in the basement. They became great friends through Cub Scouts and youth baseball.

Approach to Skeeter Hill Little League Baseball Field

Izzie reaches the Skeeter Hill Little League field before the others. He races past the NO TRESPASSING signs on the concession stand service windows and up to the KEEP OUT signs posted on the gate to the stairs leading to the scorekeeper's box above the concession stand. Everyone calls the lofty scorekeeper's perch the Skeeter Hill Press Box. The misnomer brandishes a kind of ambiance instead of an undignified name of scorekeeper's box. The Skeeter Hill Parks and Recreation allows only staff and adults to enter the scorekeeper's box in order to avoid distraction during a game. All season long, a volunteer stands guard by the gate to enforce the strict rule. A warning on the gate indicates fines for unauthorized use of the premises. In Willie's estimation, the signs serve as a warning and not a deterrent.

Many times, he capitalized on the opportunity to observe Officer Higby stripping the shackle from the padlock case without a key. Because the locking cam does not work properly, the padlock will open with a strong downward jerk. The flimsy padlock on the gate was more for show than security. Since Izzie could outrun everyone else he had the responsibility of being the gatekeeper and unlock the gate.

Izzie jerks down on the padlock as hard as he can. The shackle pops open. Methodically, he twists the shackle through the hole in the gate latch and thrusts open the gate. Anticipating Willie and the others, he retreats to the corner of the concession to watch for any bystanders. Willie sprints by and skips up the steps.

At the landing, Willie grabs the combination padlock attached to the bottom portion of the Dutch door (split door hinged separately. The top half will open and a bottom half will open, separately) leading to the scorekeeper's box. He pauses to recall the numbers to enter for the combination. Ironically, Izzie accidently discovered the numbers to the combination lock. When his mom painted the comical baseball characters on the wall of the concession center, she painted the numbers for the combination on their jerseys. He discovered the secret on the paperwork in the garage she converted into an art studio.

Players with numbers on their uniforms

Carefully, Willie enters each number to match up with the indicator. Nimbly rotating the dial with each selected number, he hurries as fast as he can to open the lock. Wanting to open the lock as quickly as he can but not wanting to go past a number and have to re-enter all the numbers over again he takes his time. Out of the corner of his eye he sees Wee Bones turn the corner as he enters the last number. He pulls down. The combination worked and the paddle lock opens.

Wee Bones arrives and scampers up the steps to the landing. Removing the lock, Willie throws back the hasp from the eye loop to release the bottom of the Dutch door. Immediately, he swings the door open for Wee Bones to scamper inside. Wee Bones slides under the top half of the Dutch door and slithers inside. Willie gives a thumbs up and waits by the door for the others. Izzie pretends they're under enemy fire. Before scampering up the stairs, he sneaks a look around the corner of the concession to ascertain if there are any bystanders or people on the sidewalk, the enemy. Without further hesitation he scales the stairs. Seeing Izzie leave his post by the concession, Punzak rushes out from underneath the bleachers and darts up the steps. Gooch dashes out from underneath the bleachers and dashes up the stairs. After Gooch and Willie duck down and sneak inside, Punzak grabs the door handle and closes the bottom half of the Dutch door behind them. Methodically, he latches the dead bolt on the inside of the door. The top door of the split door is secured with a top and bottom latch to keep it secure from the inside. The silver handled door knob is more for show.

Everyone sits down in a circle and crosses their legs Indian style. Willie retrieves the game day program from the deep side pocket of his pants and joins his circle of friends on the floor. Very meticulously Willie thumbs through the game day program to the overview of the outfield similar to what he saw when he attended the game. He stops occasionally as he studiously examines a page.

"Guess what, Willie? The players went on strike," Wee Bones says.

"Just ain't right. Ain't right at all," Willie replies with his nose buried in the program. He lays the program on the floor for everyone to be able to see the pictures. Taking the palm of his hand he presses down very gently on the spine to crease the program in order to keep it open to the selected page. Extremely excited and anxious to share the firsthand experience of attending the Gunslinger game, he rises up on his knees to elaborate. With the overview picture of the outfield displayed, he begins to articulate the more interesting points he observed.

Overview of Gunslinger Baseball Field

"Guys, this is really cool." He leans over the program and points with his left hand index finger at the picture. Trying to integrate showmanship and enthusiasm, he begins his individual show and tell. "Pretend you are sitting way up high—ya know, the nose bleed section. Well, seats up here will make you feel like you're on top of the world." With his finger, he directs everyone's attention to a portion of the upper deck in the stadium.

"Wow!" exclaims Gooch. "Really, uh, really...

"Way cool," Izzie exclaims shaking his head in disbelief. "That's what my dad says all the time. Way cool!"

"...that's huge. It's so big, like," Wee Bones says groping for words.

Pointing to the box seat section by first base, Willie proudly announces, "My dad and I sat right about here." Everyone squeezes in closer to get a better look at the box seat section.

All of a sudden, they hear pounding at the door. No one knows about their secret club house, at least that's what everyone thought. Had they gotten caught? Did someone see them? Were they in trouble? Izzie and Gooch slide across the floor to the door. Willie places his index finger up to his lips to remind everyone not to talk and to remain quiet. A few moments later, the pounding resumes.

"Come on, guys. Let me in!" comes a squeaky girl's voice.

Willie grabs his game day program and hides it underneath an overturned wastebasket. Carefully, he pushes the wastebasket underneath the scorekeeper's shelf. Gooch takes a couple of short breaths. Izzie tries to cover Gooch's nose and mouth thinking Gooch might sneeze. His response happens too late. A sneeze shatters the silence exposing the group. "It doesn't matter, Gooch. It sounds like Weezie," says Willie.

Weezie lives next door to Willie. The two went to pre-school together and have been chums through elementary school. Weezie has an older sister but does not have any brothers, so she adopted Willie as her brother. At the same time, Willie does not have any siblings, so he has an on-again off-again sister in Weezie. He adores her smile and ability to take a good tease. Best of all, he likes her tomboy ways, but he does not share that with the guys.

Tomboy Weezie

Weezie manages to shadow the boys everywhere. This freckled face, sandy-blond, tomboy does everything she can to belong to Willie's merry band of friends. When they play a baseball game, she always wants to join. In spite of her persistence, the boys refuse to let her take part. After they play sandlot games, the boys usually meet at Chelsea's soda fountain. Weezie generally manages to walk into Chelsea's Drug Store on "an errand" and sits down at the soda fountain. If they are comparing baseball cards at the library, she always has her deck of baseball cards at the ready. No matter what they did they couldn't discourage her. She ignores every message the boys send. For some reason, the boys enjoy teasing Weezie as much as she seems to enjoy being the brunt of their tactful games. It is like a game within a game they play back and forth. Punzak once sent her to get a left handed bat. She was gone all afternoon and came up empty handed.

"I know you guys are in there. Now let me in," Weezie begs, leaning up against the door.

"Not on your life! Go away!" Willie responds trying to get a glimpse through a crack in the slats of rough cut wood siding.

"I'm going to tell," threatens Weezie standing up and placing her hands on her hips.

"Go away, Weezie. This is guy stuff," Willie reminds her not yielding to her threat.

"Oh, alright; this time I'll leave. But remember, I can tell," Weezie reiterates slowly making her way down the steps.

A silence ensues. Punzak peeps through gaps between the slats of the siding overlooking the stairs. "She's climbing down," Punzak shares with everyone while he continues his surveillance. "She's going around to the gate between the backstop and home team dugout. I can't see her." Punzak scrambles over to the scorekeeper's counter. He unfastens the latch on the inside to release the slatted window awning. Izzie hurries over to unfasten the inside latch on the awning on the other end. Next the two turn the crank to move the awning outward, Gooch stares underneath. He motions for them to lift the awning higher, still higher. Willie skates over the scorekeepers counter and squeeze in beside Gooch. He places his one hand on top of the other on the counter then slides forward. Bracing himself with his elbows on the counter he rests his chin on the back of his hand and peeks out underneath the awning as the boys raise it.

Boys peek out from inside announcer's box

Willie watches Weezie shuffle her feet in the gravel and kick up dust as she saunters across the infield. She stops at the pitcher's mound and sheepishly glances back over her shoulder at the scorekeeper's box. In her heart, she wishes someone might apologetically call out to her, especially Willie. She stands and lingers occasionally and looks up at the scorekeeper's box. She spies the awning on the scorekeeper side shift out from the window frame. She knows someone is peeking out from inside because she can see the awning moved out. While she loiters and stares at the scorekeeper box, Garvin and his band of devious pals march onto the visitor's side of the infield. Garvin surprises Weezie from behind. Gooch motions for the others to watch what is happening. Everyone huddles around Gooch and Willie to peek outside and see what is developing on the pitcher's mound.

On the infield, Garvin and his mischievous friends surround Weezie. The boys in the scorekeeper's box wonder what Garvin and his nasty pals might be saying to Weezie. She becomes animated and points at the scorekeeper's box. Willie and his friends' curiosity is aroused as they wonder if Weezie might be telling them about Willie hiding in the scorekeeper's box with his friends. Looking angry, Weezie tries to leave their company. Garvin steps in her way and pushes her toward one of the other boys. Laughter ensues. She stumbles. When she steadies herself, another boy steps over and pushes her back to Garvin. Immediately, Garvin pushes her to someone else in the group. The cruel taunt escalates from a pushing ordeal to shoving. Her feet tangle up. Weezie becomes scared from the bullying. "Come on guys, stop it! Quit! Stop! Stop it!"

"They're picking on Weezie. Come on guys, let's get 'em," Willie announces as he pushes the upside down wastebasket further under the scorekeeper's counter, concealing it plain sight. "I'm leaving now! You guys coming with me?"

Willie swings open the bottom door of the Dutch door and crawls out. Hastily, he bounds down the stairs. He leaps over the last three steps. In the distance, he can hear Weezie's cries for help. The boys' laughter escalates. The tone changes from humorous to smart-alecky laughter. Garvin catches sight of Willie rapidly approaching. With two fingers in his mouth he produces a shrill whistle. The boys stop bullying Weezie and step away. She staggers momentarily, catching her balance. She slumps to her knees nearly in tears. Willie rushes up to her.

"You dirty rotten ..." blurts Weezie recuperating on the ground.

"Now, now Weezie, foul language doesn't become you," Garvin teases. His buddies snicker and make snide comments in private while they watch Willie comfort her.

Weezie whimpers and sobs while Willie makes sure she is okay. Wee Bones, Izzie, Punzak, and Gooch arrive at the pitcher's mound and lend their help.

"Weezie, your boyfriend's back," taunts Garvin. Willie rushes up to Garvin. "That's close enough, Willie my boy. Stay right where you are..."

Standing several feet away, he stops. "Garvin, I ought to..."

Garvin paces back and forth taking only a couple of steps at a time. Willie stands with his fists clenched at his side. "You and your big top friends... " Garvin sarcastically laughs. "Come one, come all. What we have here is the wannabe Little League Circus." He orchestrates a modeling gesture toward Willie's friends. "In the center ring for your amusement is a world famous baseball-catching midget. In the far ring, we have a human bean pole, a genuine stilt walker." He points directly at Izzie. "In the ring closest to the trapeze safety net is Fu Manchu from the far reaches of China." He graciously bows toward Gooch. "I now direct your attention to Mr. Wince Jr., our future Little League king of clowns. A clown of..."

"You ketchup drool! We ain't no circus! And you leave Weezie alone! She ain't done nothing to you," Willie rants at Garvin's degrading remarks.

"Ya know, Wincey my boy, you might be right. You ain't no circus 'cause there ain't gonna be no Little League season for you this year for your act. You guys will have to parade all over town instead in search of a team. Ha, ha, ha," jokes Garvin spitting in the direction of Willie's prized Gunslinger running shoes. "Now get outta here. This is our field. You guys are not invited, *capiche*?" Garvin flicks his fingers off his chin portraying a gangster mannerism. Garvin pretends to jump rope like Muhammad Ali.

In Willie's mind, he must stand his ground against the enemy regardless of the consequences. Garvin decidedly is the enemy. Unafraid of any impending confrontation, Garvin sneers at Willie as he continues to pretend to jump rope. Occasionally he stops pretending to jump rope and spits on the ground. Repulsed by Garvin's act and crude behavior, Willie kicks dirt back at him like a coach contesting an umpire's call. Dust billows up and disappears in the brisk summer breeze.

"Ya hear me? You clowns ain't gonna have a season." He pauses. "Clowns, sounds better all the time. You know what people do to clowns? They laugh at them. You'll be the laughing stock of the of Skeeter Hill 'cause no one will have ya."

A tingling sensation travels up Willie's spine. His legs tremble. His palms become clammy. He starts taking shorter breaths, almost like panting. Garvin continues to laugh. Willie's heart starts to pump faster and faster. His anger escalates changing to rage. Someone has to teach Garvin a lesson. Willie motions with his hand for Weezie and the others to stand back. Garvin waves his fists in a boxing rhythm in front of Willie's face.

"Sting like a bee..." Garvin teases. "You're not a champ. No, not the great Willie Wince..."

Willie desperately wants to refrain from a fight because the scales tip in Garvin's direction at least twenty pounds. Willie does stand four inches taller than him but he never heard of a fight being won by a pugilist's height. Garvin boasts about taking boxing lessons at the YMCA. Maybe that is where he picked up on the Muhammad Ali lingo. Willie cannot take his ridicule and humiliation much longer. Sensing the conversation may be escalating to physical confrontation, he decides to walk away and avoid an altercation.

"Aw, look. He's going home to tell mommy," taunts Garvin.

In a split second, Willie bolts toward Garvin. With his arms outstretched he wraps up Garvin and drives him to the ground like a tackling dummy in football. Garvin tumbles to the ground. His head lands on the hard ravine made by the pitcher's stride foot. Garvin's all-star baseball cap flies off his head. The wind toys with the baseball cap tossing it back and forth. It tumbles across the infield like a kite a few feet above the ground as the wind twists and turns the ball cap.

For a split second, the two boys lay motionless on the ground catching their breath and recovering from the element of surprise that gripped both of them. All of a sudden, Garvin begins to thrash his feet trying to wriggle away from underneath Willie. He throws short jabs in a futile attempt to free himself. The jabs translate into the two grappling back and forth tussling on the ground. Garvin and Willie jockey for a fighter's advantage. Willie's friends scream and holler showing their support. Garvin's friends inch closer together and join in the hollering match throwing support for Garvin.

Amid the mayhem, Weezie casually slips away. After reaching a safe and clear distance from the scuffle, she turns to run toward the outfield. Her eye catches sight of Garvin's hat cartwheeling in the wind. She decides to pursue the baseball cap.

The wind tosses it toward second base. She starts to chase the baseball cap toward second base. The wind changes the path. It sails in the direction of left field. She zigzags through the outfield in pursuit of the elusive baseball cap. Finally, the baseball cap flutters on the ground and jumps up in a final whirligig performance pouncing into the privet hedge that outlines the outfield boundary. At that instant, she races up and snags the elusive baseball cap. The logo on the cap seems oddly familiar. She studies it and tries to decide if the baseball cap belongs to Garvin or Willie. It's not a distinctive team logo she remembers Willie having worn in times past. Apparently the baseball cap must be Garvin's. In the distance, she can hear the boys' encouraging and heckling. The boys shield her line of sight from Willie and Garvin as the sound of screaming and hollering escalates.

At that moment, she spies a police cruiser moving around the end of the chain link fence beyond the home team bleachers. She watches the police car roll through right field and park on the infield between the area of first and second base with strobe bar lights flashing red and blue with intermittent white lights. Officer Higby, a heavyset patrol officer about fifty years old, occupies the driver's seat in the car. Weezie convinces herself it's not her fight. Wadding up the cap in her hand, she strolls through the opening in left field in the privet hedge and disappears in Rayner Park.

Willie and Garvin continue to wrestle and throw punches. Officer Higby sounds the siren on the patrol car. The bystanders keep hollering and heckling in spite of the presence of the patrol car a short distance away. Officer Higby exits the car and stomps across the infield. He pushes Izzie and Gooch aside.

Methodically, Officer Higby places his arm under Willie's arm and snakes his arm up and around on the back of Willie's head in a half nelson. "Break it up! Now, I mean business!" Officer Higby orders.

Willie kicks and tries to worm his way loose. Realizing he cannot escape, he cries out in agony. "Ow! Let me go. He started it!

Officer Higby exerts more pressure with the half-nelson grip. Garvin remains on the ground coughing up dust and spitting out dirt. "Both of you! Stop it! Now! I mean it! Break it up!" Officer Higby takes a few steps back dragging Willie backward to distance the two gladiators. Garvin rolls on his side and gradually stands up. Realizing Officer Higby has the better of him, Willie quits squirming and calms down.

Upon being released from the head lock, Willie brushes the sand and gravel off his elbow and rubs his sore neck. As he cleans the blood-caked sand from his elbow, he notices his dangling Gunslinger Jersey shirt pocket. Evidently, it ripped during the altercation. "Damn you, Garvin. See what you did!" Willie yells, tugging on the torn piece of cloth.

"So, what's it to you, punk?" replies Garvin, brushing off gravel from his pants. "They're a losing... "A drop of moisture beads up in the dirt. Garvin attributes the darkish moisture to sweat as a result of the exertion during the fight. Another drop lands on the first drop. He dismisses it. Then another drop falls to the ground. The drops appear in rapid succession. He touches his right cheek with his fingertips. It is sore and tender. It's moist and tacky. The presence of moisture on his cheek cannot be easily explained. He does not have a fat lip to cause slobbering during the course of the fight. That's a different kind of moisture and would not be increasing with intensity.

Removing his hand, he stares at his fingers. His eyes capture a mixture of wet sand and presence of what appears to be the color of blood. Tenderly massaging his cheek releases more blood to journey down his cheek unobstructed. The blood flow runs past the corner of his mouth down to his chin. The sand no longer blocks the flow of blood like a band aid or scab. The amount of blood indicates he does not have a minor cut. Instead, he has endured a laceration. Quickly, he presses his hand against his cheek. Immediately he hollers at Willie, "We were just funning with Weezie. You came along and did this, punk! You started fighting'."

Garvin and his pals rule the roost in the south-side neighborhood. Usually, Garvin's opponents back down. No one ever confronted Garvin let alone hurt him in an altercation. Never before had he witnessed such a bold and audacious maneuver by a lesser opponent. Blood continues to flow through his fingers and trickles down his arm. The droplets form a pool on the ground and splatter his clothes and shoes.

In his heart, Willie did not mean to harm Garvin. He merely wanted to teach him a lesson. What Garvin said about his friends and the Skeeter Hill Little League were blasphemous. Garvin has expectations to play in the Junior League next season and thinks his dad will coach the same Junior League team to a metro-championship. Regardless, his actions did not justify him making such disparaging remarks.

Suddenly, Garvin charges Willie unabated and pulls him to the ground throwing body jabs as fast as he can trigger each hand. Officer Higby grabs Garvin's arm and drags him aside. Willie rolls over onto his hands and knees massaging where he was pelted repeatedly. Timidly, he stands up apprehensive if there might be another wave of retaliation. Officer Higby spins Garvin around and puts his index finger under his chin. He applies pressure tilting his head upward and pushes his forehead back with the other hand to examine the laceration. Everyone stands patiently waiting and watching while he inspects the wound. Shaking his head, he places Garvin's hand against the wound. "Keep your hand right there until I tell you different!"

Officer Higby stares each one of the kids in the eye beginning with the boys that were standing around Weezie. Tension mounts with his pensive manner. He devotes time studying Punzak, Gooch and then Izzie, individually. Then he gives his eagle eye to Garvin's bunch in the same selective fashion and says, "Will you kids ever amount to anything more than trouble makers? That's all I see in you day after day. Decide what you want to do and put your mind to it! Make something of yourselves!"

Willie observes Gooch and Izzie elbow-nudge each other. It can't be about Officer Higby's lecture. Gooch's eyebrows arch as he nods toward Willie. His actions tentatively reinforce Willie's inclination that he'll be considered the victor in the battle. Izzie directs his field of vision down at his shoes with a shameful look in his eyes. Something does not measure up. A hand comes to rest on Willie's shoulder. Now he knows why Gooch and Izzie's actions seemed peculiar. He stands shamefully embarrassed at the thought his father may have observed the scuffle. How much trouble had he gotten into because of picking a fight? Willie slowly turns around and exchanges eye contact with his dad. Ashamed, he hangs his head anticipating a well-deserved scolding from his father. He never knows what his father's frame of mind might be.

Officer Higby exchanges eye contact with Mr. Wince and says, "Wilfred, I got an urgent care on my hands. I've got to take this boy to the emergency."

"Willie, you son of a..." blurts Garvin spitting blood as he talks.

"None of that language, ya hear, son!" cautions Officer Higby as he shoves Garvin in the direction of the patrol car.

"Stop! Wait a minute! He ripped my face with his damn sports ring. The fake one he's always showing off 'round town. Charge him with assault with a weapon or whatever you call it," Garvin babbles trying to implicate Willie in more trouble than a squabble.

"You've been watching too many police shows on TV," Officer Higby quips as he halts to check Willies' hand. "Hold out your hand, son." Willie holds out his hands to show the sports ring cannot be seen on any of his fingers on either hand. The absence of the ring on Willie's hand causes Officer Higby to dismiss the allegations by Garvin. He resumes escorting him to the patrol car.

"Maybe he lost it in the dirt when we was fightin'. Check the pitcher's mound. It's gotta be there!" demands Garvin, seeking to place blame on Willie. "Stay right here, ya hear, Willie!" his father says scrambling over to the pitcher's mound. Kneeling on the undisturbed ground, he pitches twigs and gum wrappers aside to scour the area. A bright illumination catches his eye. To avoid an injury from the obscure object, he removes the handkerchief from his back pocket and picks it up. He returns to Officer Higby and hands him the handkerchief.

"I don't think we should be concerned about a harmless sports ring. What you have there is a shard of glass. Found it on the ground where the pitchers plant their foot. In the kicking stride, their foot lands there."

"We don't have to keep searching for a ring is my guess," Officer Higby replies as he receives the piece of glass.

"Probably the hard ground held the piece of glass in place until he landed on it cutting his cheek," Mr. Wince explains, brushing his hands against each other to remove sand and gravel. In the background, Gavin's pals disperse in separate directions. Willie's friends disband in the direction of the concession stand by way of the home team gate opening.

"I'll have the lab examine it at the station. Thanks, Wilfred. Gonna take Mr. Fisticuffs to Skeeter Hill General. I'll follow up with an investigation later." He forces Garvin to proceed in the direction of the patrol car.

"Hey, Wincey baby. You're gonna pay for this. Don't you ever forget it! I'll get even with you," threatens Garvin as he reluctantly marches ahead of Officer Higby in the direction of the police car.

"Zip it. You don't have much to talk about." Officer Higby quashes Garvin's temper as he jerks him back and forth on the way to the patrol car.

"You can't take me to juvy. I ain't done nothing'. It's that Wince kid. He started it. Ask the others," Garvin protests as they approach the patrol car.

"Get in the car before I change my mind. I can put you in juvenile detention with very little effort. Don't test my patience," cautions Officer Higby as he pushes down on his head to force him to slide into the back seat.

Willie's father escorts Willie in the direction of the car where the street fans out into the parking lot for the Little League baseball field. On the way to the car, Willie sets his eyes on the old Victorian house with several windows overlooking the Skeeter Hill Little League baseball field. Often, he thinks he sees a man peering out from one of the windows inside overlooking the baseball field. The occasional reflection through the limbs on the towering oak tree obscures what might be a figure behind the picture window facing the baseball field. "Dad, who lives in the house over there?" asks Willie pausing to stare in the direction of the Victorian house on the hill.

Victorian House

"I don't know, son. Folks say he moved here from the big city. Heard something about him being laid off by some big company for health reasons. Rumor has it he might have been someone famous at some time. Stays shut up in the old Skeeter Hill Mansion like a hermit. He keeps to himself. Something you should have done today," Willie's father replies indirectly referencing the altercation with Garvin.

His father's judgmental attitude thwarts any thought of further conversation. Willie decides not to say anything else all the way home. He thinks about Weezie and wonders if she is okay. It was not right how Garvin and his pals mistreated her.

After everyone leaves the Little League baseball field, Weezie emerges from her hiding place behind the privet hedge in Rayner Park. She candidly makes her way through the gate opening in the chain link fence between the privet hedge in left field and strolls toward the infield. When she reaches the infield, she searches the shadows to make sure none of Garvin's pals observe her. She is worried what might happen if they catch her wearing Garvin's baseball cap. She nonchalantly paces herself through the infield until she reaches the opening in the chain link fence between the back stop and the home team dugout. At the gate, she scampers over to the stairs and skips up the steps to the landing by the Dutch door. The altercation involving Willie and Garvin did not grant an opportunity for anyone to return and replace the lock on the door.

Anticipating someone might attack from the inside, she opens the door by pushing it with her toe. Nothing happens. The door opens wide enough for her to peek inside. No one is there. The scorekeeper's box seems to be empty inside. She sneaks inside underneath the top half of the Dutch door. Nervously, she pokes around for what may have been the big a secret. Lying around the room are a couple worn out metal-framed kitchen chairs, wadded up papers on the floor, and little pencils like the ones at the miniature golf course for the score cards. What could have been so secretive? There were not any posters on the wall. She opens one of the drawers underneath the scorekeeper's shelf and finds blank scorekeeper sheets. In the corner, she searches the announcer's table. She wonders if the boys may have been looking at a girlie magazine. Next, she lies down on the grubby, grimy floor and rolls over on her back. Pushing with her heels, she gyrates to slide up underneath the scorekeeper's shelf. During her acrobatics, Garvin's hat falls off her head. Thinking that the hat is more of a nuisance than a trophy, she does not retrieve it. After diligently searching underneath the scorekeeper's shelf, she rules out that anything secret might be hidden there. During the course of standing up, she knocks over the upside down wastebasket. The unexpected sound scares her. The wastebasket tumbles end over end and travels across the floor. Her eyes behold a magazine on the floor.

Immediately, she crawls out from underneath the scorekeeper's shelf and sits up in the middle of the floor. Curious, she flips the magazine over to feast her eyes on the front cover. Much to her surprise, it's a game day program for the Gunslingers. It must be the program from the Gunslinger's game that Willie attended with his father. She reasons the program might be what she needs to use to get on Willie's good side. She decides to keep it a secret, at least for the time being. Glancing over at what must be Garvin's all-star baseball cap, she decides to leave it underneath the scorekeeper's shelf on the floor. The odd positioning of the cap makes the appearance less conspicuous than if she decides to let it rest in the middle of the floor. Weezie craftily theorizes that Garvin and his cronies will receive the blame for breaking into the scorekeeper's box. She thinks to herself that the baseball cap would be the perfect clue for Officer Higby to suspect Garvin. Smiling with a devious smirk, she gloats regarding the turn of events. While summarizing the events, she realizes that the longer she stays in the scorekeeper's box, the more opportunity there is for a recreation worker or one of Garvin's buddies to accidently discover her there. Clutching tightly to the game day program, she hustles down the stairs, races through the chain link fence gate by the dugout, and across the infield to reach the outfield boundary and enter Rayner Park.

ODD MAN OUT

When the car comes to a stop in the driveway, Willie jumps out and hustles around the car to the back yard gate. He flings open the gate and sprints around to the steps. Quickly, he scales the porch stairs and bulldozes through the screen door to the porch. Angry, he storms across the screened in porch to the two-seat swing and sits down. Sullen, he oscillates on the swing while picking at the sand and gravel imbedded in the wounds on his elbows.

His mother peeks through the kitchen window and casts her eyes on Willie's scratched-up arms. She grabs a clean terrycloth towel and brings out a large bowl of lukewarm water. She places the bowl on the wicker table and dabs his elbows with the towel to clean the abrasions.

His father casually enters the porch from the kitchen door, and strolls over to sit down in the wicker chair next to the table. After a refreshing sip of ice tea, he begins the discussion. "Well, son, I think you have some explaining to do."

"Dad, I did nothing wrong," Willie defends himself. "Garvin was picking on Weezie. I tried to stop him by talkin'. Garvin started calling us names. Gooch was a Fu Manchu. He said there won't be a Little League expansion this year. I lost my temper and railed on him."

"You know fighting never settles anything?" responds Willie's father. "You prove who can win a fight that about sums up fighting. Whatever started the fight still remains unfinished business afterward."

"Nope, only wanted to teach him a lesson because he was putting my friends down. I don't like for anyone to put people down 'cause they're different. That's what you taught me!" explains Willie in his defense.

"Well, son, you may have taught him you're the better fighter. You didn't teach him a lesson. And, you certainly didn't settle anything. In my opinion, you may have stirred the pot. He might be head hunting and you're head will be the one he wants more than anyone else," his father says before enjoying a drink of iced tea. "If you were me, what would your punishment be?"

"I guess; I uh." Willie struggles with his answer. "I think maybe being stricted for a week."

"If you fight again between now and the end of the year, that's after Christmas, then you leave me no choice. I'll put you on full restriction. That means no TV, no telephone, and no friends visiting..." He thinks momentarily then qualifies his statement. "The restriction might be for only a week, maybe more. Do you understand?" questions his father.

"Yes, sir. I do." Willie accepts the terms of the restriction. He raises his elbow and cleans more grit from the wound using the damp towel.

"I can't say for sure, but I think you both may have been wrong trying to resolve a disagreement with a fight. Check with a counselor at the YMCA. He might have some suggestions for you," Willie's father says, offering another avenue to settle his differences with Garvin. "And, son, fighting will not get you on a Little League team. The Junior League has an opportunity to bring home a Metro-League Championship for Skeeter Hill this year. They should put together one hell of a group of teams with the planned expansion. Everyone in the Downtown Business Association has thrown their support that way." Willie's father explains his reasoning for supporting the Junior League expansion.

"So? Wha...what about the Little League?" Willie quizzes his father concerned that Garvin may have been right.

"Well, the Little League might not get any expansion teams this year. The Youth Sports Authority plans to expand the Junior League. Some of the boys who played Little League last year will be allowed to play Junior Youth League ball if they relax some of the rules. That will be more Junior League players and fewer players for Little League. That means Little League will keep the same number of teams. Not enough money for both Little League and Junior League."

"Dad, we can raise more money—car washes, selling candy, can recycling."

"Won't matter; we'll need a lot more to pay for at least four more teams for Junior League first. The decision will be made in the fall meeting to budget and plan for next spring."

"I can sell my baseball cards!" Willie suggests enthusiastically to part with some of his precious collection.

"That's pretty generous on your part. Won't be enough, son. Money will be tight adding more Junior League teams with new uniforms, bats, and catchers' equipment." Willie's father explains the monetary complexities of the expansion.

"What you're saying is that without Little League expansion, I might not get on a team... that means my friends might not get on a team! ...and worst of all we won't get on the same team."

"Baseball teams are expensive. Junior League expansion will be this year; maybe expand Little League next year." His father reiterates.

"That's rotten. I always have to wait until next year. Wait until next year, Willie. First, the professional baseball players go on strike. Now, I learn all the grownups care about is the darn Junior League for a rotten trophy to sit in a display case downtown." Willie blasts the monetary formulary. "I can't believe they want to take our Little League money and give it to the Junior League!"

"Willie, this year might be the last chance we will have to capture a metro-championship because Remcore Technologies is shutting down and people will move away. That's the youth baseball in a nutshell: economics and politics."

"You're saying Junior League is more important! Well, I'm running out of opportunity to play in Little League with my buddies. And I want to play with my friends! May not have next year 'cause some of them might be moving away thanks to that fricking Remcore..." Willie insinuates according to his father's logic.

"Son! You watch your language! The fall Skeeter Hill Town Hall planning meeting will decide on expansion and the future of next spring's Little League program. By deciding on the expansion teams now, players can work together to raise more money for their team." He pauses to weigh his words. "My guess is the Skeeter Hill Junior League will have some great players coming up from Little League. We'll know what the Youth Sports Authority has to say next Saturday night."

"Just ain't fair. It's wrong, all wrong! It's coming down to the Junior League or me!" Willie warns as he bolts into the house from the porch, runs through the kitchen, and rushes across the living room and up the stairs. Sniveling, he continues his journey down the hallway into his bedroom. Inside, he slams his bedroom door. The WILLIE'S LOCKERROOM sign swings back and forth and eventually falls to the floor. Overcome with heartache and disappointment, he curls up on his bed.

Burying his head in a pillow, he bursts into tears. More than anything Willie wants to strike out against the world. A sense of betrayal wells up inside. His thoughts drift to the fond memories about the hopes and dreams he had during the days he played T-ball at four years of age. Every week he got excited about going to practice. Moreover, during the games he could show off in front of his mom and dad as well as his teammates' parents. No one could take that away from him. He concludes Skeeter Hill needs to support T-ball. He can't suggest eliminating T-ball to save money.

Next, he recalls the days of Peewee ball. Fielding and hitting in the Peewee League were an unequalled highlight. Batting rules proved to be a different story. After three strikes, the coach let the batter hit off an adjustable batting T. He felt he had outgrown the adjustable batting T by the time he could play in Peewee. Willie thought an adjustable T did not develop anything except a crazy, outrageous blind swing. If a batter didn't get it in T-Ball, then Peewee play was too late. The coach said, "Peewee baseball is intended to develop the skills of baseball." At six years old, Willie played in the Slow-Pitch league. It was different from the Peewee league because coach did not pitch the ball or use the adjustable T. No one really knew how to control a pitch throwing over hand so the pitcher delivered the pitch underhand. Peewee ball helped him learn skills of batting and throwing. Doing without Peewee ball won't save much money.

The Slow-Pitch and Fast-Pitch league proved to be more fun and the games move along faster. Those were good times and the city should give them support. Now, he has attained the age to play real baseball: Little League. The idea of Izzie, Wee Bones, Punzak, and Gooch on different teams shatters the dream they shared since slow pitch. Without his friends, it would not be the same. Sure, in Skeeter Hill Little League he got a uniform and wore shoes with rubber cleats. Wee Bones and Izzie played T-ball with him and the tee shirt inspired the same connotation as having a uniform. Gooch joined the "threesome" during the first year of Peewee baseball. They joked about being the "four amigos" and sometimes "three amigos plus one." He remembers graduating from Peewee ball to Slow-Pitch. When Punzak played on the same team in fast-pitch, the band of friends changed the name to the "fabulous five." Each of the players contributed to team play. The Coyotes did not have a reputation of being a team to be reckoned with but the boys enjoyed playing youth baseball and had a fun time. He convinces himself players need slow-pitch and fast-pitch if they really want to go onto Little League baseball. How many years must a player have to endure before he can play on a Little League team with his buddies?

Willie recalls standing in the batter's box at the Skeeter Hill Little League baseball field and pretending to be Hank Aaron, Sammy Sosa, or Tommy Tomlinson. He re-lives the dream of making the final out to win a championship game like Javon almost did two years ago with the Lumberjacks. He hopes someday it might not be merely a dream.

Unable to hold back his emotions and confusion, Willie bursts into tears crying profusely in his pillow. His aspiration of playing with his friends in Little League means more than words can express. Just once he wants the opportunity to point to center field like Babe Ruth and try to hit a home run. When the dust settles, the last out made, he wants to be carried off the field as the most valuable player. *Those old fogies don't know anything,* he thinks. Again he buries his head in the pillow to cry and cry and cry.

Playing in the Skeeter Hill Little League means a coming of age, a graduation. All of his hopes and dreams rests with the town hall meeting.

Unexpectedly, the bedroom door bursts open like a cyclone struck it. Willie pops his head up to cast his eyes on Gooch, Izzie, Punzak, and Wee Bones invading his bedroom privacy. Without hesitation he sits up and dangles his legs over the side of his bed. Using the sleeve of his jersey, he wipes the tears away from his eyes. Gooch hands Willie the sign that fell on the floor. He continues to saunter over to the chair. Casually he turns the chair around and sits down resting his arms on the top of the back rest of the chair. Izzie lands on the baseball beanbag, Punzak sits Indian style on the floor, and Wee Bones finds his usual place on top of the empty plastic crate Willie often uses for his dirty laundry.

"Guess you didn't get grounded. Your mom let us in. Saw your sign saying 'out,' but we knew better," Gooch surmises with a grin.

"Did ya get walloped?" asks Punzak with an impish look on his face.

After a few deep breaths and a sigh, Willie gains his composure to speak. "Naw, didn't get nothing," Willie answers.

"If ya didn't get walloped, then what's the water works all about?" Izzie questions with a puzzled look on his face.

Willie clears his throat. "Garvin said there might not be enough Little League teams. My dad told me that Garvin might be right because the Skeeter Hill City big wigs will support the Junior League expansion 'cause they want a trophy, real bad. In my opinion, the Junior League teams should pay to play. They have their own metro-league championship in the big city. Gotta get more Little League teams."

"Gee, we're benched before we get a chance to step onto the field," Wee Bones elaborates.

"Only the best players will be selected by the coaches to play on a Little League team with only a few teams. They will apply the cut rule for Little League because there's not enough teams for everyone to play." Willie sniffles while describing the Little League scenario. "We don't have a chance. When I was nine, Dad didn't think I was old enough to play against the twelve-year-old players. Then I broke my leg when I was ten. Ruled me out that year. The next year, Tornado season in April took insurance agents like my dad and church people like my mom. I had to quit baseball and stay with my Aunt Judith Ann in Texas."

Gooch says, "Yeah. My mom wouldn't let me play none when I was nine, remember? When I was finally nine, I got told I couldn't play 'cause I'd get hurt. Then we went to Japan when I was ten to visit her relatives," Gooch explains. "They play real young there. When I came home this July, she said I could play if I could get on a team. Well guys, I'll be eleven next year in April and an old man before I get to play any Little League."

Wee Bones jokes, "I played on different teams all the way through... thought you guys didn't like me." He laughs thinking someone might say something. "I've played every year without you guys. Been playing since fast ball."

"I've played on and off," says Izzie. "Coaches don't seem to want to let me pitch. They'd play their own kid instead. You know how that goes," complains Izzie.

"You think you got it bad?" chimes Punzak. "Well, try being dragged all 'round the country with your ol' man for a boss and being his pack mule. I'd rather have been playing Little League any day of the week."

"Life gets tough when you get older," Wee Bones quips. "I bet if we all got on the same team we could prove ol' Officer Higby wrong. We could show him we can do something and make something out of ourselves. I bet we'd be better than the other teams."

Willies says, "Well the way I see it, we're all about eleven or twelve and have one or two years to play Little League. Remcore moving people outta town is our biggest problem. This year is our only year!"

"Anyone wanting to play Little League should be able to play," insists Gooch as he shuffles through the baseball cards he picked up from the floor. "Never heard of not having enough Little League teams to go around. Shoulda stayed with cousin Yuuta."

"What ya say we round up all of the Skeeter Hill Little League players to show up at that town hall planning meeting on Saturday night," Punzak suggests as a measure of protest.

"Everyone could wear their baseball caps and chant, 'Who are we for? Little League!' Kind of catchy, isn't it?" Izzie recites his made-up protest chant.

"Yeah, and holdup those signs like we see on TV when people walk in front of places they don't like," suggests Gooch.

"I like, 'We will rock you.' Then we stomp our feet on the floor like at the big team games." Wee Bones chimes in with his idea to help with a protest.

"That's it," Willie shouts. "I've got it!"

"What—we stomp on the floor? Won't your parents get mad?" Wee Bones suggests while thinking they might practice in Willie's bedroom.

"No, we do like the adults. We'll have a campaign," Willie declares.

"But, there's not an election. Besides, none of us are old enough to run for office or anything important," Gooch replies confused how a campaign figures into playing baseball.

"No, this ain't an election. We'll campaign for the Skeeter Hill Junior League!" Willie blurts out with an anxious tone.

Gooch replies, "Now, I think you've lost it. You want us to support the Junior League. Come on, Willie, get real." Gooch flings a card toward the waste basket in the corner.

"Yeah, they've got enough support without our help," objects Izzie.

"Listen up. I'm not saying we campaign for them to win anything. What I'm saying is we campaign for them to lose." urges Willie as he slide off the bed to stand up.

Punzak says, "Did your mom give ya any of that pain type medicine? You know the powerful drugs your doctor says you can get? You're talking kinda funny. Way out there kinda funny."

Willie ignores the comment and says, "Izzie, you go home and get as many cans of that powder kind of paint your mom uses for her projects. You know the kind of paint she mixes with water. Get as much white paint as you can get; colors will work just the same. Gooch, you need to go by your dad's grocery. Grab about three of those small blocks of dry ice; that's about how many my dad used for Fright Night last Halloween. Remember to wear those big rubber gloves, and bring them along. Wee Bones, meet Gooch at the grocery with your wagon and bring the biggest hammer from your dad's workshop—the bigger the hammer the better. Gotta break up the ice, and grab one of the plastic hand sprayers he has us use to spray around your yard. Punzak, you stop by Smitty's Hardware. Yesterday, they spray-painted their front window for the Labor Day specials. Get as many of the empty spray paint cans you can get from the dumpster out back. They usually put all of the spray cans in a trash bag. Grab the trash bags; they should make your job easier. The fall PTA planning meeting is tonight. Meet me in the alley behind my dad's insurance office. Be there about seven o'clock tonight. Don't tell a soul! Say, you're going to Chelsea's for ice cream or something. Find an excuse."

The conspirators talk in confidence as they exit Willie's bedroom. They question if Willie's plan might get them into trouble. Apprehensive, Wee Bones whispers going down the steps to the living room, "What does dry ice have to do with a sprayer or empty paint cans?

Punzak wonders out loud in the hallway, "Yeah, what good are the empty paint cans? His plan is a little looney if you ask me."

Gooch asks, "How will this help the Skeeter Hill Little League? I think we're heading down the road to getting into trouble."

They clam up and scamper down the stairs and march single file out the front door. From his chair at the dining room table, Mr. Wince observes the peculiar behavior. He is perplexed by their early departure. *Perhaps the altercation with Garvin played a role in the more subdued demeanor. Must be the reason,* Willie's father concludes before he *returns to the PTA business.*

After dinner, Willie's father calls up the staircase to Willie. "Son, your mom and I are going to PTA." Willie opens his bedroom door and steps into the hallway. "It's the school year planning meeting. Might take a little longer than when school is in session. Should be home a little after ten o'clock. Take the trash out, close all the windows, and get to bed early. Might need your help at the office in the morning. Be good! Remember our understanding."

Willie's mother and father walk out the front door. He hears the spring on the screen door creak and then the screen door slams against the door jamb. Wasting little time, Willie rushes downstairs and locks the front door and flicks off the lights to the living room. Spinning around, he returns up the stairs to his bedroom.

Willie slides across the floor to his bed. Reaching under his bed, he pulls out the plastic storage under drawer and opens it. Quickly he sorts through the magazine pages he saved and tosses selected pages on his bed. He takes the scissors from his desk and then cuts out headlines and photos from the magazine pages. The clippings of photos are set aside in one pile and lettering clippings in another pile.

Finally, Willie slips his dark blue Cub Scout hoody over his head and twists his body and wiggles back and forth for his head to crown in the opening at the top. He tugs and pulls until the hoody finally slips over his head. After slipping into his jogging shoes, he grabs his navy blue knit ski cap, obtains his Cub Scout pocket flashlight, and rushes over to the bed for the clippings. He uses the front side pockets of his hoody to keep the clippings separate. Without any additional preparation he races out his bedroom door, skips down the stairs, and runs through the house turning lights off and closing the windows in the living room, dining room, and kitchen. With all the windows closed and only the living room light on, he prepares to leave for downtown. In the back yard, he snatches the trash can and drags everything to the street. He puts on the dark blue ski cap. Hugging the shadows, he sneaks toward the downtown to Pioneer Square.

After arriving at the alley behind his father's office, he shines the flashlight ahead of him to scare off raccoons, cats, and mice scavenging the trash. He hurries to the back door of his father's office. Once he retrieves the hidden office key box, he locates the key and unlocks the office door. In reverse fashion he replaces the office door key in the designed hiding space by replacing the brick to conceal the key.

In the distance, Willie recognizes the silhouettes of Gooch and Wee Bones as they trudge down the alley. Changing his point of view to the other direction in the alley he casts his eyes on Izzie and Punzak plodding down the alley in his direction. When everyone joins him at the door he sets the plan in motion.

"Gooch, bring the wagon with the dry ice inside. Don't want anyone seeing it."

Next, Willie orders, "Everyone get inside." One by one the boys single file into the insurance agency office. Willie follows Punzak and closes the door. "Don't turn on any lights. Be extra careful what you touch. Only things on the break room table can be outta place. Keep the light pointed down on the floor at all times. Everyone follow me to the break room door and wait there until I come back."

"We ain't gonna get in trouble are we, Willie? Are we?" questions Wee Bones afraid there might be consequences should they get caught.

"Not if everyone listens and minds their own business. Don't go messing with things in the office!"

The band of conspirators trail Willie down the hallway until they reach the break room door on the right. In the break room, Willie turns the flashlight upside down in the middle of the table to rest on the flat end of the handle like a lamp. The flashlight illuminates the room enough without having to turn on the ceiling light. Willie leaves the motley group in the dimly lit break room. He departs and then returns moments later with his arms full. Grabbing the bag of tempura containers from Izzie, he sorts through the paint containers. He lines them up carefully on the table.

Willie says, "There are four cans of white, a blue, a green, a couple of red, and a couple yellow tempura containers." He matches the paint cans up with empty water bottles. "Fill the sprayer with white paint. Use a lot of powder paint. Then ya fill it up. Put the colored powder paint in the empty water bottles to the line here. Then fill them up with water." He points to the ring above the bottom of the disposable water bottles. "I can get you more because Jasmine recycles them. She doesn't count them. There's a bunch in the box.

There's a faucet in the large sink inside the closet in the hallway. I've got to make flyers. If you need me, I'll be at the desk by the copier."

Willie gets a couple sheets of blank paper from the copier to use for his project. At Jackie's desk, he removes the clippings from his pockets and spreads them out on top of the desk. Without delay he searches through the collection of clippings with bold type to use for a headline. In no time at all, he spells out, JUNIOR LEAGUE RULES. After taping the letters to a blank sheet of paper, he sorts through the pile of photographs for a player of his choosing. After deliberating, he selects a picture of the Minnesota Avengers team celebrating the World Federation Championship defeating the Atlanta Sharpshooters. Across the bottom of the page, he tapes the selected words, "Little League sucks." Underneath the phrase, he puts in larger lettering, "Junior League Rules." He arranges a photo of Conrad Schmidt from the New York Generals in the left bottom corner of the flyer. In the right bottom corner, he places Darrel Driskell from the Lumberjacks. He scampers over to the hallway and calls out to the break room. "Hey guys come in here." He collects four different ink pens from the receptionist desk container and places the mock up flyer in the center of the desk. The foursome meets him at the desk.

"I want you to come up with two Junior League player's names. Everyone must have two different names of players from last year or going to be players this year. Then, take two different pens. On the paper wherever you want to write, in a place on each side of the picture of the Minnesota Avengers picture one name. Write each name with a different pen. It'll look like different people signed their name on the flyer."

Izzie tries his hand by scribbling a name with one pen on one side of the picture and with the different pen on the other side. Gooch follows and picks up two pens. He studies the names Izzie wrote and writes two names of his own. The two remaining boys switch off writing the names on the posters. Willie scribbles *Garvin Hackworth* on top in the middle. Taking two different pens, he writes *Huggable* and *Turk* on opposite sides of the picture of the Minnesota Avengers.

"Thanks guys; we got it," proclaims Willie putting the pens away. In the meantime, the boys pass it around for approval.

Resolutely, Willie walks over and places the flyer on the glass top of the copier and closes the cover. After making his selection for fifty copies, he watches as the copier scanning light illuminates to

47

scan the flyer for each copy. Without warning he notices the flicker of a light flash through the front window facing the Pioneer Square. Repeatedly, the bright laser from the copier streaks across the ceiling piercing the darkness. Willie drops to the floor and scrambles around the copy stand to search for the wall plug behind the copier. Izzie rushes down the hall to the break room to turn off the flashlight. Willie gropes around for the cord connected to the copier. Punzak immediately peels off his coat and places it on top of the copier to shield the spray of light through the glass. Wee Bones rushes to the wall by the front window to be the lookout. "It's a cop. He's walking up to the window."

The copier continues to produce copies. After finding the cord behind the leg of the copy stand, Willie desperately jerks it trying to release it from the outlet. The cord pops out of the wall outlet and the copier stops scanning. Immediately he crouches down behind the copier in the shadow by the wall. The blue hoody and dark pants blend into the darkness.

"It's the cops," whispers Wee Bones as he crouches down by the window. "Get down!"

"We're screwed," mumbles Gooch. "We're screwed. I knew it!"

"Get outta sight. Go down the hall!" whispers Willie as loud as he can.

Instead, Gooch and Punzak hide in the shadows of the room behind desks. A flashlight beam reflects off the wall behind Jackie's desk. Willie eyeballs the magazine clippings, tape dispenser, and scissors on the desk. The light beam rests on the desk. Next, the light travels over toward the copier. Willie reaches up and snatches Punzak's jacket. Half a second later, the police flashlight beam scans the copier stand. The beam continues to dance around the room. The officer switches off the flashlight and saunters down the sidewalk. Darkness fills the office. Willie crawls over to the window and pulls back the blinds and watches the officer open the car door and slide inside the patrol car. The car backs up and moves down Miner Street. The patrol car shines the search light into selective stores along Miner Street. He waits until the patrol car turns at the corner at Miner Avenue.

"All clear!" Willie makes known as he stands up. Without delay, he returns to the copier. He plugs it back into the outlet.

Willie instructs Gooch on what to do with the flyers in his absence. He grabs a handful of flyers and goes to the break room.

In the break room, Willie takes Izzie and Punzak aside to give them their instructions. "I want you to put the water bottles with mixed paint in these trash bags you brought. Use these bags for the containers with unused or partially used powered paint to take back home."

He demonstrates to Punzak how to adjust the nozzle on the sprayer to get a direct spay instead of broadcasting a mist. "Go to the Skeeter Hill Little League baseball field with the sprayer, bottles of mixed paint, and some flyers. With the direct white spray, write "Junior League Rules" everywhere you can on a flat surface like the dugout or concession," Willie suggests. "Paint on the walls of the concession, on the dug outs, and on any flat surfaces that are big enough. Be artistic when you splash with the bottles and when you write "Junior League Rules" with the sprayer. When you're finished, take the enamel spray cans from the hardware and scatter them all over the area where you painted. Drop them on the ground. Don't be neat!" By indiscriminately littering the area with the enamel paint cans, Willie figures the first impression will be tagging. "That stuff in the cans will need the paint removing gunk to get off. The powder stuff in the water bottles can be washed off." Willie stresses before they leave. "Guys drop off the bag of containers with unused powered paint at the church on the square on your way to the baseball field. Hide them in the bushes. Be sure you bring back all the bags with the empty water bottles of paint and Wee Bone's dad's sprayer. When you're done, meet us at the church with the empty water bottles and the sprayer."

Willie continues, "Wee Bones, fill the empty water jugs with really, really hot water. Take your wagon with the dry ice, water jugs, and the hammer to the church on the square—you know, on the other side of the courthouse? Hide the wagon in the shadows by the steeple house and wait between the bushes until Gooch and I get there."

"Gotcha," replies Wee Bones, snugging up his coat for the long journey.

Inside, Gooch divides the remaining flyers up into two piles to distribute. Willie carefully removes two rolls of tape from behind the rolls stacked on the front on the shelf. He surmises Jeanine will not discover any rolls missing until ordering. Removing the rolls of tape from behind would leave the other rolls flush with the edge the way she arranges them.

He instructs Gooch to tape at least one flyer on every storefront going along Pioneer Street to the left of the Wince Insurance Agency. At the corner, he should continue down Wagon Trail Street to the church on the square. Gooch departs and goes about his assigned task to attach the flyers to the stores.

Willie knows the office must be left the same as when he arrived. Not knowing how the chairs were arranged in the break room, he turns the chairs upside down on the break table like the janitors does when he decides to wax the floor. Last but not least, he brings the mop bucket from the cleaning closet and leaves it next to the sink in the break room. The mop leans up against the wall by the doorway. Willie wants to suggest the janitor did not finish his job. Grinning, he steps back to admire his handiwork.

After a final walk through, Willie determines that everything is in its place with the tables and desks cleaned off. The desk chairs must be arranged properly or someone might suspect an intruder. Jackie wants her desk chair positioned back from the keyhole enough to see the seat. After sitting down on her birthday cake, she has a fetish about having her chair being positioned away from the desk. Jeanine wants her desk chair parked under the secretarial leaf that pulls out from the left side of the desk. She visualizes her chair in that position represents a dedicated work habit. Vonnie wants her chair pushed all the way into the keyhole of the desk. She likes everything nice and tidy. There is no evidence of the boys being there.

Satisfied everything has been cleaned up and in place, Willie grabs a roll of tape and his handful of flyers. He runs out the back door and makes sure it is locked before he dashes down the alley. Along the way, he tosses the trash bag with clippings, paper towels, and other trash into the dumpster behind Horace's Print Shop. Usually the print shop has to rush several printing orders the first of every morning. The trash from the print shop most likely will bury the trash bag he tosses into the dumpster. Willie squeezes through a tight crawl space between Jessop's Barber Shop and Chelsea's Drug store to reach Pioneer Street. The short cut saves valuable time.

Systematically, he moves from store to store taping the flyers on every storefront without exception. Occasionally, he waits in the shadows because of a passing car or on account of someone walking on the sidewalk. Gradually he works his way to the church in the square.

WHERE THERE IS SMOKE

In no time, Willie finishes his mission of distributing flyers on storefront windows and on the doors. Much to his surprise, he arrives at the church before Gooch. He has one flyer left when he approaches the church. A sneaky grin comes over his face as he starts his journey up the church lawn. He scampers around to the front door of the church. After applying one strip of tape on the top of the flyer, he decides another on the bottom of the flyer might be better. Then he affixes another piece of tape to the side. Before long he has plastered every side of the flyer with multiple pieces of tape. Satisfied, he makes the journey down to the sidewalk to meet up with Gooch.

Puzzled by the reason why Willie visited the front door of the church, Gooch questions him, "What were you doing at the front door of the church? You know they lock it at night?"

"Ya, I know. You remember the tour we had at Our Savior Lutheran Church as part of getting our merit badge?"

"I do, but what's that got to do with you taping that flyer to the church door?"

"You remember Pastor Michaels telling about that guy who used ninety-five nails to put a letter on the church door?" replies Willie with a smirk on his face.

"Yes. But what..."

"Well, I just stuck a flyer on the door with about ninety-five pieces of tape." Willie laughs at the stunt. The meaning of Willie's stunt confuses Gooch. He merely chuckles to humor him unaware of any hidden meaning. "Maybe Pastor Pennington will think it's funny. Anyways, I want Pastor Pennington to find it and think Garvin was the trouble maker. He's the 'Dennis the Menace' type at church."

Hearing the two exchange conversation, Wee Bones emerges from the darkness. "What took you so long?" asks Wee Bones with the wagon in tow.

Not expecting him, the stir startles Willie. "We-Wee Bones, you scared me! Whew! Guys, meet me at the steeple house door with the wagon. I'll be right back," Willie calls out as he jaunts toward the end of the driveway. In a flash, he disappears by the juniper bushes next to the shed. Moments later he returns with a thirty-two gallon aluminum trash can he wrestles with trying not to make any noise. Trying to keep as quiet as he can, he holds it up in the air as he takes a couple of steps at a time. Every other way he maneuvers the trash can to carry it is awkward and makes noise.

Izzie and Punzak race around the corner and meet Willie in the church driveway. Willie speaks up, "Hey guys, keep the containers of unused powered paint to put back on your mom's shelves that you hid under the bushes. Throw the empty water bottles in the dumpster over there, and give Wee Bones the paint sprayer for when he leaves."

"Gotcha, on my way," Izzie says arranging the bags in his hand before he sprints toward the dumpster. "I'll come back for the sprayer and the other bags in the bushes."

"Pastor kept this beat up old trash can behind the shed. We use it for garbage and trash when we mow the lawn. It'll be perfect for what I've got in mind. Give me a hand, Punzak; grab the handle and run with me over to the steeple house door."

Willie glances up at the clock on the courthouse tower. The clock reads, fifteen minutes after nine o'clock. He knows they do not have much time to complete his last and most important Junior League prank. At the steeple house sidewalk, Willie prepares to transfer the dry ice to the trash can.

"Bring the wagon over here on the sidewalk by the steeple house door." Willie instructs Gooch. Before proceeding, he acquires the oversized rubber gloves from the wagon. The gargantuan rubber gloves for the dry ice slide over his hands and above his elbows. His appearance with the hoody, a surprised expression on his face, and the oversized rubber gloves with his glasses resembles a mad junior scientist. The group laughs, and laughs, and laughs.

With the wagon in place, Willie takes the aluminum trash can and lowers the rim to the underneath the side of the wagon. "Okay, guys. Got it! Now, tip the wagon over. The blocks of ice should tip out of the wagon and fall into the trash can. Izzie and Punzak, you steady the bottom of the trash can so it won't roll. Gooch, hold the top of the trash so it won't tip. I will watch the dry ice to keep it from falling out. Everyone ready? One, two, three, let's go!" orders Willie. Wee Bones tilts the wagon for the three large blocks of dry ice to tumble out of the wagon past the lip of the trash can and slide down to the bottom of the trash can. *Thunk!* And a milla-second later, another *thunk!* Then the blocks jostle around the bottom of the trash can for a moment.

"Wee Bones, you got the hammer and the jugs of water?"

"Sure do," he replies scrambling over to the Juniper bush. "Got the water jugs here. The hammer is in the grass by Punzak next to the wagon."

Punzak spies the hammer in the grass. "I got the hammer. It's over here."

Willie cinches the hood of his hoody to avoid being pelted in the face by stray pieces of dry ice. On his knees, he cinches his hoody to prevent being pelted in the face with ice chips, and then he fumbles with the humongous gloves while he steadies the dry ice with one hand and chips away at the blocks of ice with his other hand. Gradually the three bricks of ice reduce to a pile of large chunks. "Hey, guys we did it!" Willie exclaims.

"Okay guys, we gotta stand it up!"

Punzak and Gooch grab the metal handles and hoist the trash can upward to stand it up. "Now, guys, carry the trash can up to the steeple house door."

Gooch and Punzak grunt and groan as they wrestle with the awkward trash dragging it up sidewalk leading to the steeple house door. Wee Bones runs ahead to open the door.

Willie glances up at the courthouse clock to see thirty-five minutes past nine o'clock. He worries the PTA meeting might adjourn early. He decides not to say a word. "Wait up guys. The door is locked." Immediately Willie drops the humongous gloves and hurries over to a large juniper shrub next to the steeple house and retrieves an oversized rock. Gripping the rock, he twists his hands in separate directions. The fake rock separates. Right away he removes a key from inside and runs over to the steeple house door. After he unlocks the door, he returns the key to the inside hallowed out space in the rock and hides the rock by the bush.

"How did you know a key was over there?" asks Izzie.

"I rang the church bell every Sunday morning for about a year. That was before I became an altar boy. Guess you can say it pays to go to church," Willie jokes as he swings the door open.

"Or, don't trust your local altar boy," quips Punzak laughing. The others join in the laughter.

Willie gives orders for his plan, "Take the trash can inside the steeple house and wait for me. Izzie, you grab the jugs of water from Wee Bones. Don't want you lifting that there trash can. Need to protect those precious pitching hands. Take my Cub Scout flashlight to shine up the steps to give us light. Wee Bones, you post guard." Willie rushes over to grab the gloves for the dry ice and slides them on over his hands and above his elbows.

Gooch and Punzak stand on the first step with their hands poised on the handles of the trash can. Willie steps inside the steeple door with the large rubber gloves to lift from the bottom. "Punzak, Gooch, let's do it, lift!" Punzak and Gooch move their heels to the next step and haul the trash can up the first step. Willie helps lifts from the bottom of the trash can until it slides onto the next step.

"Wee Bones, close the door," Willie calls back down the steps before he grunts lifting the trash can up to the next step.

"Shut up and lift," yells Gooch lifting on his side of the trash can.

Izzie shines the Cub Scout flashlight upward to illuminate the staircase. The boys slowly advance up the steps one at a time.

"Come on, Gooch," hollers Punzak. "Hey, Willie! Lift up your end."

Gooch replies with a grunt, "I'm lifting, dag gum it! Come on you're lagging on me!"

The sounds of the trash can banging against the steps, the grunts, and the groans echo in the dark eerie winding staircase. Occasionally, the boys take a break and exercise their fingers and rest their tired arms. Twisting and turning while balancing makes the journey with the trash can a little more difficult around the slight curves of the steeple house.

"Hey, Gooch, slide over to the side and push up on the handle while I lift from this side," instructs Punzak.

"I think we got it made once we get around the next turn," declares Gooch as he repositions his hands. "Willie, you're gonna have to push real hard because the last step is higher than the rest."

"Gotcha, I will bend over and put my back against it. Count off one, two, and three."

"Ready?" asks Gooch.

Punzak counts off to the appointed time for them to coordinate their efforts together, "One, two, three, lift!"

"Ungh, ooooha, ungh..." the boys grunt and groan in unison. All of a sudden the bottom lip of the trash can slips by the top step and onto the landing and slides across the plywood flooring. Punzak and Gooch nearly fall down but manage to keep the trash can upright. Gooch and Punzak set their feet on the belfry landing and stand up.

"Slap me five!" exclaims Gooch as he raises one hand about head-high, and pushes forward to slap the flat of his palm against the flat palm of Punzak's hand. They give each other a high-five over the top of the trash can.

"Made it! We're at the top!" declares Gooch shivering from the cold air rising from the cavity in the steeple house. "It's cold up here," he calls back down to Izzie.

"Take it over to the window. Haven't got much time," instructs Willie as stands up from the crouched lifting position and grabs a gallon of water from Izzie. "Drag it across the floor to the window opening. You can see the little window openings."

Punzak pulls on the handle and navigates. Gooch gently pushes from the other side. The two push and drag the trash can across the floor to the platform where the bell ringer stands to tug on the rope in order to ring the bell on Sunday mornings. They snug it against the window sill below the wood-louvered panels of the window. Willie hands Gooch the gloves for the dry ice. Izzie arrives with the other jug of water and the flashlight. After setting the water jug by the trash can, he inches over to the railing and directs the flashlight beam into the darkness below. The darkness swallows up the bright beam.

Amazed Gooch tells everyone, "Wow, that's a long way down," he comments as his voice echoes in the darkness.

"Racks my nerves. It's spooky up here. Let's get this over with," Punzak urges snatching the gallon bottle of water.

Willie twists the cap and holds up his gallon for Punzak to pretend clink for a toast. Punzak twists off the cap, clinks, and splashes the water over the chunks of dry ice in the bottom of the trash can. He leans back so the water does not splash up into his face. Willie raises and lowers the jug pretending to be a mixologist of sorts as the water splashes into the trash can. Everyone finds his performance comical.

"Okay, guys. Get the hell outta here! Everyone go home. Don't get caught. Remember, no one knows anything!"

"Willie! Catch." Izzie tosses the Cub Scout flashlight to Willie underhand. He cups his hands around it before losing it over the edge and leaving them in the dark.

"Good catch." Quickly Izzie scampers down the staircase ahead of the others. Willie shines the beam of light into the steeple house shaft ahead of them. Everyone follows in the shadows on their way down. All the while Willie hopes the small flashlight will illuminate the stairs enough for everyone to see in order to get down to the bottom of the stairway safely. One by one they file out of the door. Finally, Willie exits through steeple house door. He leaves the door open.

"Guys don't close the door. I'm leaving it open on purpose. I want 'em to think whoever did this left in a hurry," explains Willie.

"Gotta get going. Night." Wee Bones leaves with the sprayer and hammer pulling the wagon and disappears in the night. Izzy grabs the paint can bags and jogs into the darkness in order to catch up to Wee Bones.

"Hey, Gooch! You better get going. Don't want anyone seeing you. And drop off the gloves at your father's store tomorrow."

"Too chancy with everyone working—they might see me. Got enough time, so I'll run by and drop them next to the dumpster. Louie takes his smoke break there," suggests Gooch. "He's a little absent-minded. He'll think he left them by accident."

Willie throws the empty water jugs in the dumpster and jogs down the driveway. He jaunts across the courthouse lawn to Wagon Wheel Street. Short of breath, he slows down to jog at a steady pace. The clock in the tower of the courthouse begins to chime the hour. He looks up to view the back lit face of the clock that symbolizes the pioneer beacon of spirit. His eyes become drawn to the face on the clock that reads ten o'clock. He picks up the pace jogging home. Again, he jukes in and out of the shadows.

Courthouse Clock reads 10:00 pm

At the same time, Tyson Pemberle saunters out of Prospector Bar. Having enjoyed the hospitality of the bar since happy hour, he pauses on the sidewalk teetering back and forth trying to achieve a sense of balance. While standing on the sidewalk, he gazes up at the courthouse clock as it chimes the hour of ten o'clock. Something looks peculiar. He rubs his eyes and returns his stare at the clock. Nothing looks different about the clock then his eyes drift toward the church and are drawn to the smoke pouring out of the church steeple windows in the background. Alarmed by the smoke, he drops his keys and staggers back inside the bar. Unable to collect himself he stutters, "F-fa-fire cha-church, fa-fire." He turns and scurries outside to verify what he saw moments ago. He hopes someone will follow him.

"Ah, forget it; it's just another of them Tyson's jokes. Don't waste your time," Jeb comments as he sips on his beer. Carl observes the erratic behavior and wonders if there might be something worth investigating. He strolls over to the door and steps outside to gaze in the direction of the church in the square.

"Cha...cha...church," Tyson stammers and slurs his speech trying to draw attention to the cloud of smoke rising out of the steeple. The plumes of mist billow aimlessly out the window and float up against the star lit sky. "Fa...fa...fire!"

"Okay. I got it!" Carl responds. Immediately he races back inside Prospector Bar. "It's an emergency! Call 911. Have fire and rescue come, smoke is pouring out of the church steeple. Could be real bad! All volunteers over to the church!" The volunteer firefighters quickly evacuate. Sounds of sirens fill the tranquility of the late summer evening.

Two fire engines drive up onto the front lawn of the church. An ambulance pulls into the church driveway and parks. Pickup trucks and sports utility vehicles park catawampus in the street. In spite of the haphazard parking there is a lane to allow enough room for the police cars and emergency vehicles to snake in and out. The Skeeter Hill Police Patrol car maneuvers through the vehicles in the street to reach the church lawn and park. The bar lights on the vehicles illuminate the area. The fire department volunteers set up a perimeter in front of the church. Fire Chief Loomis surveys the church steeple. What he sees confuses him.

Fire Chief Loomis directs for the flood light on the ladder truck to shine on the top of the steeple house, "Gentlemen, something's odd about this. There's not any smoke scarring the louvers. Should detect some smoke damage and smell. I need a flashlight! I don't trust the staircase even in the daytime. Gotta do what I gotta do. Only one man suit up."

He straps on an oxygen tank and acquires protective headgear. Followed by a single firefighter, Captain Vince Barret, they enter the steeple house together. Inside he cautiously tests the strength of the first step to hold his weight. With an assuring nod he navigates the steps one at a time as he ascends to the church belfry platform.

At the top, he directs the flashlight beam across the platform landing. Through the foggy mist he sees the trash can next to the outside wall of the steeple below the window. Fire Chief Loomis scales the last step and reaches the old wooden platform in the belfry. Captain Barret follows close behind. Fire Chief Loomis takes off his oxygen mask.

"Vince, does it seem hot in here?" asks Fire Chief Loomis perplexed.

"Not at all. That's odd," Vince replies beginning to understand the reality of the situation.

"I think we've got a hoax on our hands," Fire Chief Loomis exclaims. "Gotta check this out. Trash can has intentionally been placed there for our benefit." Fire Chief Loomis surveys the interior of the steeple with his flashlight. A continuous cloud of mist rises up and tumbles out through the opening in the louvers.

Captain Barret quickly removes his glove and pats the side of the trash can with his bare hand to test for temperature. "Chief, check this out." He holds his hand on the side of the trash can a little longer than expected if it were hot. He steadies his hand to indicate the trash can is not hot to the touch.

"That's odd? The trash can is a little bit cold if you ask me." mentions Captain Barrett.

Simultaneously the two men shine their flashlights into the trash can. Their investigation becomes clouded by the mist from the dry ice and water fog.

"I'm going to get to the bottom of this," says Fire Chief Loomis as he advances to the staircase. "Bring that dam trash can with you." The two men descend the stairs.

Volunteer firefighters guard the perimeter outside the steeple house and wait. Spectators point at the steeple while engaging in conversation. Tension no longer fills the air because the dry ice fog has abated no longer wafts out of the louvered windows. Pastor Pennington stands next to the fire truck and waits for word from Fire Chief Loomis.

Mr. Wince saunters up the driveway approaches Pastor Pennington, "The Elders figure the steeple would have to go sometime, always suspected a fire might be the reason why." Comments Mr. Wince staring up at the top of the steeple.

"Ya never know, Wilfred. God works in mysterious ways. Wind or fire? Who knows," replies Pastor Pennington looking away from the steeple into the night. "Might be a message."

Mr. Hackworth joins the conversation. "Might have to relocate the church bell closer to the ground. I've seen church bells on a pedestal. Don't look too shabby."

"Have to give it some thought," answers Pastor Pennington. "Found this on the front door, Mr. Hackworth. Has your son's name on it. He's given top billing. Know anything about it?" inquires Pastor Pennington with a stern look on his face.

"He's pretty worked up about being in the Junior League next spring. Didn't think it would come to this. Gotta talk to that boy," casually comments Mr. Hackworth. "Boys will be boys."

The men continue to converse while they watch the activity around the steeple house.

Fire Chief Loomis exits the steeple house door and marches through the perimeter of volunteer firefighters and says, "Ladies, Gentlemen, everyone can go home. There's no fire. False alarm! You can go home, now. Church is not on fire. Put away the marshmallows."

"I beg your pardon, Chief. But in my book, where there is smoke there's fire," objects Gus Iverson pointing toward the steeple.

"Take a deep breath, Gus. Tell me, do you smell wood burning?" Chief Loomis decides to color what he says with a touch of humor as he surveys the audience. "Tell me if it's oak or pine?"

Captain Barret carries the trash can out of the steeple house. "Gus, I'll show you the fire," responds Fire Chief Loomis as he grabs the lip of the trash can and flips it upside down on the grass. Water splashes in every direction leaving the dry ice to sit on top of the lawn. A mist engulfs him and the firefighters next to the dry ice. Fire Chief Loomis retrieves his flashlight from his firemen's belt. He scrolls the beam on the remainder of the dry ice on the grass. The crowd sees the remains of the chunks of dry ice as the mist dies down. "This may be someone's idea of a prank but its serious business. Tonight we had an impromptu fire drill thanks to whomever." He turns off his flashlight and approaches Pastor Pennington.

"Well, Pastor. What we have here is a fog like mist with dry ice mixed with water. Have your insurance agent check with the fire department examiner to verify the integrity of the structure. Need to verify if the steeple is structurally sound. I doubt anything will be significant. Just the same maybe something else might turn up," suggests Fire Chief Loomis.

"I certainly will have the integrity of the structure checked. We have young boys climb the stairs on Sunday morning to ring the church bell. It's a little old-fashioned or maybe nostalgic in my book. I always have said, if you ring it, they will come." The pastor chuckles as he jokes

Trying to go to sleep proves to be another story for Willie. The exploits with his friends replay in his mind over and over. He thinks through every detail of the pranks in case there might be a clue that could get them in trouble. Finally, he drifts off to sleep with visions of Little League dancing in his head.

In the morning sleepy eyed Willie steps across the hallway to the bathroom, he hears his father's voice. He takes a moment to eavesdrop. He's curious who his father might be talking to instead of being at his office downtown. He tip toes down the hallway to the steps. Continuing to eavesdrop, he slides down a couple stairs to listen.

"I tell you, Wilfred, these kids are nothing but a bunch of juvenile delinquents. They plastered my downtown with flyers, created a fire hoax, and trashed the Skeeter Hill Baseball Field," details Officer Higby. "It'll take a lot of elbow grease to remove that paint on the concession and in the dugouts."

"What do you mean trashed the baseball field?" asks Wilfred.

"First of all, there are the crudely made handouts plastered everywhere, on the concession, the trash cans, and the dugouts. The boys had the gumption to sign the dang thing. At least the department knows who to round up. Then there is the matter of paint—"

"Wait a minute! What was printed on what handouts?" Wilfred inquires nursing his hot cup of coffee.

"I thought you might ask. I brought one of those handouts like things."

Willie sticks his head between two of the banister rungs in the staircase and cocks his head to peer around the corner into the dining room. He observes Officer Higby remove a flyer from the inside pocket of his police jacket. A brief moment of silence interrupts the conversation. He unfolds evidence and slaps it down on the table. "See here, it's pretty simple: Junior League Rules. Look at all them signatures!"

"...and you said paint?" Wilfred recalls somewhat confused about the order of the mayhem.

"Yes, they painted the concession, the dugouts, and the trash cans. Now get this. They did not throw the paint cans in the trash cans. No! No! No! The paint cans were scattered all over on the ground. Real mess to clean up if you ask me. Must've been ten or twelve by my guess, maybe more. There's downtown, the ball field, and the church."

"Somebody's got a big head. This definitely must be discussed at the town meeting next Saturday night," Wilfred suggests intently eyeing the flyer. "Boys had this planned out ahead of time by my guess."

Willie hears the grandfather clock downstairs chime nine times. Confident he will not be needed at his father's office, he decides it's time to go to Chelsea's. Willie wriggles his head back through the rungs on the staircase. Once he has freed himself, he runs back down the hall to the bathroom.

The soda fountain serves as a hangout for the kids and teenagers after school or following sports contests. In the front of the store Chelsea stocks cigarettes, pipe tobacco products, and cheap cigars for C.J. Heinze and his friends. Everyone calls it the tobacco corner. Throughout the day the men congregate in the in front of the store in the tobacco corner to crank up the rumor mill and banter about the most popular subject.

Excited about hearing the stories and rumors pertaining to the pranks orchestrated last night, Willie runs into the bedroom and changes out of his pajamas into his Gunslinger shirt and pants. Before leaving he grabs his sunglasses, Gunslinger baseball cap, and a stack of baseball cards as a cover story for his reason to go to Chelsea's in case his dad asks. When he approaches the stairs, he hears Officer Higby ranting and raving about the events around the downtown. Apparently Officer Higby deems the pranks to have priority over any other pressing police business to investigate. Willie decides to continue to eavesdrop.

"You know we found an All-Star baseball cap in the corner of the scorekeeper box. It's an Atlanta Braves baseball cap, not Atlanta Sharpshooters. It's got a Fred McGriff patch stitched on the back. I happen to know that one of the Junior League expansion teams might be named the Braves. I'm not sure but I'm thinking it belongs to the Garvin kid, a junior team wannabe. Must admit there's a strong connection. See his name on top of the flyer?"

"I think you're jumping to conclusions based on circumstances." Mr. Wince cautions Officer Higby's concept of guilty before proven innocent.

"You want circumstance and coincidence?" Officer Higby angrily replies.

"Well, I think you're trying to build a case by reading into the evidence. Be objective," charges Mr. Wince as he tentatively slurps up a little more hot coffee.

"Wilfred, listen to this: 'Crime Dog' happens to be the nickname of a professional baseball player named McGriff who reluctantly adopted the name because of a cartoon dog created that the police used to raise awareness regarding crime prevention."

"Wendell Higby, where are you going with this?"

"Hear me out. The story goes that McGriff preferred the nickname 'Fire Dog' because of a fire in the press box on the day the Atlanta Braves signed him to a contract from the San Diego Padres. It's a bit of a coincidence finding an Atlanta Braves All Star cap in our press box, don't ya think? Press box fire? Atlanta team cap?"

"Well, Wendell, that sure is coincidence. Great stuff if you're writing a book," jokes Mr. Wince slurping up his coffee.

"That boy figures into a lot more than a little tussle with your son. It's odd he picks a fight with your son on the same day there's a breaking and entering of the press box at the baseball field, not to mention vandalism. We have another breaking and entering at the church on the square. I don't know what you call the distributing of those handouts. No permit? Well, then I call it littering." Officer Higby continues to build his case.

"I'm still trying to make sense of the handouts. Clearly, it's not a sales promotion because there's not any mention of a Labor Day sale or a new product like Mean Mountain Accident Picker Upper. It's not introducing a service like winterizing a home or car. It's not arguing a point of view like abortion rights. It's plain and simple: the Junior League blowing their horn."

Willie decides there's nothing more to hear and scrambles down the last eight steps to the landing at the bottom. "Going to Chelsea's. Bye!" He skates through the front screen door, sprints across the porch, and skips down to the front steps to the walk below. Since no one calls to him to come back to the house, he continues to Chelsea's.

On the way to Chelsea's Drug Store, Willie ponders what the outcome of the pranks will be. Will the police department charge Garvin with a crime? He knew once the events were set in motion there was not any way of stopping the rumors and gossip except with the truth. The problem with divulging the truth meant his friends would get in trouble.

On a lighter note, maybe Chelsea's Drug Store might prove to be intriguing. Perhaps the rumors might provide him with an answer. During the middle of the day, C.J. Heinze usually holds his provocative discussion session at the tobacco corner in the store. Bystanders, onlookers, and businessmen crowd the tobacco corner to listen to the pillar of the community expound on his views and perceptions. He served as mayor of Skeeter Hill twice. During his first term, he promoted the construction of a one-stop shop multipurpose superstore retail center with a grocery and department store combined in the same building surrounded by a shopping plaza. The multiplex shopping center would carry the name, Homesteader Shopping Plaza, and be the most innovative shopping experience of any town in the metropolitan area. Retired members of the community could get all of their shopping and personal errands managed in the strip mall and grocery complex. As a public figure, C.J Heinze is a person to promote a subject, topic, or an idea. At the same time, he is not a person to have champion against a cause. Smitty's Hardware provides another soapbox for the men to visit and discuss issues and topics of the day. At Smitty's Hardware, men engage in a mutual discussion instead of being led exclusively by a prominent discussion leader like C.J. Heinze. Usually the men do not have the luxury of time to stay and visit because they need a part or tool to complete a job or task. The only discussion occurs over the cashier counter or may last as long as a styrofoam cup of coffee.

Aunt Bea's Beauty Salon, on Miner Street, around the corner from Chelsea's Drug Store, serves as the ladies' gossip and rumor center in the downtown. Faster than the speed of light, a rumor flashes through the downtown stores and into plazas and shopping centers. The moment C.J. Heinze addresses an issue, the women manage to hand off the details faster than a baton in a relay race. A story or rumor spending any amount of time in the beauty salon will have a personalized embellishment before walking out the door. The beauty salon functions as the social media center for Skeeter Hill.

Today, Willie speculates whether the discussion will concentrate on the Junior League or juvenile crime. In the distance, he can see the orange and white sign with black Rexall Drug Store letters. He has chills of excitement. He can hardly wait until he strolls inside and hears the news of the day.

Inside the drug store, Willie observes epic volumes of customers. Walking straight ahead he is surprised by the number of women shopping for stationary products and greeting cards. Must be more in that department shopping than he witnessed during the Christmas holidays last year. Veering to his right, he must pick a path through the congestion of customers browsing for cold and allergy medications or the always popular vitamin supplements. He threads his way through floor displays, from one aisle to the next until he reaches the soda fountain in the back of the drug store.

All of the stools are taken at the soda fountain. Kids stand in line three deep behind the stools waiting to be served engaged in heated conversation. Desperately Marla tries to accommodate as many of the orders as she can in a timely fashion. While waiting everyone talks about the mysterious pranks and wonder who may have orchestrated them.

He catches sight of Garvin's friends playing interference in front of Garvin as he stands on a step stool. He gazes out over everyone with a flyer in his hand.

"I tell you this is not my signature! I don't write my name like that. I know Officer Higby will say I made it look like I did not write my name... Come on really?"

Willie turns to leave the awkward situation thinking it might culminate in an altercation. "Hey, Willie my boy, what's up?" comes a voice obscured by the crowd. Willie merges into the plethora of shoppers on his journey to the front door.

"Coming thru! Coming thru!" Willie hears behind him. Toad wrestles his way through the shoppers to catch up to Willie. Toad tries to associate with the most popular person at any given moment. He is a walking social media billboard. None of Willie's circle of friends associates with Toad because of his annoying habits. His coke bottle glasses, conservative slicked back hairstyle, and incessant nasal twang while talking keeps all the kids at a distance. Outside on the sidewalk, Toad catches up with Willie.

"Toad, strange meeting you here." Willie tries the tactic of surprise. "Haven't talked in a while. What's up?"

"What's up? The biggest thing since the courthouse clock, that's what my boy is up," responds Toad totally amazed as he hands Willie a folded up flyer. "Check it out. Junior League propaganda if you ask me. Garvin has his name center page. Go ahead—check it out."

Attempting to be taken by surprise, he carefully unfolds the flyer and studies the pictures and the names. Gooch, Izzie, and Punzak join Willie. "What ya got there?" asks Gooch flicking the flyer with his finger. Willie is impressed how good the flyer looks in daylight.

"Toad said it's Junior League propaganda. Give it a look, Gooch." Willie hands the flyer to Gooch. "Toad, where did you get this?" Willie asks trying to appear ignorant. "It's got Garvin, Huggable, and Turk written on it."

"From Tony Samoni's front window. They say Chelsea's Drug and your dad's agency are the only stores on the square not plastered with one of these." replies Toad with a jittery giggle as though he let out a secret.

"What's your point?" Wee Bones questions with a nervous twitch in his voice.

"My point is they must have run out when they got to this side of the courthouse square." Toad explains himself extremely serious.

"Makes sense to me. I bet that's what happened. They ran out," Punzak agrees nodding his head trying to get everyone's approval.

"That's not all! There was a fire in the church house steeple last night. Did so much damage the police had to tape it off until inspection," Toad adds in his customary jittery style. "And, there was the ball field!"

"That happened last night?" Punzak plays along listening closely to every detail. "I had to stay home and watch re-runs of "Jeopardy" and "Who Wants to be a Millionaire?" You know, 'cause of my parents' going' to the PTA planning' meeting."

"They vandalized the Skeeter Hill Baseball Field and tagged the concession stand," Toad starts to elaborate. "Old Officer Higby taped it off and covered up the home team dugout 'cause it got tagged real bad. Didn't want no more vandals doing more stuff. You know, tagging."

"Wow. This happened last night?" Wee Bones exclaims acting surprised. "I watched repeats of Wheel of Fortune on TV."

"Ya! Hear this! They broke into the press box. Ya know, where the scorekeeper sits, and tried to start a fire," Toad adds. "These guys were real firebugs if you ask me."

Out of the corner of his eye Willie catches sight of Weezie strolling down the sidewalk in their direction. As she walks up to Willie, he spontaneously announces as loud as he can, "Okay guys let's do that thing Izzie suggested. Okay, Gooch?" Suggests Willie trying to distance himself from Toad and Weezie. Immediately Gooch hands the flyer back.

"Gotta do some talking to Garvin. Thanks," yells Toad as the boys walk off and leave him behind. "Going ta California! My dad's gonna move there with Remcore."

Willie, Gooch, Punzak, and Wee Bones head toward Wagon Trail Street walking as fast as they can to leave Toad turns to talk up a storm with Weezie.

Puzzled Wee Bones inquires, "Do what thing Izzie suggested?"

"Whatever he's doing right now! Needed an excuse to get outta there," Willie explains. "What if Weezie saw me sneak out last night?"

"Izzie is helping his mom clean up at the baseball field," interjects Punzak. "You want to go help?"

"Let's go to Rayner Park and play in the creek under the bridge. We can help Izzie later," suggests Wee Bones rolling up his sleeves.

"Willie, you sure are quiet. Something on your mind?" asks Gooch walking a double step to the corner to keep up the pace with Willie. "You're kinda nervous like."

"Something just came to mind. I overheard Officer Higby and my dad talking this morning. He said they found what he thinks is Garvin's baseball cap in the scorekeeper's box." He stops at the corner to catch his breath and to let the others reach the corner and join them.

"What's so unusual about that? They must have poked around there after we all left."

"That's not it, Gooch. I left my game day program in the scorekeeper's box. My dad might ask to see it. What am I to do? I can't go back to the baseball field and check."

"Tell ya what ya do. Go to Wasserman's…"

Punzak and Wee Bones reach the corner. "Gooch wants to go all the way to Wasserman's." announces Willie motioning to walk in the direction of Wassermann's.

"Ah geez, guys," complains Wee Bones. "That's gotta be half a mile to Homesteader Plaza. "Count me out."

"Listen, guys, we can't go to the clubhouse any more. It's off limits for good. Don't want any of us getting caught. It'll ruin everything."

"Gooch, you go to Wasserman's with Willie; I'm going to the park," Punzak says as he jogs down the street in the direction of the park.

"Hold up! I'm coming with you," calls Wee Bones.

"Willie shrugs his shoulders and starts to jog behind Wee Bones. "Why not?" Gooch does not object and jogs alongside Willie.

Later in the day, Willie finds the time to call Wasserman's from the privacy of Punzak's house. During the telephone call he knows he can talk without fear if either his mother or father might overhear or listen in on the conversation. Mr. Wasserman informs him about the Gunslinger game day program. Much to his dismay, the game day program becomes more of a dilemma than he anticipated. He must purchase one as soon as he can, but the price is more than he can afford. On the other hand, Mr. Wasserman only has one on hand to sell. At the same time, he must have someone else buy the program for him in case his father or Officer Higby asks Mr. Wasserman if Willie bought the program to replace the program his father purchased at the Gunslinger game. He hopes Mr. Wasserman did not recognize his voice.

The downtown rumor mill cranks out gossip all day changing the version with every listening ear. The happy hour crowd at the Prospector Bar becomes a welcome center for gossip. "Did you know Garvin and his cronies burglarized the press box?" mentions Hazel from Murphy's Ranchette Supply Store.

"Yup, they meant to start a fire," summarizes Ben Shacklesford at the end of the bar.

"I heard Garvin's pals broke in to the press box to drink his dad's moonshine and smoked a joint," interjects Chris Jacobson.

"And get this—rumor has it they 'flew Mexican airlines.' Ya know, slang for taking a trip on wacky weed. Junior Leaguers are going wild. Get this—they white-washed the concession stand and the dugouts," mentions Seth Ryerson between swigs of his Continental Divide Ale.

Ben interrupts from the other end of the bar, "They dropped the cans on the ground where they ran out of paint." He chugs his beer. "Those tagging..."

"The church steeple was their second attempt to start a fire after smoking that south of the border stuff. Remember last year? The guy with the Braves wanted to be called fire bug," says Chris guzzling a Lakeside Beer with a shot of Oaken Bucket Whiskey.

"No, wasn't fire bug. It was 'fire dog'. Get it right, would ya," corrects Seth before grabbing a handful of pretzels.

"Yeah, all around town they're calling it 'the Skeeter Hill eternal flame,'" Ellen Dunsmore jokes as she serves a chilled Cherry Rum Cola to Katlin at the end of the bar.

MEETING OF THE MINDS

Over the next several days, more stories surface and the original stories become exaggerated. The pranks are the major topic at Chelsea's, Smitty's and Aunt Bea's. The conversations at Prospector Bar create more rumors with each passing day. Stories include hazing by a nearby college, Junior League initiation for prospective players, and end-of-the season mayhem.

On Saturday evening, the townsfolk gather at the Derwood Dickinson Events Center for a potluck before the fall planning meeting. Willie and his friends play catch on the grass area beside the town hall events center. Between tosses, Willie pokes fun at the terminology pertaining to the name of *potluck*.

"What makes it a potluck when there is the same food to choose from at a dinner? Is it lucky if you find the one that doesn't wrench your gut!" He laughs to himself. "Or if you find something that surprises your taste buds, that's lucky?" He tosses the ball to Izzie.

"At least three tables are devoted to salad trays with celery, carrots, black olives, and radishes. A carrot is a carrot, no matter which way you slice it."

Willie tosses a pop fly to Punzak and continues, "Next you come to the three bean salads. From the looks of it, there's more three bean salads than the number of ants on an ant hill." He catches a toss from Izzie and throws to Gooch.

"There's at least two tables with macaroni and cheese dishes, maybe more. The old-fashioned macaroni and cheese that Grandma Spika makes is gone before you get to it. What's lucky about that? Then you're left with all the imitations of her macaroni and cheese besides the scalloped macaroni, three cheese macaroni dishes, and from there, the list goes on forever."

"Hey, Willie! Throw it in here," calls Wee Bones crouched down in catcher's stance.

Willie continues to elaborate, "When it comes to potato salad, Grandma Ella Jane's is still the best in the West. By the time I find her potato salad bowl, it's empty. I don't feel so lucky about that!" He throws a ground ball to Izzie.

Willie catches a ground ball and throws it back to Gooch. "Now, potato salad comes in more varieties than bees in a beehive. The list goes on forever beginning with the Southern potato salad, German Potato Salad, red potato salad, mustard potato salad, deviled egg, and there is more yet to come. They're inventing potato salad names faster than I can eat them."

Willie fields a ground ball from Gooch and tosses a line drive to Punzak before continuing. "Finally I get to the meat dishes. No one wants to bring meat to a potluck because everyone gets full on potato salad, macaroni, and tuna dishes. Aunt Bertha's country fried chicken resembles Kentucky Fried Chicken but not in a bucket. The variety of meatloaf dishes is not a variety at all. Every one of the meatloaf dishes will be smothered in a different tomato sauce called Heinze 57."

Willie glances over and spies Weezie skipping down the steps as he says, "Before I load my plate with the five food groups, I think about the missing food group: desert. Usually, the first two tables contain different Jell-O deserts. Next there are at least two tables with different kinds of cake: chocolate, Dutch chocolate, devil's chocolate, butter pecan, pineapple upside down and…*uhhh*," Willie groans as he stretches to catch the ball from Gooch, pausing briefly from his monologue. "Whatever Betty Crocker or Pillsbury dream up you'll find on desert tables one through five." He snags a pop-up throw from Izzie.

Willie concludes, "I guess by now you'll know what's lucky and what's not lucky about *potluck*. Basically what's really lucky is the ice cream afterward."

The pounding of the wooden ladle against the bottom of a two-quart sauce pan serves as the signal that the food tables have been arranged and the time to eat has arrived. Willie and his pals scamper into the events center hall. Before he tracks down his father, he does a fly-by of the desert tables.

Reverend Farnsworth delivers the invocation. Conversation about the antics played around town by the Junior League group prevails as the most important topic. Everyone wonders who the culprits might be.

Following dinner, the women rapidly clear the tables. The Boy Scouts join other older teenage boys from the Skeeter Hill Youth Ministry to fold up the tables and arrange the chairs in meeting layout. In preparation for the meeting, Mr. Wisenhut places the team rosters in the glass case at the back of the event center by the door.

The men gather on the front porch to discuss the concerns and business agenda. The kids and young children play on the playground or on the grass. With all the preparations for the meeting completed, Mayor Polkinghorn steps to the podium and rings a tarnished brass school bell to call everyone to their seats.

The mayor and other dignitaries sit on either side of the podium on a stage riser in front. "Ladies and Gentlemen, we will dispense with the minutes of the last meeting since City Council approved them. Anyone interested can grab a copy of them on the table along the back wall by the glass bulletin board case. We'll begin with the Labor Day events."

Mayor Polkinghorn proceeds to explain the plans for the Labor Day parade. He details a two-day miniature golf tournament with prizes for families, teenagers, and multiple divisions for ages under twelve. A "Taste of Skeeter Hill" is to be held on Saturday and Sunday with restaurants selling food samples, a la carte items, and dinners, at designated tents arranged around Pioneer Square on both sides of the street. The weekend will conclude with a concert on the lawn at the Skeeter Hill Memorial Park. The crowd cheers and applauds, and then Mayor Polkinghorn outlines the events for Halloween including Fright Night around Pioneer Square to take place on the weekend preceding Halloween.

Irritated that the meeting more pomp than business and avoiding the most important issue many of the men are waiting for, Brian Huddleston interrupts. "This is all well and good, Mayor. We don't need to know about the Saturday of Caring Thanksgiving Meal for low-income families and the homeless or the Gobbler's Trot on the Friday after Thanksgiving. We have that every year. What we want to know is what are you doing about the Junior League rampage that happened through downtown last Tuesday night?"

Willie springs to his feet and says, "Yeah, and what about the Little League? We gonna play or not? I want to be on a team with my friends."

Motioning to Willie, Mr. Waldron interjects, "Gentlemen, you can't ignore this young boy. A little over a week ago, this town witnessed more foul play by the Junior League players than I can ever recall by youth in our community. It cannot be ignored! Tell us about Little League."

C.J. Heinze stands up, clutches on to both of his suit coat lapels, and gazes across the audience before addressing the meeting, "You described in detail the wonderful festivities and events planned for the holidays. But, you have not enumerated any plans for our kids to have an opportunity to play organized baseball next spring. It's America's pastime. Tell me, are these kids going to have the right to play Little League? Are the rumors correct that you plan to expand the Junior League at the expense of the kids who want to play Little League?"

"Excuse me, Mr. Mayor, ladies, and gentlemen," says Officer Higby as he approaches the podium. "The police department has not completed our investigation. The chicanery appears to be the doing of Junior League wannabes. In the meantime, the Parks and Recreation Department has a tentative plan in place for next spring's youth baseball league programs. Mr. Mayor—"

Mayor Polkinghorn interrupts and announces, "It is my privilege to present to you the director of the Recreation Youth Sports Authority." And with a bit of flourish, he says, "I give you Mr. Wisenhut.

The director steps up and greets everyone, "Good evening, ladies and gentlemen, T-Ball, Peewee, Slow Pitch and Fast Pitch have a solid youth league program in place with the necessary appropriations in the budget. These programs are relatively inexpensive. Every child will have an opportunity to play.

C.J. Heinze raises his voice, "Let's get on with it. What about the Junior League roustabouts? Let's get to the point. Are they going to get away with it?"

"Let's not rush to judgment. Officer Higby told us the jury is still out." Mr. Wisenhut takes a moment to shuffle through papers on the podium. "The Parks and Recreation and Youth Sports Authority met with Mayor Polkinghorn's staff several times this week. We drafted a twelve-team Little League plan for next spring. In order to hold costs to a minimum, we are strictly enforcing the age requirements for Little League and Junior League. A player must be at least nine years of age at the start of the season to play starts in Little League. If a player wants to play in Junior League, that player must be thirteen years of age"

Mr. Hackworth jumps to his feet and angrily interrupts, perturbed at the enforcement of the age requirements. "That's not right! My son, Garvin, has his heart set on playing in the Junior League. His birthday is the middle of May. You can't change the rules now! He's played in Little League for nearly three years now. He's put in his time and should be able to play Junior League ball!"

"The rules are the rules. We are not changing the rules; instead, we are enforcing them! The Youth Sports Authority members' decision is to go strictly by the Little League International rules for the age brackets. There will not be any latitude for a player to transition to Junior League unless they meet the age requirement. No exceptions! We performed an inventory of equipment and made the decision to expand Little League to twelve teams and keep the four Junior League teams."

Willie shouts, "Yippee!"

"Hooray!" yells Gooch. "We Did It!" He cowers down in case he may have been heard over the commotion.

"All right!" screams Punzak.

"Yahoo!" comes a voice from the other side of the room before other boys, wondering if they might play or not, join in the chorus and cheer.

The announcement offers a glimmer of hope for parents and boys wanting to get into the Little League program. Many of the boys who were unsure if they would be able to play Little League sense an opportunity to get to play. An aura of excitement and great expectation fills the air in the meeting hall. On the other hand, some parents introduce an atmosphere of disdain and ill will because they anticipated their child would play Junior League but cannot because of the age requirement. Instead their son/daughter must play Little League. Consequently, the room erupts with cheers and celebration mixed with anger and trepidation.

Mr. Hackworth jumps to his feet and says, "Hold on! Stop right there! Are you telling me there's nothing I can do? Garvin can't move up because of his blankity blank birthday?"

Mr. Wisenhut responds, "He cannot play Junior League until he reaches thirteen years of age. He must be thirteen on or before April 30th—not twelve going on to thirteen. With that being said, I would like to direct your attention to the bulletin board in the back of the room where the projected team rosters have been posted."

The boys jump out of their seats and stampede to the back of the events center and swarm around the bulletin board in the display case.

Mr. Wisenhut frantically pounds the gavel, "Everyone, quiet! Boys, come back to your seats! Now! Sit down! Quiet. Everyone, quiet down!"

Izzie reaches the bulletin board before anyone else. "There's my name. I'm on the Chieftains."

"Look, Wee Bones is on the Sharpshooters," exclaims Gooch jostling back and forth.

"There's Gooch. He's a Gambler," Punzak shouts pointing at the page on the bulletin board. "I'm a Rustler," Punzak proclaims saddened realizing he will be on a different team.

"Willie, you're on the Rebels," Izzie announces.

"Guys, step outside! I think we've got a problem!" Willie summons his friends to join him. He takes a few steps away from the bulletin board and begins the arduous task of weaving through chaos in front of the glass bulletin board case.

At the same time, parents rush up to the swarm of boys in order to sort through the crowd and find their child to go back to their seat and sit down. Willie's father muddles his way through the commotion and finds him before he has the opportunity to venture outside. "Come on, son. We have to get back to our seat. The meeting is about to resume."

Officer Higby with the assistance of a couple of other officers coral the other boys and directs them back to their seats.

"Dad, we're not on the same team! The eleventh team called the Rebels team has eight players. The sheet for team twelve does not have a name or players." Willie gestures toward the bulletin board. "I'll show you. Look!"

"Let's get back to our seats. There must be a simple explanation." He gently tugs on Willie's arm to step away and return to his seat with him.

"It's just not fair, Dad. You gotta do something."

Mr. Wisenhut continues to pound the gavel on the sounding block, calling everyone back to their seats. He turns the gavel over to Mayor Polkinghorn. "This is your mayor. Attention everyone! Will everyone please find a seat! The meeting is about to resume," announces Mayor Polkinghorn showing signs if aggravation.

Mr. Wisenhut resumes the meeting with an explanation, "Ladies and gentlemen. There will be twelve Little League teams and four Junior League teams. The Youth Sports Authority will provide the Little League teams with batting equipment and uniforms for each player except the head mask and knee guard equipment for the catchers. The teams will have to provide four new baseballs for each game. Should there be additional costs, the teams will have to manage by raising money on their own."

Mr. Hackworth shouts, "Expand Junior League and let me coach a Junior League team with my son on it. I'll bring home a trophy. Give back to the Little League after Remcore Technologies moves everyone out of town. This is the year for us to win the Metro Junior League trophy."

Mr. Waldron disputes the logic, "That hardware has no purpose, no practical use; it will only collect dust in a display case. A young boy's or young girl's self-esteem goes a hell of a lot farther if you ask me. The Junior League is parents wanting to worship a trophy."

Mr. Wisenhut interjects, "Mr. Hackworth, you are out of order. I assure you the Youth Authority will not engage in the practice of trophy worship. Remcore Technologies is shutting down. There will not be a need for as many teams the following year, especially Junior League. The Junior League will rule."

The room grows quiet. Heads turn and murmurs of conversation escalate. "The Junior League will rule their own destiny and have to fend for themselves. How they do it does not really matter. We fielded four teams this year. Next year will be no different, and there will be four Junior League teams. Our office will arrange with the Metro Inter-City League for scheduling. Equipment and uniforms will be the responsibility of the respective Junior League teams. If the Junior League wants to rule, the coaches can captain their own ship." Mr. Wisenhut pounds the gavel and says, "Ladies and gentlemen, now that we've gotten that out of our system, we will take a break and come back to talk Little League baseball."

Willie makes tracks for the door. Gooch, Izzie, Punzak, and Wee Bones leap off their chairs and quickly thread their way through the crowd. On the porch they search for Willie. In the distance, Punzak sees Willie pacing underneath a lamppost by the utility shed next to the parking lot skipping ricks across the parking lot.

"There he is over there by the lamppost," exclaims Punzak. One by one they scramble down the porch steps and run across the lawn over to Willie.

"Hey, Willie, we did it. We won. Just like you said..." shouts Izzie.

"You're a genius. Everyone thinks Garvin did those things," Punzak adds. With a grin of surprise and satisfaction.

"I can't believe we pulled it off. I thought we'd get caught," exclaims Gooch in disbelief. "Junior League rules."

"How are we gonna get on the same team?" Wee Bones asks with sad eyes. "We need a ... "

"Sounds like we have to talk to that guy, Wisenhoot, or whatever. You know who I mean," mentions Gooch as he skips stones across the parking lot like Willie.

"Yeah, our parents gonna have to talk to that Wisen...ya know—the guy with the hammer in the meeting," agrees Punzak with wishful thinking. He picks up a handful of stones to join the others in nervous stone-skipping.

"There's gotta be a way, right, Willie?" Izzie questions aloud. "You're the one with all the ideas."

"Can't think of a thing," laments Willie as he skips a stone across the asphalt of the parking lot. "I'm stumped. We've made it this far. One for all," Willie charges the group for their devotion to the cause.

They raise their hands up simultaneously and yelp, "All for one." The light on the veranda porch of the events center flashes calling everyone back to the meeting. The boys jog back to the events center. Inside Mr. Wisenhut sounds the gavel to call the meeting back into session. "Ladies and gentlemen, it's getting late. Please return to your seats."

Mr. Wince stands up and says, "Excuse me, Mr. Wisenhut, but may I offer a suggestion?"

"Proceed, Mr. Wince. Anything constructive at this time is welcome."

"Looking at the postings on the bulletin board, you have allocated twelve teams with sixteen players on each team based on registrations from last year."

"Yes, sixteen players based on registrations," agrees Mr. Wisenhut nodding his head.

"Then I suggest each coach from the ten teams move two players to round out the eleventh team and partially fill the roster for the twelfth team. Then you'll have twelve teams with fourteen players on each. With fourteen players on each team, you'll have a twelve-team model to work from." Mr. Wince scans the room for anyone wanting to comment on his suggestion or elaborate.

Willie jumps down from his seat and says, "I'll be on team twelve. Ya know, the one with no name. Take me off the Rebels!"

Wee Bones shouts, "I'll join Willie. I don't want to be a Sharpshooter. Put me on team twelve."

"I'm with Wee Bones. I don't want to be a Chieftain." Izzie yells over the clamor.

"Count me in. Don't make me a Rustler," yells Punzak.

"I'm in. Take me off the Gunslingers." Waving his hand for recognition, Gooch joins the chorus.

"I see that it won't be too hard to arrive at twelve teams with fourteen players," exclaims Mr. Wisenhut. "See my secretary Mavis to fill your name in on the roster."

"What do you know about that? We'll have our very own Bad News Bears right here in River City," jokes Mr. Hackworth. "All the also ran players will be the twelfth team cast offs from the other teams."

"I fail to see the humor in that, Mr. Hackworth. Granted the players released by the ten coaches might not be all-star material. You have no right to ridicule them," criticizes Mr. Waldron. "Take my son off the Rustlers. Kippy will play for the team with no name."

"Playing against a team of losers will be like batting practice against these rascals," Mr. Hollingsworth sarcastically jokes.

"Bad News Bears ain't right 'cause they'll stink," Comes a suggestion from a man seated in the back row of seats.

"Ya, let's call them the Bad News Skunks!" ridicules another member of the audience.

Mrs. Engle stands up and says, "You don't even have a coach for this group of misfits. Already you're poking fun at these poor rascals."

Mrs. Avery adds, "There's not a coach in the world to step up and volunteer for this lost cause. He'd have to be some kind of Casey Stengel, if yeah ask me."

"Ladies and gentlemen, I believe we are overstating the situation. I realize we need a coach in order to field a team. Maybe you, Mr. Wince?" asks Mr. Wisenhut expecting a positive reply.

"No, I'm afraid not. I have a hard and fast rule about coaching a team in the same league that my son plays, let alone a team he plays on."

Heads turn, secretive conversations ensue and murmurings grow louder and louder. The commotion escalates. Mr. Polkinghorn steps up to the podium and pounds the gavel three times. He gazes across the room at the audience. Silence fills the meeting room in the events center.

"It's easy to have a loose tongue when it comes to a winning team. We all shy away from a team with low expectations. It's not surprising that a volunteer will not come forward to coach a team with little promise. Every team—the Yankees, Los Angeles Dodgers and even the Detroit Tigers—no matter how good they are, will at some stage go through a season of losing game after game before they get back on track. I would like to put everyone's mind at rest. The twelfth expansion team will not be the "Bad News Bears"! That name is reserved for Hollywood and does not have any place in the Skeeter Hill recreation program. Keep in mind that we have two teams that will need a coach. What about you Mr. Hackworth, since you won't have a Junior League team?"

Mr. Hackworth stands up and says, "I believe you requested during break I coach the eleventh team called the Rebels. I know most those boys already on the Rebels roster. Some of them I coached last year. If you can maneuver to have my son, Garvin, to be on the Rebels, then I will volunteer to be the coach. "

"Mr. Hackworth, I accept your kind offer to coach the Rebels. Anyone willing to volunteer for the twelfth Little League team? Anyone interested in coaching, let Mavis or myself know. We'll take a break for Mavis to register the names of the boys changing to team twelve." Mr. Wisenhut sounds the gavel.

Willie and his pal's jump to their feet and race to the back of the room in order to register their change of team with Mavis. After everyone has made the change, they rush out of the events center through the crowd of men congregated on the porch and down the steps to the lamppost by the parking lot.

Willie says, "Listen up, guys. Luckily, we'll all be on the same team. It's gonna be our team. Anyone with a name, blurt it out."

"Well, Skeeter Hill Skunks has been ruled out," jokes Punzak. Everyone shows their amusement and laughs.

"Better yet, Skeeter Hill Thunderbirds," suggests Willie. There is a brief silence as Gooch Izzie, Punzak, and Wee Bones exchange glances.

"Thunderbirds," Gooch reluctantly agrees and nods his head.

"Yes, Thunderbirds I guess," proclaims Izzie.

"Me too. It's better than skunks." Wee Bones throws in his support for the name.

"Not my first choice but Thunderbirds it is." Punzak gives his support.

"If we have a catchy name for the team, maybe we can get a coach to step up to the plate," interjects Willie with a hint of excitement in his voice.

Garvin comes out from behind the shadow of the utility shed next to the light pole. "Well, well, Wincey. Everyone sort of expects us to mix it up a little before this night is over."

"What do you want, ketchup drool?" asks Willie on his way back to the events center.

"See these stitches?" Garvin points to the cut on his cheek. "I have a score to settle."

Willie steps up to Garvin and pokes him in the chest and stares him in the eye. "The only score I have to settle will be on the baseball field."

Garvin steps back. "Watch who you're poking." Garvin cautions with rage in his eyes.

"I bet being a Little League for another year is a put down for Mr. Junior League wannabe. See ya on the diamond, ketchup drool." Then Willie intentionally bumps shoulders as he walks by Garvin toward the events center.

The porch light flashes, signaling for everyone to come back inside for the meeting.

"Wincey, you're lucky I can't fight with these stiches. Otherwise I'd knock your block off." warns Garvin.

After Willie is a safe distance away he gives a sigh of relief and keeps walking as the conditions of the restrictions he agreed to with his father about fighting come to mind. He does not give Garvin the pleasure of him looking back.

After everyone settles down in the folding chairs, Mr. Wisenhut announces, "Our last business for this meeting is to establish a volunteer for the twelfth Little League team."

Heads swivel back and forth searching the room for a volunteer. The whimsical joking mood suddenly changes. Murmuring grows louder and louder. At that precise moment, Mayor Polkinghorn raps the gavel twice. "Ladies and gentlemen, come to order. I have no intention to stay here all night bickering and arguing. If no one will volunteer tonight, the Parks and Recreation Youth Activities office will make some telephone calls Monday. I don't want to embarrass anyone."

"Mayor, what you have here is the Skeeter Hill Skunks. Not a sane person in this room would volunteer to coach a team of Little League players without any skills or promise at all," states Carlton Hubbard nodding his head as he looks around the room. "It's a lost cause."

The meeting decorum is shattered by a thunderous sound that emanates from the back corner of the room by the folding chair carts. There is a brief silence in the audience. Several more chairs clang to the floor.

At that instant, a man emerges from the shadows in the back corner of the events center. He is unfamiliar and strangely dressed, and saunters in the direction of the audience. He has a tattered and torn New Jersey Generals baseball cap; unshaven and bushy eyebrows fill out his distinctive facial features. He stops at the center aisle. Uncomfortable, he tugs on straps of his old faded pair of overalls.

Taking one-step at a time, he slowly strolls down the center aisle toward the podium. When he reaches the middle of the room, he stops and removes his baseball cap. The stodgy old figure of a man does not seem to be a threat or dangerous, only unfamiliar, and all eyes in the room are trained on him.

"Ladies and gentlemen, allow me to introduce myself. I'm Aaron Swatkowski. My great grandfather was one of the standout catchers in his era. Baseball was his life. My father's father followed in his footsteps and my father in his father's and me in his. More succinct, I come from a long line of baseball standouts in professional baseball."

His opening statement and well-groomed handlebar mustache elevates him from unshaven to the more familiar first generation of baseball. The bushy eyebrows reflect a kind of baseball savvy. His posture portrays a first base coach with years of supporting his weight with his hands on his knees, leaning forward in anticipation of the next pitch to pounce on the moment. His facial expression characterizes an underlying sanguine. The deep creased crow's feet around the outside corners of his eyes testify to the days on end, playing and coaching baseball in the unforgiving elements of sun, wind, and rain.

His raspy and somewhat gravelly voice resonates years of yelling as a big league coach and yield to a mysterious but inviting wisdom.

Willie questions Gooch and Wee Bones sitting a few rows in front of him. "Hey guys! Do you know who he is? Two years in a row he batted over .400 for the season. He's played in more professional baseball play-off games than any player in the last twenty years. He's...he's..." Willie's mother places her hand on Willie's lap to communicate to him to quiet down and listen.

Gooch's eyes light up as he completes Willie's sentence. "He's a baseball legend!"

Mr. Swatkowski continues, "I stand before you and question your wisdom, downgrading a proven system for organized baseball. The Skeeter Hill Youth baseball slogan—the one the city ornately painted across the bottom of the baseball field sign—contradicts everything that has been discussed in this meeting. The sign reads: OUR CHILDREN ARE OUR MOST IMPORTANT RESOURCE. Do you folks recall those words?" He takes a moment and looks around the room. Before he resumes, he saunters the remaining three rows to the front of the audience. "It's all about winning. Parent's winning, not the players winning. You have asked coaches to cut players just like the professional leagues do. In your heart, you know they are not the cream of the crop."

Mayor Polkinghorn interrupts, "Sir, where are you going with this? It's getting late. We need to be adjourning sometime soon."

"Let me tell you a story." Mr. Swatkowski strokes his mustache in preparation to impart a tidbit of wisdom. He steps up on the platform riser and sits down on the chair vacated by Officer Higby. The strange man has captivated the attention of everyone, young and old alike.

"There was a little boy, his uncle nick named him Sparky after the comic strip horse called Sparkplug. He never did outgrow the nickname given him by his uncle. Sparky struggled in school. In fact, school proved to be practically impossible for him. Every subject in school Sparky found not only to be a challenge but extremely difficult. In high school, he flunked physics. Granted, it's a difficult subject. The teacher gave him a zero for a grade. The grade wasn't any failing grade. It represented the worst grade for a student to take the class in the history of the high school. He not only had a difficult time with physics; he also failed Latin, algebra, and English. Imagine that—

English! Academics were not his only shortcoming. He struggled socially. He never could ask a girl out because he was too afraid he'd be turned down. Social situations proved to be awkward for him. Sports did not prove to be much better. He managed to qualify for the high school golf team. Somehow, he managed to find a way to lose the most important golf match of the year. He was given an opportunity to play a consolation game. The outcome remained the same—he lost again. Yes, Sparky was a loser in the land of mediocrity. He resigned himself to a philosophy that if things were meant to work out then they would."

"So, do you have a point, Mr. uh...Sa...? Saw..." Mr. Wisenhut stammers trying to remember the man's name.

"Yes, as a matter of fact I do. Sparky, took pride in his ability to draw. During his senior year of high school, Sparky submitted some cartoons to the staff preparing the class yearbook. His cartoon drawings were unacceptable and rejected. Again, he failed by a tribune of his peers. Nevertheless, he still believed in himself. In his heart, he believed he could draw. He wrote a letter to Walt Disney Studios. He received an invitation to send some examples of his artwork. Sparky spent hours and hours drawing the cartoons as specified in the request letter. After submitting the cartoon portfolio to Walt Disney Studios, a response came back to Sparky. He had been rejected, again. Turned down as the case may be. Yes, another loss for the loser, a failure."

All eyes are trained on Mr. Swatkowski. The room grew so quiet that the creaking rafters can be heard above the occasional murmur. Mr. Swatkowski wipes his forehead with his handkerchief and gathers his thoughts.

"Still believing in himself, he decided to draw his own autobiography in cartoons. He drew his childhood of an inept little boy. He depicted the chronic under achiever as a cartoon character. The entire world would come to know and love this little boy's failures frustration, disappointment, and shortcomings. In a matter of time, people would come to love the man known to most of us as Charles Monroe Schultz. Yes, he created the Peanuts comic strip for the entire world to know his entire life's struggle in strife, mediocrity, and constant rejection punctuated with failure and misfortune. Everyone has come to know and love Charlie Brown, the little boy whose kite never would fly and his football that never would clear the goalpost!"

"Wow!" Willie gasps.

"That's cool!" exclaims Wee Bones.

"Unbelievable," Punzak marvels at the surprise ending.

The audience begins to clap, and clap, and clap. The applause grows louder as they rise to their feet in appreciation of the oratory from the unfamiliar face in their midst. He has shown them wisdom and insight. This strange, odd, old man unified the town hall meeting.

Peanuts characters often grace the Halloween and Christmas programs at the community schools. The high school cafeteria displays the name "Snoopy's Place." Charlie Brown characters promote the reading program at the library. Charlie Brown, Lucy, and Snoopy are a large part of everyone's daily lives in Skeeter Hill.

He strokes his mustache as the applause subsides, and then Mr. Swatkowski continues to address the town hall meeting. The captivating old man clears his throat before elaborating further. "These boys you have selected to round out the twelfth team on the Little League program are no more losers than Charles Schultz. Given half a chance, they will prove all of us wrong in our initial estimation of their ability to play youth baseball. Many of these boys are not losers; rather, they are future Little Leaguers in love with the game of baseball. At their impressionable age they live their lives through baseball cards and fantasy. Day in and day out their imagination carries them to new heights fanaticizing about being the next Nolan Ryan or Jack Hargrave or to play in Candlestick Park. Allow me a moment to ask how many parents have heard their child announcing a stand out play for a game? It's the bottom of the ninth, two outs, losing by one run and it's your child's turn to step up to bat. Day in and day out they put themselves in a professional baseball player's shoes to hear the crowd and re-live the drama. These are not losers. These boys are not cast-offs. These baseball-loving boys and girls belong to a mother. These aspiring Little Leagues belong to a father. And most importantly, they belong on a baseball field living out their fantasy!"

"Excuse me! Mr. Baseball or whatever your name is. I do not intend to spend the rest of the evening listing to some unfamiliar face expound on the virtues of Little League Baseball," interrupts Mr. Hackworth. "I do not see how eloquence with words will turn a hand full of rascals into a Little League caliber team. I dare you to practice what you preach. You be the coach of these rascals on the team with no name! In fact, I double dare you, old man. You coach these little rascals!"

"Dare is an interesting word," responds Mr. Swatkowski. "If my mind serves me well, we have a program in the schools called DARE. It's a program to teach kids to resist drugs, be an individual, and think for themselves. Kids are taught to walk away from what is bad for them. In other words, kids learn not to be a loser. I understand kids learn self-esteem, self-worth, and how to make decisions. DARE has a lot in common with baseball. Come to think about it, I would be proud to coach in the Skeeter Hill Little League. We'll call the team the Rascals! Yes, it'll be Skeeter Hill Rascals! I dare you to beat the Rascals!

A collective applause of approval ushers up from the members of the audience. Officer Higby walks over and shakes Mr. Swatkowski hand. Mayor Polkinghorn claps enthusiastically as he steps over to the microphone and says, "Ladies and gentlemen, boys and girls, I think our meeting has concluded. The Skeeter Hill Fall meeting is officially adjourned." He receives the gavel from Mr. Wisenhut to sound on the sounding block and bring the meeting to a close.

In spite of the joyous moment, a suspicion prevails in the minds of some of the members of the audience. The tattered Boston Red Sox jersey suggests Mr. Swatkowski could be delusional. The eloquence of his oration parallels the famed Professor Hill from "The Music Man." Maybe he intends to solicit money for uniforms and equipment with the promise of an All-Star Little League baseball team then continue on his way. His motivating address raises questions. If he had ulterior motives, he did not express any intentions after concluding his acceptance of the coaching position. Time will tell if he is an old charlatan or an authentic coach.

Promptly, the women carry out ice cream cups from the kitchen and prepare for the ice cream social festivities. Willie searches through the crowd for his new coach. Mr. Swatkowski is nowhere to be seen. He's mysteriously disappeared in the same fashion as he appeared during the meeting.

As the boys enjoy their ice cream, Willie and his pals harbor the belief the Little League won out over the Junior League. The mission of the night marauders last Tuesday evening has proven to be a success in their minds. The Junior League did not rule. With the addition of Little League teams, Willie and his pals manage to finagle the registration process enough for the fabulous five to be on the roster together. Moreover, their coach has a big league reputation.

After finishing his ice cream, Willie heads for the door. He stops in his tracks in the doorway. Resolutely he marches to the glass case that houses the bulletin board. Struggling with the glass, he slides it back, reaches up, and snatches the wide marking pencil dangling on a long piece of yarn. Standing on his tip toes he writes in broad strokes across the bottom of the twelfth team roster, **"BEWARE OF THE RASCALS!"**

TICKET PLEASE!!!

The Skeeter Hill Parks and Recreation holds the annual Halloween program at Pioneer Square on the Saturday night before Halloween. On Fright Night, the Rascals team sells cider, donuts, and cookies to raise money. The Little League players and family members dress up in baseball-related Halloween costumes. Gooch selected Willie McCovey, first baseman for the San Francisco Giants in Major League Baseball. He adds a Halloween twist with large Elmer's Glue image in the pocket of his glove on his catching hand for sure-handed catching. He wears a countless number of fake medals for glove handling like 'Golden Glove Award' on his chest. Wee Bones favors Jerry Benchly, a Chicago Gangster's catcher in the United Federation of Baseball. He fashions a catcher's mitt with a honey label in the pocket for his sweet spot and a baseball wedged into his catcher's mask to highlight his facial disguise. Punzak created a bat with a large charred cavity and burn marks up and down the barrel of his bat. He put together a Detroit Road Runner uniform resembling Orlando Rodriguez—a power hitter with fangs and piercing eyes. Izzie wears a Los Angeles Monster's uniform of Hershel Greystone with his arm in a sling and a blood-soaked shoulder. The San Francisco Monster player broke his arm while pitching a championship game in 1991. Willie chooses to be Ty Cobb. He selected his father's golf shoes as the slashing baseball cleats. He designed a championship belt with the saying, "The best baseball player to wear diggers." Because of the humor and unusual costumes, the fabulous five in the Rascals concession receive more patronage than any of the other concessions on Pioneer Street. Weezie attributes the reason to her make shift cheerleading costume luring customers to the booth.

Garvin parades around in a costume portraying the Slasher from the movie "Halloween." He constantly strolls by and stares aimlessly toward the back of the concession, giving everyone an eerie feeling. Every opportunity he can manage to intimidate Willie and his friends he tries by making his presence known. Dressed in a twenties baseball uniform with the name NOTORIOUS on his back, Coach Swat finds different ways to scare off Garvin. One of Coach acquired some water balloons. At the end of the evening of the players were given a water balloon. When Garvin intentionally tips over one of the last glasses of cider the players immediately aim at him with water balloons. Rev. Michaels finds great amusement in the antic by the Rascals because of the known the menacing image of Garvin.

On the Saturday before Thanksgiving, Skeeter Hill's community churches host the Day of Caring. Coach Swat and the other coaches greet people at the door. The Rascals team helps with seating and beverages. Afterwards, the *Skeeter Hill Gazette* reports that the Thanksgiving Day of Caring served a record number of people in the community. It is not considered a fundraiser but serves as a medium for the teams and coaches to give back to the community.

At the Gobbler's Trot, on Friday after Thanksgiving, the boys sell raffle tickets for drawings to be held at the lighting of the Christmas Tree Ceremony on Saturday night. Each ticket during the Gobbler's Trot festivities raises money for the Disabled Youth Recreation and the Little League programs. The merchants donate prizes to be given away at the Christmas tree lighting program.

On Saturday evening after Thanksgiving, Skeeter Hill residents gather at Pioneer Square for the celebration of the Christmas Tree Lighting. Merchants set up tents around Pioneer Square inviting everyone to take the opportunity to make a different craft. Before the tree lighting, children create their own candles, Christmas cards, ornaments, and small wreaths. Mr. Wince sponsors a tent to make a Christmas necklace or bracelet. Willie and Gooch trade off with Izzie and Punzak selling hot and cold cider. Situated at the table on the side of the tent, Wee Bones sells his mother's oatmeal raisin and pumpkin spice cookies. Knowing the nibbling habits of his friends, he does not trade off watching the table. It is a cheerful fund raiser for the Rascals players.

Skeeter Hill Pittinger Elementary School and Hartwell Elementary School won honors to participate in the Christmas music program. Melodaires, a select group of talented and accomplished acapella singers from Mount Edington High School, entertain the gathering with familiar Christmas songs and conclude with a sing along.

Following the Thanksgiving festivities, Christmas tree lots can be found on nearly every corner in Skeeter Hill. Among the organizations there are the Boy Scouts, Skeeter Hill Varsity Club, the Knights of Columbus, Kiwanis, and American Legion. After school on Monday at four o'clock in the afternoon, the boys decide to meet at

Murphy's Feed Store on the west side of town, which is nearby the tree lot.

As they approach the store and then see the tree lot, they notice something looks different. The Christmas tree lot does not have the same drab appeal with all white lights strung haphazardly like Little League teams have done in years previous.

"Guys, hold up! The tree lot looks...well, it doesn't look like it always did," comments Willie a little perplexed.

"Guys, they strung up new colored lights," exclaims Wee Bones. "That's different..."

"Look! The warming shed has been painted," Izzie notices. "Maybe we got new digs. "I like the huge candy canes to hold up the lights in the center of the lot."

"Who's that old guy in the overalls and scraggily beard?" Punzak asks as he observers an odd-looking character with overalls, a Santa Claus beard, and engineer hat.

"Don't know. He doesn't look familiar," Gooch answers in a wispy voice.

"You guys can stay here yakking, but I'm gonna sell some Christmas trees," announces Wee Bones as he sprints across the street.

The boys run into the tree lot and stop to look around. "Well, well. What do we have here?" the odd-looking old man rhetorically asks.

"Rascals Little League volunteers reporting for duty, sir," replies Gooch as he gives a military salute.

"You can call me..."

"I know now. You're Coach Swat! You talk different and look like Santa just rolled out of bed with that all-white long scraggily hair," exclaims Willie half laughing at the sight of Coach in disguise. "Your craggily Magoo voice almost fooled me. Wow! I remember them overalls now. You wore them at the fall meeting."

All at the same time, the other boys recognize Coach Swat through his disguise of white curly hair, near perfect theatre style white beard, and rosy red cheeks. The overalls help him fit the part of a counterfeit Santa Claus.

"I'll teach you how to raise lots of money selling Christmas trees."

"We already know how to sell Christmas trees, Coach. Don't need any lessons," Gooch asserts objecting to the suggestion of taking lessons on how to sell Christmas trees. "We did it as Cub Scouts."

"I've some Christmas tree salesmanship to teach ya that might help," mentions Coach Swat.

"What's Christmas tree salesmanship? I thought we just ask what kind of tree?" Punzak explains. "Then we take them to where those kinds of tree are stacked. They pick one out and that's about the size of it."

"Ya and how tall they want it," Izzie suggests. "Isn't that good enough?"

"It's a start. Let me explain. Let's say Mr. Smith comes into the tree lot shopping for a Christmas tree. We have a greeter, Gooch. Our greeter says out loud, 'Merry Christmas, Mr. Smith.' The second boy standing out of sight, let's say that's you, Willie. When Willie hears the name, he writes the Christmas tree shopper's name on a tag. He waits and listens for Gooch to repeat the type of tree and the height: 'You want a five-foot spruce. Did I hear you correctly, Mr. Smith?' Immediately, Willie will secretly run over to the Christmas trees and find a five-foot spruce. Gooch will tell Mr. Smith how much he hoped he might stop by the tree lot because he had chosen a Christmas tree especially for him. The greeter, Gooch, walks the shopper directly to the tree beside the tagger, Willie. He reaches down and checks the tag on the tree to reveal the shopper's name. Next he will verify the kind of tree and height. He will repeat everything for our shopper. Gooch will say, 'What I have here is a five-foot spruce just like you wanted, Mr. Smith.' He will proudly say the tree has been reserved for him. Your tree shopper will be impressed and buy the tree. What ya say, guys? Let's give it a try. I'll be Mr. Smith."

Coach Swat scrambles through the opening in the fence for the lot entrance and circles around to re-enter the tree lot. The boys practice in teams with this folksy sales approach. This proves to be a very successful way to sell Christmas trees. Shoppers find the approach of a pre-selected Christmas tree impressive. Sometimes, the Christmas tree shopper may not select the tree that has been tagged with their name on it. Nevertheless, the shopper usually buys one of the trees because the showmanship impresses them.

After the holiday season, pancake breakfasts and spaghetti dinners are on the menu for fundraising. The man affectionately called Coach Swat manages to make each event special. He wears unusual

Italian costumes to accentuate the spaghetti meals and his overalls for the pancake breakfasts to look like a lumberjack. He teaches the boys how to make animal balloons. The kids love the animal balloons as a gift to take when they leave. Parents manage the kitchen by cooking and serving up the meals.

Warmer weather means car washes. Coach Swat arranges for Chelsea Drug and Tony Samoni's Variety Store to give coupons good for candy up to a quarter. Buster's A-1 Auto gives an air freshener to each customer paying for a car wash. At first, the mild winter weather seems a bit too frigid for the car washes. Butane heaters from Murphy's Farm Supply help keep everyone warm at the Kwicky Car Wash. Weezie shies away from the combination of cold air and the frigid water. Instead, she patrols the corner waving a sign for driver's to read. Occasionally she will set the sign down and flash a car passing by showing her two-piece bathing suit under the choir robe that keeps her warm and then direct the driver's attention to the big sign for the car wash.

Copyright Registered

Spring Training!!!

POSITIONS EVERYONE

"Little League registration forms must be turned in by March 1st," reads a large sign inside the display case outside the Dickinson Events Center by Delhi Township Hall. Religiously, the boys check the updated rosters for player's names. After March 1st, the Youth Authority Activities Committee hands out equipment and practice jerseys. The twelve-team schedule is confirmed for the season and displayed.

Coach Swatkowski wastes little time getting to know all of his players and families after the fall meeting. Within a week from the Parks and Recreation posting of the baseball players rosters, he sends a personal letter to welcome the players to the Rascals team and requests a family meeting before the first practice. The letter exhorts the players and families to enjoy the youth baseball season as a good time to be among family, friends, and especially teammates.

Coach Swatkowski uses the opportunity to describe the not-so-illustrious career as a professional baseball player. Fame and fortune were illusive thieves in disguise. These culprits took him away from him his treasured family and closest friends where he lived while he grew up.

During the familiarization meeting, he fields questions from the parents in order to help them feel more comfortable with his role as the Rascals coach. The rapport between the Rascals coach and the family grows with each player-family visitation. Coach Swatkowski utilizes a very diplomatic approach to win the confidence of his players and their parents. Before concluding a family visitation, he hands the Rascals player a hat with personal instructions to be carried out. "Wear this hat at all times. You'll recognize other Rascals players by the hats, and they will recognize you. In time, you'll begin to seek out Rascals players in the hallway between classes, the parking lot, or downtown while shopping. The change will be gradual. Before long, you'll recognize another team player in a fraction of a second. Your reaction and recognition time becomes instantaneous. The hats will help bond you together as a team before you become a team. Soon player's individual voices will turn your ear."

Coach Swatkowski strongly believes people do not notice the unimportant things as much as they should. He compares his way of thinking to the phenomenon of buying a car. Before purchasing a car, a buyer usually does not see many of the same models on the road. After the purchase of a car, however, the owner of a new car usually will spot more and more of the same make and model of car than before the purchase of the car. Coach believes mental preparation is a key element before addressing the physical skills of the game. Players must mentally understand their role to complete as a team. In other words, the success of the team will not be a single player but the team playing with heart and all of their ability combined. The hats were a small part of recognizing others on the team and to foster a sense of pride among the players.

On the second Saturday in March, the boys on the Rascals team meet at the Skeeter Hill Baseball Field for the first practice. Willie and his close friends left far behind the days of T-ball, fast pitch, and sandlot baseball. Now, they step into the batter's box and face a pitcher with the long awaited experience of the stretch, wind up and delivery of a Little League pitcher. Instead of wearing the customary silkscreen tee shirts with the team name made by a stencil spray painted on the back, they will wear a bona fide Little League baseball uniform.

The boys anxiously sit on the first row seats on the home team bleachers. They impatiently wait their coach's arrival. Since Coach Swat doesn't arrive on time, the boys engage in frivolous activities to pass the time. Some players play tic-tac-toe in the packed mud. The more restless depart from the bleachers and decide to play tag in the in-field or keep-away. At first glance, the Rascals team resembles a three-ring circus without a ringmaster.

"Look! Over there! Left field!" A voice comes from the bleachers.

One by one, the players stop their horseplay and group around home plate. In the distance, Coach Swatkowski trudges through the tall grass of left field burdened with several bags of equipment. Approaching the area around third base, he calls out to the players to sit down on the first row of seats in the visitor's bleachers. After arranging the bags of equipment, he stands in front of the bleachers facing the players.

"Before we take the field, I want to say a few words. Because my name is difficult to pronounce, I've already asked most of you to call me Coach Swat." He scratches his forehead before continuing.

"Some time ago, one of the great professional baseball team mangers, Tommy Lasorda, said there are three types of players. Mr. Lasorda explained himself by saying there are players who make it happen. There are players who watch it happen. Then there are players, who stand around and wonder what happened. The Rascals Little League team will be players who make it happen. The other teams can stand around and wonder what happened."

The boys clap and cheer. He continues to speak by saying, "Hard work and following the rules are the keys to making up a great baseball team. I have a short list of rules. You will be at the practices and games on time. You will bust your butt at all times, not for me but for the sake of the team. And play smart; know your next move. Playing smart means you must be alert at all times while you are on the field and in the dugout. If you want to play rock, paper, scissors, then you should be watching the game from the bleachers. Spectators do not have their heads in the game like you should as a player. Any questions?" Coach Swat places both hands inside his jacket side pockets. "I'm a firm believer that most Little League baseball players do not have any idea why they are on the field other than mom or dad said it would be fun. We'll have fun on the field at the games. I can promise you that. I want you to promise me that you will not horse around or play meaningless games with each other during practice. There's time for work and there's a time to play. Each practice session gives a coach time to evaluate what you have done at home to prepare to play in the next game. All of you will be given three drills to practice. I will leave them on home plate under a rock. You must practice every day just like learning to play the piano. A student learning a musical instrument does not just pick an instrument and knows how to play. Any skill in life begins with learning the fundamentals. The skills of the game help you stay injury-free and enjoy the game the way your mother and father intended."

Coach Swat explains the fundamentals of good sportsmanship on and off the field. He expounds on his manner of coaching that includes giving every player a chance to play. He explains that winning a game is important but regardless of the outcome of a game, every player will take the field and share in the win or the loss. "Let's play ball!"

Adjusting his hat, he motions for the players to follow him to the infield. Coach Swat saunters over to the first base side of the infield. Placing his hand on Punzak's shoulder, he positions him on the grassy portion of the foul ball area along the first base. Next, he instructs Izzie to stand on a spot at the tip of Punzak's outstretch arm and fingers. Finally all the players are lined up. There are two lines about five feet across from each other and an arm's length apart. Coach runs up to the visiting team dugout and emerges with a basket full of farm eggs. He walks between the two lines and distributes an egg in Punzak's line. "The first thing I want to teach you is that a baseball is hard to predict. Keeping your eye on it at all times is essential. If you field it the correct way, most likely it will not hurt you. Everyone, put your baseball gloves on the ground behind you. With your bare hands, roll the egg on the grass to your partner across from you. Cushion the egg and bring it in and up to your chest."

Coach Swat strolls behind the players as they roll the egg to their partner. The players repeat the exercise over and over as Coach observes the player's concentration and execution of the drill. Because the egg wobbles and rolls unpredictably, the players have a difficult time cradling the egg in their hands and maintaining possession. The boys laugh and joke while concentrating on the egg drill. The more the players laugh, the more careless they become. Some of the players drop the eggs. Instead of the egg white and yoke running out of the broken eggshell, they quickly learn the eggs are hard-boiled. All the while, the players handled the eggs so delicately, taking every precaution, thinking they were practicing with raw eggs. The players were taken by surprise and learn when they joke around they lose concentration.

Next, Coach reaches into his back pocket and retrieves a baseball and rolls the ball over to Izzie. "Now, throw the baseball back to me."

Coach Swat steps backward about ten feet. Izzie fields the ball and tosses the ball in the direction of Coach Swat. The baseball travels wildly to his left and rolls up against the chain link fence. Smiling back at Izzie, Coach Swat reaches into his back pocket and produces another baseball. He has the player form a semi-circle around home plate while Izzie remains at first base. He grips the ball slowly, placing three fingers of his right hand over the top and placing his thumb on the side. He stands with his feet positioned shoulder-width apart and throws the ball at home plate. He repeats the demonstration two more times. "I want you to see how the wrist moves, changing where the ball will travel. With your shoulder, you wind up bringing the ball back as you step through the throw by making a kind of skipping motion as you come forward with the ball. As you start to crack your wrist, you release the ball in the direction you have positioned your body. You will learn all of this before the Memorial Weekend tournament games." The boys line up to practice his hop and throw technique.

Before concluding practice, Coach Swat explains to the players how a glove should fit and the proper manner to fan the fingers of a baseball glove. He then instructs everyone to take a lap around the baseball field. After the lap they can pick up the practice sheet at home plate. At the end of the lap, players are surrounded by friends and family on the infield. Coach Swat mingles with players, family and friends at the end of the lap.

Weezie sits by herself in the corner on the top row of the home team bleachers. Silently she watches the players go through the drills during their first practice and remembers when Willie came to her defense on the pitcher's mound late last summer. In her hand she holds the rolled up game day program from the last game of the United Federation Baseball season Willie treasured so much. Today is not the day to return his treasured memento. She trudges down the bleachers and slowly plods home. She can't mingle because he will see the game day program.

During subsequent practices, the players learn catching techniques, fielding bouncing balls, and grounders. Repeatedly, Coach Swat reinforces lining up with the feet squared up with the shoulders for the catch. In preparation for the throw, he reinforces stepping out with the lead foot in order to begin the hop and throw technique. Coach Swat reviews each position on the field with the players. He explains the different responsibilities and skills required to play the various positions. As a first baseman, the players learn to place both heels against the base and not to stretch until the ball has been thrown in the direction of first base. Next, Coach has everyone practice catching the ball with one knee down on the ground. Playing in the outfield positions includes learning how to pursue the baseball by using scissor steps instead of running backward. Players learn not to run with the baseball glove held up in the air. Coach Swat helps the players learn how to judge the speed of the ball. And most importantly he instructs them how to correctly catch a fly ball and roll maintaining possession in the process.

Marty Ostrander's father, Marvin, becomes interested in Coach Swat's approach to teaching the players the fundamentals for fielding, especially the infield because of the shorter players than the other teams. Consequently, he decides to help with the chores of coaching with batting and place hitting for the more skilled players.

Each practice, Coach Swat concentrates on a different aspect of baseball. Special attention is given to the cross-over step, the shuffle toss, the shuffle step, and the body pivot. He explains how a catcher hides the sign for the pitcher by placing the glove below the left side of his knee. The players learn about a normal batting stance. Gradually, he incorporates batting exercises to establish proper timing and power with the lead side of the body, giving the hitter proper contact with the ball. The players learn hitting speed, bunting, and choking up on the bat for a Baltimore swing to a tomahawk chop with the baseball. Coach Marvin Ostrander becomes the official batting coach, allowing Coach Swat to concentrate on other fundamentals. He selects Marty, Frankie, Gooch, and Willie to learn body mechanics on how to place hit the ball. He explains feet placement, body English, and where to position the hands on the handle of the bat. How to choke up and the correct position to stand to place the ball in the opposite field for a right handed batter.

After every regular practice, Coach Swat assists with the players learning positioning their feet in the batter's box and choking up on the bat. The positioning will make a difference as to which direction the ball will fly off the bat. The batting clinic is somewhat of a secret. When the other players leave, the spectators think the practices are over. This provides the opportunity to the extend practice teaching the players batting skills or work individually with a player having difficulties with another aspect of the game such as fielding or throwing.

Word travels fast regarding Coach Swatkowski unique approach to developing the young player's baseball skills. Skepticism and rumors circulate around town about Coach Swat's ability to transform a group of unskilled ambitious boys into a competitive Little League team. Some consider the innovative coaching techniques more window dressing than grooming the players to play competitive Little League Baseball. Regardless of the rumors and gossip circulating, Coach Swat continues to work closely with the Rascals players during and after practice. Oftentimes, he stays after practice to work on the basics of baseball technique introduced during that day of practice. He demonstrates a sincere willingness to work with any player wanting more instruction and coaching. Some parents are envious because the other coaches are stern and lack patience with the players.

The home bleachers show more and more spectators watching practice. Occasionally Garvin, accompanied by his cohorts, observes from in the home team bleachers and make their presence known with antagonizing cheers and snide remarks. More and more, curiosity seekers fill the bleachers. Frankie Sternicki's father, Wayne, decides to join the team and help coach.

Finally, the big day arrives for Coach Swat to announce the team positions for the opening game of the season. The position assignment ordinarily takes place quietly during the course of practice. Instead, Coach Swat announces a barbeque in Rayner Park behind the Skeeter Hill Baseball Field followed by the awarding of the position assignments, which will take place at the Skeeter Hill Little League Baseball Field.

During the barbeque, families take advantage of the informal opportunity to become better acquainted other family members, with other players, and the coaches. The social event is great for all the members of the families because the barbeque is conducive to people feeling less encumbered. Sitting in the bleachers watching practice does not afford such an opportunity. While the adults talk the children play in the playground. Soon, the frolicsome event comes to an end. Coach Sternicki and Coach Ostrander invite everyone to migrate to the baseball field. Shortly after everyone finds a seat in the home team bleachers, Coach Swatkowski, Coach Sternicki, and Coach Ostrander amble through the gate in left field and embark on the customary journey to the infield. It's unusual seeing Coach Swat being in the company of Coach Sternicki and Coach Ostrander hauling equipment.

All the duffle bags are tagged pertaining to the equipment assignment. The coaches carry all the bags of equipment to home plate and sort them in preparation for the presentation. Finally, the uniforms are ready for distribution. Coach Swat motions for the players to line up along the first base line in the same fashion rehearsed during the previous practice. The players quickly exit the dugout and scramble out onto the infield. They anxiously line up in a single line arm's length apart. Ecstatic, the players face the crowd with anticipation. Willie exchanges eye contact with Garvin, who is sitting on the top row of the home team bleachers.

In dramatic fashion, Coach Swat strolls up to the duffle bag at first base and pulls a jersey part way out and stops. He stands up holding on to the jersey with one hand and faces his audience. "Ladies and gentlemen! Abbott and Costello popularized baseball with their humorous comedy act entitled 'Who's on First?' Today, I will address that question. Not only will I tell you who's on first, but also I will give you the entire lineup for the Rascals Team's first game. When I call out a player's name and position, I want the mother or the father or possibly an aunt or uncle to join their Rascals player on the baseball field at the position assigned.

"I will begin with the catcher. I present you The Rascals team's version of Johnny Bench!" He pauses and pulls out the rest of the jersey in the duffle bag. "None other than Wee Bones." Coach Swat hands the team jersey to Wee Bones. "Our catcher will be Wee Bones—a nickname his teammates have endearingly given to him."

Wee Bones sprints to home plate and raises his catcher's mitt. Wee Bones' mother makes her way down the bleachers to join him. At home plate, Coach Sternicki and Coach Ostrander distribute the pants, socks, and other items for his uniform to his mother.

Presentation of the Rascals uniforms carries a message like a rite of passage. The uniform presentation compares to a graduation in baseball for most of the players on the Rascals team. With the presentation of each jersey, Coach Swat mentions a famous professional baseball player known for excelling at that position on the field.

"Next will be Gooch covering first base in the same fashion as Clancy O'Rourke of the Detroit Road Runners. Second base will be Jimmy Tuttle with the ball handling of Charles Perkins of the Chicago Gangsters."

Willie tingles from head to toe waiting to hear his name being called out for the next jersey.

"Shortstop will be Willie Wince, our very own Ozzie Smith with the Sand Diego Padres."

Willie's heart races faster and faster as he nonchalantly walks up to Coach Swat. The butterflies in his stomach make him question if this experience might be a dream or if it is actually happening. He reaches Coach Swat and grips a corner of the Rascals jersey, holds it against his chest, and caresses it like a soft pillow. His eyes dance.

"On third base, we'll have an up-and-coming Dale Berra from the New York Yankees, our own third baseman Punzi Punzak. Starting in left field will be the Jimmie Aaron of Rascals baseball, the one and only Chico Martinez." He halts the presentation in order for Coach Ostrander to come over to the duffle bag.

"My favorite presentation is to my son, Marty. He will play second base and back up with the pitching duties." He drops the jersey on Marty's head and follows up with a bear hug God set blooming in his heart.

Coach Swat reaches into the duffle bag for the last time and pulls out the jersey like he is retrieving an anchor from the fathoms of the deep. He drapes the jersey over his arm and slowly sways it over in the direction of the last player standing, "Our last presentation is to the darling of the lineup in right field, the adorable Molly Mayfield."

The days of struggling to learn the skip and throw technique, or the proper way to cushion the baseball during a catch, or the excruciating manner to slide into a base seem like a distant memory as the players bask in the moment. After the players and parents elaborate on the uniforms and talk about their respective positions, Coach Swat blows his whistle. The players sprint over to Coach Swat, Coach Sternicki, and Coach Ostrander. Parents sluggishly follow in their footsteps.

"I asked for everyone to dress casual for a reason and not just for the barbeque. Boys, put on your Rascals jersey. We are going to play a friendly game of work-up. Adults will bat with one hand behind their back. All of the adults must throw the baseball underhand; no over-hand throws. Players, for your playing enjoyment, we will use a softball instead of a baseball."

The friendly family game of work-up becomes an informal gathering matched with the skill of the Rascals players. The game starts with three batters selected by Coach Swat. Coach Ostrander is relegated to pitching duties. Coach Sternicki will be the base umpire and Coach Swat will umpire behind the plate.

At the conclusion of the game, coach Swat addresses the gathering. "Ladies, gentlemen, and Rascals Players, I would like to paraphrase a great professional baseball club manager, Whitie Herzog. We need just two players to be a contender this season. I suggest those two players might be Babe Ruth and Sandy Koufax." He chuckles before continuing. "All kidding aside, I want to see all of you Saturday for our first Skeeter Hill Little League first game of the season. Players, most of you will have a sleepless night tomorrow night. I want each of you to remind yourself, over and over again, to come into the game with the mindset that you are better than the Rebels. If you think you will lose to them, then you have already lost. It's not about beating the other team. It is about playing smarter and better. In the end, you'll win and enjoy the game you played." He clenches his hand into a fist, and making a jab like a body jab similar to a boxer, he declares, "Go Rascals!"

"Go Rascals!" everyone replies in unison with the same fist-pounding motion.

The peculiar old man with an aura of confidence, charisma, and vitality remains at the center of controversy in the quaint town of Skeeter Hill. He holds an unmistakable reverence for the game of baseball. This relatively unknown member of the community stepped out of obscurity and challenged the stoic, backward thinking prevalent at the town hall meeting in the idiosyncratic city. In his own way, this strange little old man accepted a dare from the folks of the town to coach a team of cast-off Little League wannabe players, including some who didn't want to be on the baseball field but were going along with what their parents expected of them. His task is to prepare his players to compete on even terms with teams endowed with more experienced players. He accepted the challenge to take this handful of Rascals and mold them into baseball players. Because Coach Swat has a little wit and humor in his disposition he devised innovative plays that will be entertaining when the time is right.

PLAY BALL!!!

In less than twenty-four hours the Little League season will begin. Willie and his pals will step onto the Skeeter Hill Baseball Field to play their first Little League game. He mulls over in his mind if the professional baseball players experience butterflies and nervousness the night before a big game. His stomach feels like he has the flu but he know he doesn't. He feels queasy but he's not. He stares at his baseball card of Eric Densmore and imagines him in the batter's box taking practice swings. The slapping bedroom window shutters remind him of fans stomping on the bleachers to distract the pitcher before a momentous pitch. His imaginings turn to the other baseball cards on the wall and the ceiling. The bright moonlight shining through the blinds offers enough light for him to focus on posters and memorabilia. His imagination runs wild. He tosses and turns in bed unable to get comfortable. Eventually, he drifts off into a restless slumber.

Water in the half-acre pond at Pioneer Park glistens as the sunlight skips across the surface. The Glenn Haven Dairy trucks weave up and down the cozy neighborhood streets making the daily dairy deliveries.

Sy Chalmers and his son travel up and down the streets in a re-conditioned 1956 Ford pickup truck delivering newspapers. From the back of the truck, Sy slings newspapers in the direction of subscriber's porches. Noise from the modified exhaust system wakens Willie from his restless sleep. Everything appears like an ordinary Saturday morning with the usual sounds outside his bedroom window. The exception: this is not an ordinary Saturday. Today will stand out as his Little League debut on the Skeeter Hill Baseball Field. It is the day of his dreams.

Willie opens one eye and directs his line of sight toward the Rascals jersey he carefully draped over the back of his chair in front of his desk. He slips both legs over the side of the bed and pulls back the covers. Drowsy, he stands up and staggers through the maze of baseball items on the floor and finds his way to the chair by the dresser and faces the mirror resting on the wall.

He switches his pajama top for the jersey and then strikes a batter's pose envisioning himself at bat. He cracks a smile at his pillow hair in the mirror. While he stares at the reflection in the mirror, he remembers Coach Swat's recommendation that the first impression a batter can make will influence how a pitcher sets up. He turns to face the mirror like he would stare down a pitcher. After several imposing attempts to strike a mean demeanor, the door to his bedroom opens and his mother pokes her head through the opening.

"Better get ready breakfast in ten minutes. Have to get to the ball field."

"I'll be down." More awake, he questions whether the Rascals team will demonstrate the skill set to measure up against the precision of the Hackworth fine-tuned Rebels. Then, he recalls the words of Coach Swat: *When you believe the other team is better than you are, you have taken the first step toward losing. It's not about merely trying to beat the other team. Instead, it's about playing smarter and better, and that will translate into winning at the end of a game.* The speech keeps playing over and over in Willie's head.

The season inaugural game between the Rebels and the Rascals teams occupies much of the soapbox conversation at Chelsea's Drugs Store in the days leading up to the opening game. Smitty's Hardware and Aunt Bea's Beauty Salon entertain the scuttlebutt as well. Coach Hackworth's Rebels are the favorite of the Downtown Business Association. Consequently, many groups and even players on the other teams have decided to support the Rebels.

The inaugural game is highlighted with banners and streamers that decorate Pioneer Square and accentuate the charm of the quaint little town. At the baseball field, team moms and volunteers finish lacing blue and yellow crepe paper for the home team and maroon and gold crepe paper around the top bar of the chain link fence behind the visiting team dugout. Helium balloons are tethered to the fence. The concession booth becomes a bustle of activity as the volunteers for the Youth Sports Authority program make preparations for the inaugural event. A banner stretches across the back of the visitor bleachers that reads: BEWARE OF THE RASCALS. By late morning, most of the preparations are in place.

Willie arrives in time to watch the finishing touches for the game. Quickly, he releases his hold on the handle bars of his bike and dismounts dropping his bicycle next to the bicycle rack. In the distance, he views the home and away team bleachers as well as the concession. Speechless, he takes a moment and stands in awe.

Willie jogs toward the baseball field. Passing the concession, he slows his advance in order to study a banner stretching the length of the back of the dugout. He eyeballs the depiction of a Rascals with a smirk on his face and a tattered baseball glove wearing a baseball uniform showing the Rascals colors. Not a very impressive mascot in his estimation. The gangly figure is bracketed with shadow lettering: BEWARE OF THE RASCALS. The words he left as a reminder at the fall meeting. He continues past the backstop to the baseball diamond. Caught up in the moment, he stares at the playing field in the distance. He thinks to himself that the Skeeter Hill Baseball Field resembles a pasture in comparison to the United Federation Gunslinger baseball outfield.

The players for the Rascals team arrive and situate their backpacks and arrange their bats with the team equipment at the on-deck circle before they start warm-up drills. Coach Swat leads them out onto the field. At third base, Coach Sternicki hits fly balls and grounders to the outfielders. At home plate, Coach Ostrander hits infield grounders and bouncing balls to the players. Coach Swat saunters around giving pep talks to the players. Periodically, he stops to give a fielding pointer when necessary.

As the Rascals players exit the field following warm-up exercises, the Rebels players take their opportunity to warm up before returning to the home team dugout.

"Good afternoon, ladies, gentlemen and fans of all ages. On behalf of the Skeeter Hill Youth Recreation program, I would like to invite you to the inaugural game for this year's Little League season between the Rebels and the Rascals teams." The players for both teams line up in front of the dugouts.

Reverend Blissfield, Mayor Polkinghorn, Mr. Wisenhut, Coach Swat and Coach Hackworth congregate between the pitcher's mound and home plate. Mayor Polkinghorn raises his hands up in the air above his head in order to quiet the crowd.

"Ladies and gentlemen, players and spectators of all ages, I invite you to join Reverend Blissfield of the First Presbyterian Church in the blessing for the Little League Skeeter Hill season." Following the invocation, four cadets with the Junior Reserve accompany Emily Beaverson with her trumpet cradled under her arm. Emily leads the group as they march onto the field. They journey down first baseline to the flag pole landing by the home team dugout. The four cadets pair off on the landing and stand in formation to unfold the flag.

Emily splits off from the cadets at the flag pad and continues to travel to the join the coaches and dignitaries on the baseball diamond at the pitcher's mound. Facing the crowd, she raises the trumpet and proceeds with a trumpet solo of the "Star Spangled Banner." The pole runner prepares the flagpole ropes and clips while the three remaining cadets unfold the flag. The pole runner methodically places a clip in the grommet at the top of the flag. Keeping in pace with the playing of the national anthem, the other clips are fastened to the flag as it is hoisted by the pole runner. Emily concludes the National Anthem trumpet solo at the same time the last flag reaches the top of the flagpole. The crowd claps and whistles. She traces her steps to join the cadets.

As Emily and the Junior Reserve Officer Cadets march off the field, Mayor Polkinghorn exclaims, "Emily, that trumpet rendition of the 'Star Spangled Banner' was arousing and touching," He pauses momentarily while Mr. Wisenhut steps up to the microphone. "I turn the Little League inaugural season proceedings over to Mr. Wisenhut."

"Ladies and gentlemen, I welcome you to the season opener for the Little League season. It's time for everyone to meet the coaches." A round of applause ensues with intermittent whistling. "The Rebels will represent the home team." He waits as Coach Hackworth joins him at the microphone. "Their coach is none other than the renowned Coach Eugene Hackworth."

Coach Hackworth waves to the home crowd. He faces the Rascals bleachers and recognizes the fans with an abbreviated wave. The Rebels team players sprint onto the field. In military fashion, the players line up along first baseline in front of the home crowd bleachers. Coach Hackworth walks over and stands behind each player, announcing their name to the spectators. With each introduction, the player tips his baseball cap. Following the final introduction, the players jog back to the home dugout.

"Ladies and gentlemen, today we have the Rascals team as the visiting team with Mr. Swatkowski as their coach." Coach Swat steps forward and removes his ball cap and waves to the crowd in the visitor's bleachers and then the home bleachers.

The Rascals race onto the field and line up arm's length apart spanning between first base and third base. Coach Swat walks over and places his hand on Gooch's shoulder encouraging him to take a step forward. He introduces Gooch and announces the position he will be playing on the field during the game. He continues down the line introducing each player. When he completes the introduction of the players, he steps over to the pitcher's mound and addresses the spectators. "Mr. Fred Sternicki is the Rascals fielding coach." Mr. Sternicki waves from his place on the field at third base. "And, Marvin Ostrander leads the team as the batting and base coach." Mr. Ostrander waves to the spectators from first base.

"Ladies and gentlemen, Yogi Berra once said, 'Little League Baseball is a good thing because it keeps all the parents off the streets.'" He chuckles and takes a moment for the spectators to respond. "I'm glad to welcome you here today. Thank you for attending the season opener for our Skeeter Hill Little League season. Let's play ball." He bows his head reverently to the spectators. He raises his head and shouts, "Go Rascals!" The team reiterates the same cheer, "Go Rascals!"

As the players exit the baseball field, Weezie and a couple of her girlfriends weave through the visitor bleachers and distribute a game day program Willie's father assembled from pictures taken during the walk-through when Coach Swat distributed their Rascals uniforms and candid pictures of the game of work up afterward.

"Good afternoon, ladies and gentlemen. This is your friendly insurance partner, Wilfred Wince from the Wilfred Wince Agency on Pioneer Square in greater downtown Skeeter Hill, and I will be your announcer for today's baseball game. Our home plate umpire will be Mr. Dale Friedan." Umpire Friedan simultaneously removes his cage mask and baseball cap in order to wave to the fans in the Rebels bleachers and then to the fans in the Rascals bleachers. "The base umpire will be Herb Sellars." The spectators and players usher up applause and cheers. Umpire Herb Sellars waves to fans in the home and visitors bleachers. "The first batter for the Rascals team will be Tyler Kushihashi." Mr. Wince's voice can barely be heard over the cheering fans. Confetti streamers shoot up into the air from the home and visitor bleachers.

Umpire Friedan brushes off home plate. Tyler Kushihashi enters the batter's box. All of the coaches watch with great anticipation.

"Let's play ball!" Umpire Friedan announces as he positions himself directly behind the catcher in order to get a bird's eye view of the pitches.

Tyler goes through his usual routine to prepare himself for the pitch. First, he pulls up his left baggy pant leg. Next he pulls up on his right baggy pant leg. Then he positions his feet shoulder width a part and swings his bat a few times before he raises the bat for the pitch. Garvin reads the signs from Turk the catcher. He shakes his head and nods before he removes the baseball from his glove. Instantaneously, the Rebels bleachers erupt with the customary Little League banter, "Heybattabattabatta! Heybattabattabatta!"

Garvin goes into his wind up and delivers the first pitch of the season. The errant throw speeds toward the outside of the strike zone. Using a tomahawk swing, the end of his bat connects for a squibber, creating an odd spin as the ball speeds toward the first baseman. Hitting the grass, the ball takes an unexpected bounce away from the first baseman. He gives chase as Garvin races over to cover first base. In the meantime, Tyler keeps pulling up on his pants as he runs for the first base. The first baseman tosses the ball to Garvin in time to make the force out. Tyler does not reach first base in time.

Mr. Wince announces, "The next batter for the Rascals team will be, Marty Ostrander. Remember, you can't get a hot dog at home like a Skeeter Hill dog on game day. Visit your Little League youth concession today."

The fans start the banter, "Heybattabattabatta! Heybattabattabatta!" The chatter becomes intense as Garvin begins the wind up.

"We gotta cheer. You're the big high school cheerleader. Come on!" Weezie pulls on her older sister's arm coaxing her to come down and help her lead some cheering.

Reluctant, her sister refuses. "I came to watch the game. I do cheerleading all the time. You should know that by now."

Disappointed, Weezie skips down the bleacher seats by herself to the ground below. She bounces up and down, swinging her arms in large circles with intermittent claps to coax Rascals fans to join her cheer, "Garvin, Garvin, and Garvin."

The unrehearsed routine does not stir the fans into joining her by cheering. Weezie's chin begins to wiggle and her eyes well up with tears and spill over as they trickle down her cheeks. She sits down on the first row of bleacher seats with her chin uncontrollably quivering as she tries to hold the tears.

Feeling sorry and sensing her anguish, Cheryl debates if she should scamper down the bleachers. Having been in her shoes, she recalls not knowing the correct cheering footwork and manner to synchronize her arms can be embarrassing and humiliating as well as look goofy to the fans. Cheryl resolving to support Weezie she bounds down the bleacher seats in a hurry and sits down beside her.

"Hey tear buckets, take it from me—cheerleading is a lot more than jumping up and down and yelling out some made up cheer you want people to repeat. You've got to work the fans."

"But I thought you didn't..."

"Just hold on, sis. Doing jumping jacks and screaming at the top of your voice will give cheerleading a bad name. It will give Miss Varsity Cheerleader a bad name."

"But, you wanted to watch the game..."

"Sometimes a big sister has to do what a big sister's has gotta do."

"You mean...?" wonders Weezie.

"I'm a varsity cheerleader, so what'll people think of me if my little sister looks like some kind of wind up cheerleading doll?"

"You... You..."

"Zip it! If you want to learn, then pay close attention! Listen to me. I'll start out slow and we'll and see what you can do."

"Cheryl, you're the...the bestest ever!" says Weezie as she gives Cheryl a big hug.

"First thing we're going to do is bounce on our toes. Stand up and start bouncing! You have springs in the toes of your shoes. And move our arms in circles round and a round. Watch me!"

Weezie watches Cheryl's toes as she lines up beside her. Together, they practice with simple footwork and motion with arms moving back and forth, cheering, "Garr-vin! Garr-vin! Garr-vin!" The fans respond right away. Weezie smiles with her eyes. It's game time!

Marty sets his batting stance to send a line drive to right field. Garvin pulls his arm back, kicks out with his leg, in order to deliver the pitch. "Heybattabattabatta! Heybattabattabatta!"

The ball accelerates toward the strike zone. It seems like a hundred miles an hour. The catcher thrusts his catcher's mitt in the line of the speeding sphere. *Thwwaaap!* The once speeding ball lands in the catcher's mitt.

"Strike!" announces Umpire Friedan. Marty stands in awe at the speed of the ball as the catcher returns the ball to Garvin at the pitcher's mound. After reaching the full count with three balls and two strikes, he chokes up on the bat. Marty remembers the words of Coach Sternicki: *...choking up and clutching the bat an inch or two above the neck of the bat will sacrifice power for control.*

Garvin reads the sign and throws the deciding pitch side arm. The banter in the Rebels bleachers begins. Weezie starts the Garvin cheer under the direction of her sister. Marty swings hitting a worm burner down the third base line. The ball slows down by the time the third baseman fields the ball. He fires the ball to the first baseman. Marty is thrown out at first. He trudges back to the dugout trying to put the season's first experience at bat behind him.

"Punzak will be the third batter for the Rascals team. Remember, everyone! Ice cream is in season year 'round at Tasty Twist on Wagon Wheel Street across from the Skeeter Hill Library."

Garvin reads the signs and winds up to deliver the first pitch to Punzak. The familiar chatter begins. "Heybattabattabatta! Heybattabattabatta!"

Coach Hackworth yells from the sideline, "Garvin! You're better than these skunks. Strike him out! Rock 'em, Rebels!"

"Ball one!" declares Umpire Freidan. Excited, Cheryl and Weezie introduce a sarcastic cheer to the Rascals fans. "Hoo-ray Garr-vin. Hoo-ray Garr-vin."

After improvising a couple cheerleading routines with the help of her sister, Weezie begins cheering solo. "Garrr-vin! Garrr-vin! Garrr-vin!"

The Rebel's fans chant the tried and true cheer, "Heybattabattabatta! Heybattabattabatta!"

Punzak anticipates the fastball. He adjusts his stance and swings. He drives a bouncing ground ball to second base. The second baseman makes the catch in time to throw to first base before Punzak reaches base.

"Rascals first at bat is three up and three down, just as advertised. The first batter up for the Rebels will be Lefty Carlson. Don't forget to pick up the best special occasion surprise any time of the year at Judith Ann's Cakes by Design."

During the transition from the top to the bottom of the first inning, Girl Scouts walk up and down the bleachers selling popcorn and peanuts.

Lefty reticently steps into the batter's box. Izzie reads the signs from Wee Bones and delivers the pitch. Lefty jumps away from home plate.

"Strike!" declares Umpire Friedan.

Izzie delivers the next pitch. The Rebels fans start the cadence, "Heybattabattabatta! Heybattabattabatta!"

Izzie pitching

Lefty blindly chops at the pitch and hits a blooper. Willie back peddles and Molly runs up from left field. The ball drops in for a base hit. The next batter hits a ball into shallow right field.

Coach Swat calls time and journeys to the pitcher's mound. "Izzie, I haven't seen you off your game like this. These are not their power hitters. What's the problem?"

"Playing in a real game with another team freaks me out! I'm afraid of making a mistake." He pauses taking several deep breaths avoiding a show of emotion and bursting into tears. "I'm worried everyone will yell at me. It nerves me."

"Don't try to throw anything fancy. Cut 'em off at the knees if you can; then give some chin music once in a while."

"Chin music? What's that? You trying to be funny?" Izzie chuckles and shakes his head in disbelief thinking Coach Swat is cracking a joke.

"When a batter crowds the plate, throw a high, inside pitch to cause the batter to jump back to avoid getting hit on the chin. It can be the pitch of choice for a number of situations. I suggest a low pitch combined with chin music for the next pitch once in a while. They won't expect it and usually will blindly swing or jump back. Generally, the batter will jump out of the way. It will help you control the situation and exploit a batter's weakness."

"Don't know about that. I'll practice a few pitches with Wee Bones. Thanks for making me laugh. I feel better now."

"Play ball," yells Umpire Freidan.

Izzie throws the next pitch low for practice for the first strike. Since he is more confident, he wants to try the combination of a low pitch with chin music, but thinks Wee Bones should know first. Still nervous, Izzie calls time. He meets up with Wee Bones.

"Wee Bones, I'm nervous. Coach has a solution. I want to try something. Coach suggested I might wanna try some chin music."

Wee Bones glances over at Coach Swat. He sees Coach Swat smiling and nodding. He breaks out laughing and slaps his knee. Reacting to the suggestion he does not know if Izzie is joking with him or not. "Chin music? You gotta be kidding me, right? What the heck is that?"

"Chin high and inside. I'll brush my chin when I think I'm gonna throw it. I will practice with a few low pitches first to work on control, then I'll throw a few shoulder high. Got it?"

111

"Yup, chin music! Whatever you say." replies Wee Bones.

When Wee Bones positions himself behind home plate Izzie throws a low knee high pitch.

"Strike!" shouts umpire Friedan with the pump of the right hand fist.

Ahead on the count, he decides to throw chin music. He brushes his chin with the back of his hand and goes into his pitching motion. He hopes the batter will jump back because he does not want to bean him with an errant pitch. Wee Bones acknowledges by not crouching   as   low.   He   raises   his   mitt   in   anticipation. "Heybattabattabatta! Heybattabattabatta!" Rings out from the direction of Cheryl and Weezie cheerleading.

Izzie winds up and delivers the pitch. The batter jumps back checking his swing. The ball hits the barrel of the bat. Gooch sees the ball slowly bounce down toward first base. Alert he rushes up and snatches the ball. Racing ahead of the batter he reaches first base for the force out. Quickly he throws the ball to second base for the second out to turn two. Izzie continues to struggle trying different pitches but knows he can resort to the knee high and the chin music to maintain control on the mound. His pitching improves while he works on getting the third out.

"Baseball fans, after the completion of the first inning, the Rascals have not scored and the Rebels have four runs. Speaking of runs, be sure you run to Carol and Pete's Party Store for all your party needs. Pick up streamers, banners, and balloons. The party place at Happy Canyon Shopping Plaza. Or call 1-800 FUN-TIME."

In the second inning, Garvin tries to outshine the Rascals pitching. Instead, he strains his shoulder causing soreness leading to difficulty controlling his pitches. Errant pitches seem to be more common than strikes. The Rascals batters read the throwing and release of his delivery arm. During the second inning, the Rascals manage to get on base with a few hits and advance players to score. Gooch is the last player to come to bat and flies out with two runners on base.

During the Rascals at bat, Izzie and Wee Bones take the opportunity to practice pitching low and high pitches. When he returns to the mound in the bottom of the second inning, he does not feel as uncomfortable as he did in the first inning. He settles into a pitching rhythm pitching a wider range of pitches including outside, low, and chin music. Facing an opponent on another team is not as threatening as in the first inning. Coach Ostrander reminds him that Wee Bones represents his best friend and to ignore the batter. He should keep his eye on the catcher's mitt. The hype of the season opening game no longer intimidates him. The umpire's conservative dress in dark blue and calling strikes or balls does not scare him as much as during the first inning. His authority during the game is not as threatening.

"With the second inning in the books, we have the Rebels team leading with nine runs to four runs for the Rascals. Only you can customize a chicken-to-go bucket at Winging–It. Your bucket is waiting. Step up and customize your order, today. Drive on down to Wagon Wheel Street at the corner of Buffalo Avenue."

The leadoff batter in the third inning is Kippy Waldron. Garvin struggles pitching to short batters. Kippy makes the task more difficult by positioning himself in the left hand batter's box. Reaching three balls and one strike, Kippy squats to emphasize the ball floated high out of the strike zone. His ploy results in ball four, giving him a base on balls. Coach Sternicki's strategy works. Willie chokes up on the bat with an open stance. The first pitch is low and inside. He hits a ground ball double that rolls past the third baseman into deep left field. Izzie steps up to the plate next. He takes a few practice swings and stares down Garvin. Usually, Garvin does not worry about pitching to a pitcher because pitchers cannot hit very well. Izzie is an exception to the rule. He winds up and throws a fastball. Izzie steps into the pitch and hits a ball deep into left field. His hit moves runners around the bases and concerns the Rebels coaches. The Rascals score six runs by the end of the top of the third Inning giving them a total of ten runs.

Turk steps into the batter's box to start off the bottom of the third. The first pitch is outside. He hits a pop foul ball to Gooch at first base. Gooch studies the flight of the ball and watches the descent. His sure-handed fielding makes the first out. The second batter connects with the ball for a hit into left field and gets on base with a stand-up double. A left-handed batter comes to the plate next for the Rebels and hits a worm burner to Willie. He holds up the runner at second and throws back to Izzie. Altering the chin music with other pitches becomes easier for Izzie. He begins to settle into a pitching style that is difficult for the Rebels batters to make contact with the ball. They are afraid that the next pitch might be chin music forcing them to step back in order to avoid being hit by the pitch. The batters become apprehensive when he pitches. Huggable commits the final out after scoring five runs.

"Skeeter Hill baseball fans of all ages, the Rascals team has fourteen runs and the Rebels have ten runs in the bottom of the third. Got roach and termite problems? Call your neighborhood terminator, Your Pest Is My Pest, or visit them on Highway 36 at the edge of town by the Pay 'N Go convenience store. He guarantees he won't be back." Mr. Wince reports to the fans at the top of the third inning.

The teams take a break similar to the seventh inning stretch taken during the professional baseball games. The coaches decide on lineup changes for the remaining three innings. The changes can be crucial to the outcome of the game for batting order and fielding to protect against long ball hitting and defense maneuvers in the infield. Pitching changes might be crucial decisions at this juncture of the game. The Rebels coaches become concerned that their players may not be able to beat the team that received the majority of ridicule before the inaugural season game. A defeat of that nature would be humiliating.

Jimmie Tuttle, nicknamed him Jimmie T, leads off the fourth inning. He gets a base on balls. Willie bats next and hits a bouncing ball into right field over the head of the second baseman. Jimmie speeds past the second baseman and turns the corner to race toward third base. Coach Ostrander, the players call him Coach O, sends Willie to second base. Kippy bats next. He hits a one-hop line drive to the second baseman. He checks off the base runners before deciding to throw the ball to the first baseman for the force out. With runners at second and third Izzie comes to bat. Willie keeps one foot on second base and rocks back ready to run at a drop of a pin. Jimmie T keeps one foot touching third base and rocks back and forth letting Garvin his intention to run home at any given moment. Garvin dismisses the distraction and faces Izzie in the batter's box. Out of the corner of his eye, Garvin still keeps a close watch on Jimmie T. on third base. He tries to ignore him and concentrate on pitching to Izzie.

Coach Hackworth contemplates that the Rebels need a game changer to turn the momentum of the game in their favor. He does not want to lose the inaugural game to some unknown old fuddy-duddy coach. He calls time and marches out to the pitcher's mound. Shielding his mouth with his hand, he engages in a heated conversation with Garvin. Observing the heated conversation, Umpire Friedan decides to resume the game and yells, "Play ball!"

Coach Hackworth kicks dirt toward home plate before he returns to the home team dugout.

"Play Ball!" Umpire Friedan shouts again.

Garvin checks Turk for the sign. The bleachers sing out "Heybattabattabatta! Heybattabattabatta!" He delivers the pitch.

Umpire Friedan calls out, "Ball." The count reaches three balls and one strike.

'Coach Hackworth becomes extremely irate. "Get your eyes checked, ump." Coach Hackworth removes his prescription glasses trying to emphasize a need for better eye wear, and shakes them. He bangs the side of his head with the palm of his hand to indicate to Umpire Friedan, he is crazy upstairs or insinuate something is loose by shaking his head.

Garvin removes his baseball cap and holds it with his ball glove while he slicks back his hair with his pitching hand showing his frustration. He replaces his baseball cap and prepares to throw the pitch. All of a sudden, Willie recalls the signals he watched the Gunslinger players use when he attended the game last summer. *What might the signal mean that Garvin used?* he wondered. *Maybe it was his father's signal?*

After returning his ball cap, Garvin brings his glove and pitching hand together to start the stretch motion. He pauses for a moment and stares at Izzie. Almost in slow motion, he leans back and kicks forward with his leg.

"Heybattabattabatta! Heybattabattabatta!"

With all of the strength he can summon, he throws a fastball toward home plate. The trajectory of the ball speeds toward Izzie without altering direction. Izzie realizes the baseball will not travel over the plate; he twists and tries to jump back to vacate the path of the fast ball in time. Unsuccessful, the laser pitch pummels Izzie on the side of his head. The batter's helmet flies into the air rotating in whirligig fashion on its journey toward the backstop. Simultaneously, he slumps to the ground like a rag doll.

Umpire Freidan tears off his umpire's cage and rips off the chest protector as he rushes up to attend to Izzie. Coach Swat runs as fast as he can from the on-deck circle. Izzie curls up in a motionless ball on the ground. He lays lifeless by home plate. Willie aborts second base and races toward the mound with rage in his eyes. He is intercepted by the second base umpire Herb Sellars. He wraps up Willie and tries to squelch his temper.

The Rebels fans and Rascals fans come to their feet. Angry about the beaning pitch, the Rascals players exit the dugout. Fierce tempers motivate the Rascals players to charge toward Garvin on the pitcher's mound in retaliation. Coach Sternicki and Rebels third base Coach Blanchard rush onto the field from third base ahead of the Rascals players to set up a wall of defense in front of Garvin.

Coach O hurries down the first base side of the infield to hold off Rebels players pouring out of the dugout. Izzie slowly moves writhing back and forth. Only moans of agony can be heard above the player yelling and screaming at each other and especially at Garvin. Time stands still. Mr. Wince stares speechless out of the scorekeeper's box. All cheering comes to a halt; only subdued muttering among fans fills the air.

Coach Swat tenderly braces Izzie's head before deciding to roll him onto his side. He brushes away sand and dirt searching for any and abrasion, open skin or sign of deep bruising. Gradually with Umpire Freidan's help he gets him to roll onto his back and supports his head in the event of spinal injury or to prevent the occurrence of one. Mrs. Kushihashi comes running through the open gate with an ice bag. The player's anger lust subsides. Players on both teams form a semi-circle from first base line to the third base and observe Coach Swat and Umpire Friedan examining Izzie. They do all they can until the paramedic can arrive.

Saddled with equipment, the paramedic squeezes through the chain link fence opening by the home team dugout on his way to attend to Izzie. Accompanied by two firemen, the three men make tracks to home plate. During the course of a medical examination, Izzie summons enough strength to sit up. He massages his head and appears to be dazed and disoriented.

All eyes are fixed on Izzie. Immediately the paramedic takes his vitals. After careful examination the paramedic feels confident he is not seriously injured. With the help of the paramedic, Izzie manages to stand up. Rocking back and forth he concentrates on maintaining his balance. A little light-headed, he casts a blank stare around the baseball field. "Did we lose?" he wonders out loud as he waves to the Rascals fans, then to the players by the on-deck circle, and at Umpire

Friedan. "Hi, Blue!" Gradually he becomes acquainted with his surroundings. He waves in the direction of Garvin, "Oh hi; he's the bad guy... Mr. Junior League... Shhhh, I can't tell!"

His teammates sense that even though he is a little loopy, Izzie will be okay. They call out in unison, "Go Rascals."

"Yeah Rastals!" Izzie gives a hand pump with a punchy expression on his face.

"Go Rascals!" the team responds again in unison. Coach Ostrander no longer detains Mrs. Kolinsky. Relieved, his mother rushes up to comfort Izzie. The paramedic intervenes, "This be your son?" Izzie frowns looking back and forth at the paramedic and then in the direction of his mother.

"Leave my mommy alone! Mommy, you can't play baseball." He wraps his arms around his mother's waist. "You need to go sit down, Mommy."

"Yes, this is my Izzie. My dear Izzie." She gives him a hug and a peck on the cheek. Izzie wipes off the kiss on his cheek.

"You come with me. Need to have a more thorough examination at the hospital. The firemen lead the way followed by the paramedic, Izzie, and his mother.

Coach Ostrander catches sight of Coach Hackworth leaning against the Rebels dugout with a smirk on his face. He hurries over to the home team dugout and says, "You signaled for that pitch. You good for nothing! You dirty rotten...!"

"I signaled nothing! I watched him throw the pitch just like you."

"You gave the sign. I know how shifty you are! It's all about the wins! You don't care who gets hurt!" asserts Coach Ostrander as he steps closer and gives Coach Hackworth a shove on the shoulder.

"Now, hold on there," objects Coach Hackworth. "Watch who you are shoving!"

Officer Higby and Umpire Freidan come running over to separate the two coaches.

"Your players only play for you because they want to win," Coach Ostrander insinuates.

"You don't know what you're saying. Winning is not everything," refutes Coach Hackworth as he smugly folds his arms across his chest.

"You say winning is not everything? But to you it's all that matters, even more than players' safety, more than self-esteem, more..." He collects himself and scrapes up dirt with the side of his shoe and slings his foot in the direction of Coach Hackworth.

Umpire Freidan approaches with Officer Higby by his side. Very flustered and angry, Coach Ostrander meets up with Umpire Friedan outraged. "Hey Blue, I want that pitcher out of the game! That pitch was intentional. You can't tell me any different. Take him out of the game!" he states in an ill-tempered manner pertaining to the incident involving injury to a Little League player.

Umpire Friedan summons base umpire Sellars to discuss the circumstances from Coach O's point of view. Umpire Friedan and base umpire Sellars confer momentarily. Afterward, Umpire Freidan speaks with Coach Hackworth.

The umpires cannot determine if it was intentional or inadvertent. Coach Hackworth decides to move Garvin to cover third base. Buster assumes the pitching duties for the Rebels replacing Garvin on the mound.

"Fans of all ages, according to Rascals Coach Swat, Izzie has been transported to Skeeter Hill Community for further examination. According to the Rebels coach's sheet we have changes. Garvin, the pitcher, will be removed from the mound but remain in the game. You too can remain in the game and invest wisely at the Wilfred Wince Agency on Pioneer Square, open five days of the week from nine to five."

Coach Swat sends Kevin Pritchard, called KP, toward first base to be a pinch base runner for Izzie. With bases loaded, Wee Bones comes to bat. Buster pitches for the Rebels. After struggling to strike him out, he gets a base on balls.

"Sports fans, the Rebels team has walked in a run: Jimmie T. scores from third. With one out and bases loaded, Gooch Wu-Harmon will bat for Rascals. A hair style is a creation for Aunt Bea's Salon. Treat yourself to a creation," announces Mr. Wince.

Gooch wriggles in batter's box

Buster winds up and throws outside and high. Gooch leans over and swings hitting the ball into right center field. Willie bursts toward third base with the release of the pitch. Coach Sternicki waves for him to head for home. KP steps on second base and races toward third base because he has a faster pace.

Willie charges down third base line and reaches home plate to score. Gooch reaches second base and holds up. KP stands on third. The Rascals team scores six runs during the top half of the fourth inning.

Because of the unexpected injury, the Rebels coaches ask for time out to review changes needed in the lineup. The Rascals coaches decide to designate Marty Ostrander as the pitcher in the bottom of the fourth inning. He is not as skilled as Izzie but has practiced with Izzie leading up to the season opening game. It was expected he would pitch an inning or two, but no one anticipated he would be inserted into the game on account of an injury.

Marty walks the first batter he faces, Tommy Akers. Huggable Harold bats next for the Rebels. He faces a strike first. The next throw is a wild pitch. Tommy steals second base. He tosses a strike for the third pitch. The count is one-two. The next pitch Huggable hits into left field. He reaches first and Tommy advances to third. Huggable hesitates wanting a stand up double. He settles for a base hit and stays on first base.

All eyes are on Marty as Garvin walks from the on-deck circle to the batter's box. Everyone wonders whether he will retaliate and throw an errant pitch at Garvin? He shakes off the signs given by Wee Bones. Coach Swat calls time and trudges out to the pitcher's mound. As Coach Swat approaches, he takes a moment and collects his thoughts as he stares at Garvin. More than anything he wants to throw his hardest pitch at him and teach him a lesson. At the same time, he wants more than anything to get him out at the plate and have him return to the dugout with his tail between his legs knowing he was beaten by the best. He studies his victim of prey and tries to decide. Sweat rolls down the swell of his back. He swallows hard as he prepares for the first pitch. But first, he must explain to Coach.

"Marty, what's up?" comments Coach Swat as he glances back at Garvin. "Are you going to take all day? Don't be afraid of him; that's his style."

"Coach, I know I'm not a very good pitcher. But geez... What do I do?" Marty appeals for help.

"Don't think about trying to throw one o 'them frilly pitches. You know like a nickel curve, a slider, or a hanging curve ball you and Izzie talk about all the time. Look past him. Pretend the batter does not have any clothes on. No that's not a very good idea."

"Can't do that coach," replies Marty laughing. "That's a pretty funny idea."

"I'll tell you a little trick. Don't pay any attention to him and stare at Wee Bones' catcher mitt. Don't look at anything else, just his catcher's mitt. Blaze it in there, time after time. The first few pitches might be hard, but you'll get good at it."

"Ya think, Coach?" considers Marty still uncertain.

"You've got my word on it." promises Coach Swat. "I've seen you pitch."

Before the next pitch, he nervously rubs his chin thinking. Wee Bones prepares for chin music thinking that is what Coach Swat and Marty finished talking about. He raises his catcher's mitt about shoulder high. Marty stares at the catcher's mitt position and frowns while he considers the difficulty placing the pitch.

"Wake up and smell the coffee," yells Weezie. "Smell the coffee!" Fans in the Rascals bleachers chirp with the help of Cheryl, "Heybattabattabatta! Heybattabattabatta."

He keeps his eyes fixed on Wee Bones's catcher's mitt while he recites in his mind over and over, *Garvin you have nothing on me, you have nothing on me. You're nothing but ketchup drool.* He starts the motion to deliver the pitch with all the determination he can put together in one release. Garvin leans back to avoid the speeding baseball. At the last second he decides to swing. He misses. The Rascals fans erupt with applause and cheers. Garvin angrily pounds the end of his bat on home plate. Marty catches the toss from Wee Bones. He turns and smiles and waves at the Rascals fans then steps on the rubber and goes into motion to deliver the next pitch. The first pitch was a confidence builder.

"Heybattabattabatta! Heybattabattabatta!" clamors the Rascals fans led by Cheryl and Weezie.

"Marrr-ty, Marrr-ty, Marrr-ty" respond the Rebels fans.

Ignoring the fans, he throws in the direction of Wee Bones's mitt.

"Heybattabattabatta! Heybattabattabatta!" the cadence swells from the Rascals fans as Weezie kicks up her feet and leads with hand gestures to promote the cheer.

Garvin swings at the pitch and tips the ball back out of play. Marty does not feel as ill at ease. His confidence has built up against Garvin and his threatening image. Now Garvin is not any different in his eyes than any other batter. Wavering on what pitch to deliver next, Marty rubs his chin with his thumb and index finger while he contemplates. Wee Bones's mitt positions his mitt for a high and inside pitch. Frustrated, he slaps his glove on the side of his leg. The different signals confuse Wee Bones. He thinks he remembers the meaning of tapping of the glove on the leg. He decides to go with the first signal and places his mitt for chin music.

"Heybattabattabatta! Heybattabattabatta!" rings out by the Rascals fans. Marty winds up and delivers the pitch about shoulder high.

"Out!" shouts Umpire Friedan extending his arm as his right hand fist pumps to designate the out.

Wee Bones suddenly recalls Marty's glove slap against his right leg without extending his arm means to throw to first base after the pitch. He stands up.

"Gooch! Gooch!" He points to Gooch and drills the ball to first base.

Gooch raises his glove for the catch. With a kick in his step Huggable desperately tries to return to first base because he had taken a long lead following the pitch. Unable to return to first base in time, Gooch tags him out.

Getting Garvin out means more to the team than beaning him with the ball. It's a personal victory for Marty and the team. The Rascals team shows brilliance playing smarter than the other team.

"At the end of four innings, the Rascals team has sixteen and the Rebels have eighteen. If you are ever in a pickle for your next party, visit Grandma J's Pantry for down home affordable canned goods and appetizers off Wagon Wheel Street and Ash in the greater downtown Skeeter Hill business district."

Coach O works with Gooch, Marty, Willie, and Frankie practicing the batting drills for use sometime in the next two innings, not knowing which batter will be called on to help out at home plate. The players practice foot placement and hand positioning. Coach Hackworth rotates his players from the outfield into the infield to try to protect against base hits. The rotation will bring his skilled hitters up to bat in the bottom of the sixth inning.

"We head into the fifth inning with Rebels leading with eighteen runs; the Rascals are within striking distance with sixteen runs. Facing life challenges and the unknown without the legal help you need? Don't strike out. Uncle Jon can be by your side to help with your legal problems. Call him at 517-676-5555 or visit his office on East Jefferson and Wagon Wheel, a stone's throw from the Courthouse on Pioneer Square. A word to the wise, Jon says don't throw stones."

During the fifth inning, Coach Sternicki helps the Rascals batter to adjust to the release of the relief pitcher, Buster. Gooch and Frankie get an opportunity to try their skill at placing the ball. The team moves runners around the bases and scores four runs.

During the transition in the fifth inning, Izzie returns. A precautionary dressing covers the bruised area around his forehead where he sustained the blow from the wild pitch. Players greet him and share stories about the progress of the game. He is amazed that the Rascals still have the opportunity to win the game.

Marty takes Izzie aside, "I can't throw the ball like you do. Why does Wee Bones put his glove high and inside for me to throw to his glove? That's not particularly my sweet spot to throw to but I'm getting good at it, but I am still not as good as you. Is there a certain pitch I need to know about?"

"Can't say that I can answer that. He usually follows my pitches and moves the catcher's mitt in place to make the catch. There's not a special pitch." Marty listens to Izzie's advice and tries to employ the strategy on the mound.

Throughout the bottom of the fifth inning, the Rebels' power hitters take their turn at bat. Marty and Wee Bones use made up signals to send back and forth to confuse the Rebels coaches and cause the batters to be more nervous about what pitch to expect. Marty walks the first batter and allows a hit single off the second batter.

Garvin comes to bat. Swinging fiercely at the first pitch, he sends a ball down the third baseline. Punzak catches the ground ball and commits the force out at third base. With base runners at first and second, Turk comes to bat next. He hits a line-drive up the hole between Willie at shortstop and Marty at the mound. Covering second base from his position at shortstop, Willie waits for the cut-off throw from Molly in left field. Before Garvin rounds second base, he captures the go ahead signal from the third base coach to continue to third. He steps on second base and swings wide as he opens up full steam ahead.

Garvin runs wildly passed second base

He sets his sights on Willie in the base line between second and third base waiting on the throw. With his glove poised ready to catch the ball, Willie waits. Garvin re-directs his vision from third base to Willie. Blazing full throttle ahead, Garvin lowers his shoulder and intentionally ploughs into him. He continues churning his legs and drives him to the ground. The two players tumble head over heels. The baseball bounces past Willie and rolls in the direction of pitcher's mound. Watching the collision, Marty casts his eyes on the ball bouncing toward him. He fields the ball and surveys the bases for a play to make. Punzak calls to him, "Marty, over here! Throw it!"

Marty takes aim and throws it to third base. Garvin jumps to his feet. Without delay, he resumes his base running continuing to third base. The ball arrives ahead of Garvin granting Punzak the opportunity to tag him out.

"Safe!" announces base Umpire Armbruster without hesitation.

"What! He's out! The third baseman tagged him!" shouts Coach Sternicki "Punzak, show him the ball!"

"The infielder interfered with his progress as a runner to run to third base. By obstructing the baseline, the infielder caused an infraction that contributed to what appeared to be an out. The runner is safe."

Writhing in pain, Willie rolls over and struggles to stand up. When his comes to his feet he is hunched over and favors his side because of the amount of pain and discomfort. Umpire Armbruster calls time to allow for the proper attention to be given to Willie. KP comes into the game to play shortstop. Coach Sternicki escorts Willie off the field to have a paramedic examine him in the dugout. A bouncing hit to the second baseman side allows Garvin to score. Hitting a foul fly ball to Punzak at third base commits the third out of the inning. The Rebels score five runs do to a costly error by the Rascals.

"At the end of five innings, the Rebels have twenty-three and the Rascals have twenty runs. Skeeter Hill fans, this game is moving right along. If moving is on your mind, keep in mind moving and storage is as simple as 1-2-3 at 911 Moving and Storage. Don't throw it away. Stow it away in an all steel weather-proof facility at Pioneer and Highway 285."

The paramedic rubs a sports cream on Willie's bruised ribs. He suggests a rib belt. Willie refuses the rib belt because he cannot freely rotate his upper body back and forth because the belt is too constricting. He decides he'd rather not wear it during the game because he got the wind knocked out of him. However, he does accept the elastic sports bandage for his twisted ankle. Coach Swat and Coach Ostrander defer making their decision whether he should sit out the rest of the game until they talk to the paramedic.

Coach Swat approaches Willie with a somber expression on his face, "We want to keep you in the game because you can help with your batting skills. I can put you in left field. It's not Siberia, and you will still be in the game. You can protect against the long ball."

"I'll do it. No questions about it—I want the team to win! I think I can help," replies Willie.

Punzak steps up to the plate to bat first. The Rascals team faces what might be sudden death if they do not score three runs. Should the Rascals not be able to tie the score, the game will be over. If they tie the score, they will force the Rebels to bat at the bottom of the inning before deciding the outcome of the game.

"Wake up those bats," yells Weezie. "Wake up the bats. "Come on guys."

"Wake up the bats!" parrots Cheryl cheering. "Stand up everyone, let's all cheer together!" Cheryl begs the fans.

Punzak gets a hit off the first pitch with a trailing line drive over the third baseman's head. He reaches second base to start off the top of the sixth inning. Chico Martinez steps up to bat next. He hits an infield pop fly on the third base side of second base. Buster thinks the short stop will catch the ball. The second baseman covers the base instead of running up on the ball. The shortstop rushes to field the ball grabbing it on the first bounce. Chico reaches first base.

"Way to go, Rascals. Wake up those bats. Wake 'em up! Wake up those bats!" yells Weezie.

Marty trudges to the batter's box. Buster thinks he will bunt because of his hand position on the bat handle and barrel of the bat. He tries to pitch the ball outside. Instead, the ball enters Marty's wheelhouse—one of the areas he had practiced moments earlier. He quickly changes his feet and hand position before he swings. He drives the ball into deep left field.

The left fielder plays too close to the infield instead of playing back for the long ball. He chases it as the ball speeds over his head. Punzak runs toward third base. The ball lands and bounces in the direction of the privet hedge at the outfield boundary. Coach Sternicki signals to Punzak to run home. Reaching third, he steps on the bag and charges for home. While the outfielder chases the bouncing ball, Marty heads to second. Chico reaches third base safely and charges for home, pedaling his legs as fast as he can and scoring the second run in the inning. With the throw to the shortstop, Marty gets a stand-up double.

Because of his height, Wee Bones gets a base on balls. Gooch leaves the on-deck circle to bat next. After recording a two-two count, he lifts a low pitch over the infield into right field. Marty races to third base and holds up. Wee Bones cranks his legs as fast as he can to get to second base. Gooch reaches first base before the throw to the second baseman, the relay fielder. He checks the runners. Marty stands at third, Wee Bones at second base, and Gooch waits on first base with no outs. Kippy comes to bat and hits a pop fly toward the second baseman. Umpire Armbruster tracks the flight of the ball and points up in the air as he declares for all to hear, "Infield fly." Kippy sprints toward first base knowing he has been called out. The ball descends. He raises his glove. The ball lands in the pocket of the glove and rolls out onto the ground.

"Out!" yells Base Umpire Sellars. "Infield fly rule!" He explains directing his line of sight toward Coach Swat.

"Fans of all ages! You can't ask for better sports entertainment in all of Skeeter Hill. The Rascals team has scored two runs in the top of the sixth making the Rascals Team twenty-two and the Rebels twenty-three with one out and ducks on the pond. For the baseball fans, that's lingo for bases loaded. Don't forget to load up on all your barbeque needs at the Branding Iron off Prospector Court by the Homesteader shopping plaza."

Willie takes the trip from the on-deck circle to the batter's box. In his mind, this is the perfect moment to show Garvin that his team is not the laughing stock of the town like he insinuated last summer. He looks out across the infield. For as long as he can remember, he dreamed of the day he would walk into the batter's box with the opportunity to win a game, especially against Garvin's team. Today he ponders the likelihood that his turn at bat may have disastrous results. He tries to put that thought aside. Nevertheless, a double play will bring the fairy tale beginning to an end. Looking out on the diamond, he sees the runners with their lead foot extended in preparation to run. Garvin dances back and forth vigorously to remind Willie of his presence on the infield at third base.

Coach Sternicki calls time. He runs down to the batter's box to talk briefly to Willie. With bases loaded, he decides to gamble. He explains to Willie how to stand in order to get the best result on placing the ball in the "coffin corner." Willie returns to the batter's box and positions his feet and hands.

"Heybattabattabatta! Heybattabattabatta!" The Rebels bleachers' chorus rings out.

"Buss-ter! Buss-ter! Buss-ter!" rings out from the Rascals bleachers with the direction of Weezie and Cheryl leading cheers.

Willie cocks his bat waiting for the pitch. The banter falls on deaf ears as the players concentrate on the moment at hand. Buster prepares to deliver the pitch side arm. Buster goes into his stretch. "Heybattabattabatta! Heybattabattabatta!" fills the air.

Willie aims for the coffin corner employing what Coach Ostrander taught him in practice to do like a skilled batter. He did it then why not now? Coach Sternicki has given him the go ahead.

"Buss-ter! Buss-ter! Buss-ter!" chants the Rascals fans under Weezie's much improved cheerleading style. She is enjoying the role of a cheerleader and her sister cannot believe how quickly her little sister has caught on to cheering. Evidently, Weezie must have watched her very closely when she practiced varsity routines at home because she has learned without many repetitions during the game.

Willie fixes his eyes on the speeding sphere. The ball travels outside the strike zone, which is perfect for the designation he has in mind. At the last moment, he shifts his weight to his back leg; His bruised thigh cannot withstand the weight displacement. His ribs dispatch pain. Unable to power through, he delivers his swing and drives toward the ball with as much strength as he can deliver. His hands sting from the impact. The ball strikes above the shank on the low side of the trademark. Quickly, he releases the bat and shakes his hands because of the sting to his hands. He heads toward first base gaining speed with each step he takes. The ball flies off the bat toward right field, the designated target. It gradually takes a golf ball slice in flight, which is to the right in the direction toward the right corner. The infielders watch the curious flight of the baseball in preparation to position for the relay throw to the infield. Willie dials everything else out and keeps only the base in sight. The right fielder observes the flight overhead and its fall to the ground just beyond his reach. The outfielder gives chase to the rolling ball. While he chases the baseball, Gooch charges toward second base. Wee Bones churns his short legs as fast as he can to reach third base. Willie sprints at a measured pace faster and faster until he reaches first base. Marty crosses the plate and jogs past Buster and Umpire Freidan.

"Skeeter Hill sports fans, it's time for a Kwicky update. The Rascals have gone and tied the game. The score now stands with the Rascals at twenty-three runs and the Rebels at twenty-three runs. Anytime you want a Kwicky car wash, there are five convenient Kwicky locations in metro Skeeter Hill."

The ball bounces into the chain link fence in right field and spins off like a ball in a pinball machine taking on new life in the direction of foul territory. The second baseman runs further into the shallow right field for the relay.

"Go home, Wee Bones. Run, baby, run!" instructs Coach Sternicki at third base. "You got it made, boy!"

Wee Bones rounds third base and his short legs churn and his rubber cleats pound against the hard clay surface. A puff of dust surrounds each footstep along the way to home plate. Coach Ostrander shouts to Willie, "Go to second. Go, Willie! Run, boy! Run to second, boy! What a hit! Man alive!"

Coach Sternicki yells to Gooch, "Gooch! Wake up! Come on, Gooch! Run! Hurry, my boy! Third! Run, baby, run! ... Run, baby run! Run, baby run!"

Willie sprints to second base pacing himself. The bruised ribs ache and ring out with pain with each step. Gooch streaks toward third. Puffing with every stride, he pumps his feet and rotates his hands in a circular motion to keep his momentum. Wee Bones reaches home plate with a personal triumph. Coach Sternicki sends Gooch home. He runs exhausted and out of breath.

The right fielder locates the baseball in the tall grass of foul territory. "Willie. Third! Willie take third. Run, baby, run!"

Willie pauses at second base momentarily to catch his breath. He places his hand on his ribs and takes a few deep breaths. He looks over his shoulder and observes the right fielder picking up the ball. If he intends to make third base he knows he must outrun the Rebels outfielder's relay of the ball. Gooch scores throwing both arms up in the arm to celebrate as he steps on home plate. Willie steadies himself and starts the trip to third base. Garvin straddles the front side of the base ready for the throw.

"Run, run, run." yells the Rascals fans. "Go! Go! Go!" "Willie! Willie! "Willie!" Go!"

The Rascals players have vacated the dugout and stand cheering along the third baseline, "Go, Willie! Go! Run, Willie! Run! Run! Run!"

Weezie screams, "Willie, go! Go! Go! Run! Willie, run!"

Coach Swat springs up and down on his toes, "Go, Willie, go! Run, boy! Run, Willie!"

The ball reaches the second baseman in shallow right field. He pivots and throws the ball to Buster standing between home plate and the pitcher's mound. Since Willie has not reached third base Buster's pitching arm hurls the ball to Garvin at third.

"Slide, Willie! Slide! Slide, boy!" yells Coach Sternicki.

Coach Swat rushes over to third base to join Coach Sternicki screaming with each step on the way, "Slide! Slide, Willie!"

Garvin raises his glove for the catch. Willie tucks his leg and immediately goes into his slide throwing his arms up in the air. Dust clouds up the air and obscures the visibility of the incoming baseball. Base Umpire Sellars runs over to catch the action and make the correct call. At the same time, the ball streaks across the diamond to Garvin's waiting glove. He smacks his glove across Willie's bended knee.

"Safe!" yells base Umpire Sellars as he stretches his arms out to his side. Willie rolls over on his side with his foot still resting on third base. He point toward the extended foot on the bag. Willie feels like a bundle of pain generating from his ankle and his ribs.

"Willie! You did it. What a hit! You did it! Can't believe it, the coffin corner. What a hit!" Coach Sternicki keeps repeating himself overwhelmed by the moment. Willie comes to his feet and prepares himself mentally to charge for home plate. Frankie comes to bat. Willie's success is short lived. The excitement has nearly exhausted the fans. With an evil grin on his face Buster goes into motion.

Frankie steps back with his left foot and forward. He powers forward with his swing. The ball soars into deep right field. It lands and bounces twice. On the second bounce the ball clears the chain link fence and travels into the privet fence.

"In the park double!" announces Umpire Friedan.

Willie jogs home with his hand held firmly against his ribs and Frankie sprints around to second base. Coach Swat meets him at the on deck circle. "Great hit! It's all about rounding third, then you are half way home, son."

"Seven runs score for the Rascals team and only one out. Stay tuned…. You can score today with a Coney dog or Chicago dog from the Skeeter Hill concession."

Jimmie T gets thrown out at first. Punzak comes to bat and gets a base hit with a squibber to the third baseman. Chico hits a ground ball to the second baseman to end the top half of the memorable sixth inning.

"Don't give her a package of seeds. Give flowers to that special someone. See your friendly florist at Wishing for Flowers at Bison Boulevard and First Avenue." announces Mr. Wince. "The Rascals have twenty-seven runs and the Rebels have twenty-three runs going into the bottom of the sixth inning."

Evidently Coach Hackwork has some questions regarding the validity of Willies run. Willie rests on the bench with ice on his ankle while the coach's contest runs scored during the inning. The Rebels cannot make any changes to their lineup unless there is an injury. The batting order is established and cannot be changed under any circumstances. "Willie, we have a lineup problem. Umpire Sellars will allow me to move a few players around. Your ankle okay? I need to keep you in the game," asks Coach Swat.

"Sore but I can manage, Coach," Willie replies as he grabs his glove and jumps to his feet a little unsteady.

"Against my better judgement, Willie, get out there in left field as I promised earlier, Siberia." Coach Swat details the changes in the lineup. "I need a strong arm to defend the outfield. PK, I'll leave you in center. Frankie take right field; Chico said he can't play."

Mr. Wince announces, "We are at the bottom of the sixth inning. The Rascals have twenty-seven runs. The Rebels come to bat with twenty-three. Bring your treasure-hunting spirit to Second Time Around for antiques and more. Your store for hidden treasures. Off Miner Avenue by the Old Oaken Bucket."

Huggable Harold comes to bat to lead off the bottom of the inning. Marty knows from earlier he will have difficulty facing Huggable's left-handed batting. Huggable digs in ready for the first pitch.

"Heybattabattabatta! Heybattabattabatta!" the fans in the Rascals bleachers yell out loud and strong with the direction of Cheryl and Weezie cheerleading.

The Rebels bleachers respond, "Marrr-ty, Marrr-ty! Marrr-ty!

Marty nods in agreement to the signs Wee Bones gives. He goes into the stretch and throws awkwardly toward Wee Bones. The pitch soars wide and Huggable reaches with his long arms and hits the ball into left field for a hit. Willie fields the ball on the first hop and throws to the second baseman to hold Huggable at first base.

Cliffy Cantrel steps up to the plate for the Rebels and takes a few unorthodox swings. Marty goes into his stretch and delivers the pitch. Cliffy drives the ball toward the pitcher's mound. Marty turns his back expecting to be struck by the speeding sphere. The ball strikes the rubber on the pitcher's mound and bounces back toward home plate. Wee Bones spies the ball pop up in the air. He patiently waits and catches the ball in fair territory. Huggable reaches second base. Cliffy eclipses the halfway mark down the first base line and continues running to first base to get a single off a fluke hit. Wee Bones tosses the baseball back to Marty.

"Wake up those bats," yells Coach Hackworth. "Keep it up, wake up the bats. Let's go guys."

Howie steps into the batter's box. On the first pitch, he hits a line-drive between Marty and Kippy at second base. It travels up the middle into center field. The ball is fielded on one hop by KP. Huggable tags up and advances to third base. Cliffy holds up at second base and Howie is safe at first base.

"Wake up and smell the coffee, guys." yells Weezie with the veins in her neck bulging to the point of nearly popping. "Smell the coffee, guys."

Turk saunters into the batter's box and kicks up some dirt like a fierce bull at the bull fight. Wee Bones flashes the signs to Marty. At the same time, Cliffy flashes the signs from second base for Turk to know.

The Rascals fans stand up and begin the familiar taunting chorus, "Heybattabattabatta! Heybattabattabatta!" The runners extend their lead foot ready to run as the pitch is delivered. The ball crosses the plate above his knees. Turk releases a ferocious swing missing the low pitch.

"Strike!" proclaims Umpire Freidan accentuated with a fist pump. Clutching the ball in his right hand, Marty rubs his knuckles on his chin to send a signal to Wee Bones. This time Wee Bones understands that the telegraphed signal is not inadvertent. Glancing at the runner on third, he casually tips his elbow to suggest trying to pick the runner off after catching the pitch. He delivers a high inside pitch. The Turk jumps back to keep from getting hit. His action grants enough space for Wee Bones to fire a throw to third base. Punzak snags the ball in time to tag Huggable out before he can return to base. Punzak clinches his fist and shouts, "Go Rascals!"

"The base runners are Cliffy at second and Howie at first with one out. Having trouble falling asleep at night? Visit My Dream Cloud on the corner of Prospector and First Avenue. Their prices will not keep you up at night. Sweet dreams." announces Mr. Wince.

Wee Bones steps behind home plate. Turk sneers at Wee Bones, "You sneak."

"Now boys!" interrupts Umpire Freidan. "Play ball or I'll toss you outta the game."

Marty wastes little time going into the throwing motion for the next pitch. He delivers the pitch low. Turk chops at it hitting a bouncing grounder to Jimmie Tuttle at shortstop. He fields the ball and throws it to second base for the force out. Turk arrives at first base safe. Cliffy manages to run to third base.

"Never too old until you say it's old. Try New Again to find that pair of broken-in Wrangler jeans or a vase for an unexpected bouquet of flowers. Try New Again for the first time. Stop by at Wilcox and Miner Avenue. We have runners on the corners with two outs. Baseball jargon for runners on first and third. The tying run is coming to the plate."

Buster strolls from the on-deck circle to the batter's box. Marty tries the chin music pitch to Wee Bones. Buster pivots and slides his hand down the bat to the trademark stamp on the barrel of the bat and gingerly pushes the bat into the ball. The bat sends the ball rolling slowly down the third baseline. The base umpire yells, "Fair ball!" Punzak and Wee Bones dance on each side of the baseline following the ball every inch of the way hoping the line of travel will take it into foul territory. The ball nearly comes to a stop.

Punzak snatches up on the ball. Willie covers third base for Punzak. Cliffy digs his cleats into the hard sandy clay and gravel to reverse his progress toward home plate and return to third base. Wee Bones retreats to stand guard at home plate. With bases loaded Garvin comes to bat. He arrogantly walks up to home plate and steps into the batter's box. With a stern look on his face, he tips the end of the bat toward center field similar to the noted gesture by Babe Ruth during the 1932 World Series with the Yankees and Chicago Cubs. In the fifth inning of the game, the New York Yankee batting star pointed with his bat in the direction of center field for the placement of the baseball. The famous gesture signifies an intention to hit a deep ball in the same direction. Garvin takes a few practice ' swings and gestures one more time.

"Baseball fans, here is the moment you have been waiting for, bottom of the sixth, two out, bases loaded and the winning run at bat. It's time to load up on the best smoked or barbequed ribs in town at Uncle Piggly's Smokehouse on Hwy 285 and Buffalo Trail. Or Cal 517-676-6611." announces Mr. Wince.

Marty nods his head and looks at Cliffy on third base. Without delay he goes into has pitching motion and delivers the pitch. The ball travels inside. Garvin swings exerting all of his effort to hit the ball. The ball flies over third base toward left field. Willie gives chase. He does not raise his glove in the air while running and pursues the expected line of travel. Hampered by the ankle sprain, he pursues relentlessly as much as possible under the circumstances. He keeps his eye on the ball and targets the trajectory. Almost reaching the destination, he thrusts his arm out extending his glove as far in front of him as far as he can to capture the descending ball. His bruised ribs give him extreme pain, he hesitates momentarily. With his glove wide open he pushes off his toes to make the catch. In a split second, he feels his glove bend backward. Did the ball strike the pocket of his glove? Did his glove bounce off the ground? Not willing to take any chances he pinches the pocket of his glove closed. He cannot determine if the glove has collapsed around the ball. Regardless, he must prepare for impact. Protected by his right hand, he presses the glove against his chest. All of a sudden he sees the ground coming up to meet him. Believing he caught the ball in the pocket of his glove, he cradles his arm with the glove against his chest.

As he hits the ground, he experiences more pain than he has ever experienced in his life. He screams louder than he has ever hollered before. The momentum from the chase causes him to roll on the ground tumbling over and over. After a revolution dragging his toes, he comes to a stop. He must take a moment to recover from the excruciating pain. Fans come to their feet and watch. First, he practices with a few deep breaths to relax and recover because he has the same sensation of having the wind knocked out of him. His ankle throbs and throbs. Without a doubt his ankle is injured far beyond being strained.

Silence grips the fans. The Rebels base runners must tag up if he doesn't catch it. They wait in anticipation. Garvin races down the first base line determined to reach first base thinking Willie will not make the catch; he decides not to overrun first base and turn into the foul territory. Instead he heads for second base and waits. The players for both teams exit the dugouts and stand with their eyes glued on Willie. There is no sign of the ball. Everyone questions whether he caught the ball or not. Did it bounce toward the privet hedge deeper in left field undetected? Where might the ball be? Can it be trapped underneath Willie? Willie comes to rest on his side. He raises his glove with the ball protruding partially above the fingers of his glove resembling a snow cone. Willie smiles and laughs to himself. He did not make the catch with skill. It was an accident. Regardless it is still an out.

"Out!" yells the Base Umpire Armbruster with a definitive thumb and fist raised for the last time in the game.

"Out!' shouts Umpire Friedan with a smile of disbelief on his face.

"Rascals players, you have won the first game of the season! Rascals, you are victorious! Congratulations, Rascals! Rebels and fans of all ages, the Skeeter Hill Youth Authority wants to thank you for coming to the opening game of the season with the Rascals winning by a score of twenty-seven to the Rebels score of twenty-three. Remember to stop by Wasserman's Sports Cards and Collectibles Shop. Charlie says there is a little sports fan in everyone. Located at the Homesteader Shopping Plaza."

While waiting for the Rebels team at the center of the infield, the Rascals team assembles forming a circle. Everyone extends a hand and places it on top of another player's hand. Punzak counts, "One, two, three!" Everyone raises their hand. The team yells in unison, "Go Rascals!"

Following the victory cheer, the Rebels players reluctantly trudge out to the pitcher's mound to line up across from the Rascals team players. As the players walk down the line, they shake the hand of the players on the opposing team as a gesture of sportsmanship and goodwill.

When Willie reaches Garvin, he experiences a harsh reception, "Save it, Willie. You got away with one. Got something for ya." Garvin turns his back and retrieves a can from his glove then drops his baseball glove on the ground. Curious, Willie waits with his hand extended for the handshake. Garvin pops the top off a can and pivots in order to spray whipping cream all over Willie's open hand. Players on both teams laugh, and laugh, and laugh. Coaches on both teams chuckle at Garvin's harmless prank.

"Congratulations, Rascals Little Leaguers. Rebels and Rascals, we look forward to an exciting season," announces Mr. Wince. "Some things in life we do not look forward to doing. Moving across town or relocating across the country with Remcore Technologies? The Wince Agency and 911 Long Distance Moving will be at your service. Sports, fans thank you for coming out and supporting your favorite baseball team. Your broadcast analyst today has been Wilfred Wince, your friendly Skeeter Hill Little League Baseball play-by-play announcer. Please drive safely on your way home, and come back for many more games this season."

During the announcement, Willie hobbles toward the dugout. Gooch brings him a towel to wipe his hands. Coach Swat calls out to all of the players to join him for an after game talk.

"I can't believe the game you fellas played today. Don't let that go to your heads. There were mistakes. We'll have work on that in practice. I have a brand new baseball signed by the coaches. Players pass it around and sign it or put your x on it. Willie Wince will get the game ball. Next game ball will be the Memorial Weekend tournament. Walt Disney once said, 'It is fun to do the impossible.' Today you did the impossible and, believe me, it was fun. Go Rascals!"

"Go Rascals!" replies the players in unison. Mrs. Kushihashi and Mrs. Wince with the help of volunteers bring out coolers full of sliced watermelon onto the baseball field for the players and family members to enjoy following the game.

In the sun of the late afternoon, players, family and friends re-live the excitement of the game while they enjoy the taste of ice-cold watermelon. Weezie joins the team and spits watermelon seeds with the guys as they frolic and enjoy their victory in the sun. Even Cheryl joins the group with her cheerleading supportive mood and jokes with the boys while she competes in the watermelon spitting contest trying to determine who can spit the closest from pitcher's mound to home plate. Weezie cheers for her sister to be the winner for the longest distance.

Willie hangs out with Weezie a bit, renewing their friendship that has been strained by all of the practice and fundraising from the last several months. He pairs up with her and tries to learn a few cheerleading routines. His injuries make it difficult and challenging. Regardless, Willie and the other Rascals enjoy their time away from the baseball field. The Rascals celebration continues into the early evening before everyone decides to call it a night.

LET THE GAMES BEGIN

A trophy is not awarded to a team for winning the first game of the season. Instead, the players receive blisters, bruises, sore muscles, and sunburns to show for their efforts. The Youth Sport Authority determined that Garvin's actions were questionable according to the Skeeter Hill Youth League Rules of Conduct. His actions awarded him a two-game suspension for behavior unbecoming of a player within the sports program guidelines.

Each Little League team will play all of the other Little League teams twice during the course of the season, not including the Memorial Weekend Tournament. The teams play all of the other teams once before the Memorial Weekend Tournament and the second time before the Fourth of July Season Tournament.

During the first practice ·after the victory, the Rascals compare their various cuts and bruises. Most of the players with sore muscles impact their ability to practice. Consequently, the coaches cannot have full-scale practices before the next game. The limitations cause the team to struggle during the next game against the Outlaws. Willie practices with the team on a limited basis until his sprained ankle and bruised ribs can heal. Since shortstop is more active than the third baseman, Coach Swat decides Willie should play third base. He moves Punzak to shortstop for a few games.

The Rebels defeat every team on their schedule leading up to the Memorial Day holiday weekend. The Rebels and the Rascals teams steer a collision course for the Memorial Weekend tournament.

On Saturday morning of the Memorial Weekend, the Kiwanis and Lions Clubs serve breakfast with pancakes, scrambled eggs, sausage, bacon, donuts, and orange juice, and everything for an ideal family breakfast in the park.

Families arrive early to find a spot in the shade underneath one of the sprawling maples or spreading oak trees to lay out a blanket. Younger children frolic and play in the playground on the swing sets, teeter-totters, and slides while others chase Frisbees or, on a more serious note, play catch with a baseball in preparation for the Little League game later in the day.

The Rayner softball field and the Little League field are cloaked in red, white, and blue decorations to commemorate the patriotic tradition of the Memorial Day holiday. Streamers on the bleachers flap in the wind. American flags of all sizes can be seen interwoven into the colorful decorations and bunting. A jumbo inflated Uncle Sam stands next to the large events sign on one side and an inflated baseball player the same size anchors the other side of the sign atop the concession stand at the Little League baseball field. Bunting decorations highlight the underside of the window of the scorekeeper box.

Gradually, the players and spectators arrive at the Skeeter Hill Baseball Field for the first game of the Skeeter Hill Memorial Weekend Little League Championship. Aspirations are high leading up to the championship game on Monday evening.

Weezie's mother helped her glean through cheerleading outfits at Goodwill and the Skeeter Hill Thrift stores to create a perfect cheerleader outfit for the Rascals team. She arrives with pompoms, homemade signage, and other cheerleading accessories she managed to scrounge up. By eleven o'clock, the dignitaries, umpires, and both teams wait for the commencement of the opening festivities.

"America the Beautiful" fills the air from the speakers mounted on the light poles in the infield. The Marine Corps Reserve Color Guard walks on to the field in formation. Carrying the flag of the United State of America and the state flag, they march to the flagpole next to the home team dugout. The Marine Corps Reserve runner stands in place and waits for the Capitol Aires Barber Shop Quartet to enter the infield and proceed to the pitcher's mound. While they sing the "Star Spangled Banner," the runner raises the flags. During the conclusion of the national anthem, rockets blast off from the outfield boundary. Mayor Polkinghorn, Mr. Wisenhut, and Reverend Thurston congregate at home plate. Reverend Thurston delivers the opening prayer for the player's safety and to bless the proceedings of the game.

"Ladies and gentlemen, parents and players," announces Mr. Wisenhut. "This is the first year of the expanded Little League. In order to advance to the third round of play with four teams, we will create the first Skeeter Hill wildcard team. The Little League team in the second round scoring the most runs with the fewest runs scored against them will be this year's wild card to advance as the fourth team for Monday. The final round of play will begin Monday morning at eleven o'clock at the Little League baseball field. Wins and losses are important for our championship series."

"Mr. Wisenhut, thank you for that explanation. As the Mayor of Skeeter Hill, I declare we shall play ball!" Mayor Polkinghorn, accompanied by Reverend Thurston and Mr. Wisenhut, exits the infield to join the Marine Corps and the Capital Aires Quartet. The group travels through the park to the softball field. The second game between Rebels and the Sharpshooters has been scheduled to be played on the softball field at the same time as the Rascals and Outlaws. Instead of imposing the standard time limit of two hours and fifteen minutes on a game during the Memorial Weekend Championship, the umpires allow the games to go six full innings if necessary. The mercy rule applies to the championship play but is utilized sparingly. When a team leads by ten runs in the bottom of an inning beginning with the fourth inning, the umpire has the discretion to end the game or allow the game to continue.

Izzie, KP, Kippy Waldron and Gooch miss the weekend games because of family commitments. Coach Swat must compensate and cross utilize his players. Without key players, the Rascals will be at a disadvantage to advance through the tournament. The Rascals do not have the pitching skills of Izzie. Without the hitting of KP and Gooch, scoring may be more difficult.

The scoring during the first three innings between the Outlaws and the Rascals goes back and forth. The Outlaw coaches change the lineup in the fifth inning placing older, taller players to cover the infield, which will make getting base hits much more difficult since several of the Rascals players are shorter and will likely hit ground balls in the infield. There's not a real playbook or strategy but many custom-tailored plays or lineups are designed to exploit an opponent's weakness. Coach Swat concocts a batting scheme meant to challenge their pitcher. He scrambles down the steps to the dugout and explains his game plan to the players. "In the new lineup, I will start with Chico Martinez because he is short like Wee Bones. Marty Ostrander will bat next. He is a much taller batter. Then little Jimmy Tuttle will bat. Punzak, our left-handed slugger, is next. What we will do, gentlemen, is put short batters at bat followed by a taller batter. We will get him out of rhythm by doing what we do. Go Rascals!"

"Go Rascals!" responds the players in unison.

Coach Swat's game plan plays an important role with the Rascals team's ability to get players on base and in scoring position. The pitcher for the Outlaws cannot adjust to the fluctuation in the height of the Rascals batters. The batting lineup disrupts the Outlaw pitcher's rhythm, which helps the Rascals to keep the game close.

Weezie returns to the Little League baseball field after visiting the softball field where the Rebels and the Sharpshooters are playing their game. She runs up to the chain link fence and screams, "Willie, come here! Willie, I gotta talk to ya." Reluctant at first, Willie decides to split off from the other players. "Come over here! I gotta score for you."

He jogs over to Weezie. "Hey, Weezie. What's so important?"

"I came from the other game. The Rebels are ahead seventeen to ten in the bottom of the fifth with bases loaded. Garvin is coming up to bat! No outs! Willie, they're going to win. You *can't* lose!"

"Gotcha, thanks! I'll tell the others." He waves and jogs off toward the dugout.

The news about the Rebels rallies the Rascals team. In the top of the fifth inning, the Rascals lead by three runs. The Outlaws manage to tie the game in the bottom of the fifth. A flurry of hits in the top of the sixth by the Rascals team puts them ahead by three runs. The scoring rally must be met by the Outlaws. They bat three up and three down. At the end of six innings, the Rascals team has nineteen to sixteen for the Outlaws. Jubilant, the Rascals players exit the dugout jumping up and down and congratulating each other. The players met the challenge of the first game.

On Sunday, the Rascals team plays the Wranglers. Following the opening festivities at the softball field, the Rascals players jog out onto the field representing the home team. Chico Martinez is the starting pitcher. He sprints out to the pitcher's mound as the lead-off pitcher. His only pitching experience has been in sandlot games; he has practiced with Marty and Izzie but because of being much shorter, his choice of pitches is limited. His debut proves to be a fielding exercise. The Wranglers manage to get hits off his low and inside throws. The Wrangler team scores four runs before hitting into a double play with a force out at second base and a force out at first.

The Rascals team scores six runs at their turn at bat in the bottom of the first inning. Frankie assumes the pitching responsibilities in the third inning relieving Chico. His pitching lasts one inning. Willie tries his hand at pitching and manages to protect the Rascals lead but does not show much promise. At the end of the fifth inning, the Rascals team leads by two runs.

In the sixth inning, Marty faces the top of the batting order. He mixes up his pitches with low and inside and high and outside to avoid allowing batters to hit long and deep balls. With runners on second and third, Jeff Dumont steps up to bat. His reputation precedes him. Last summer, he won the longest ball during the fall sign-up games over the Labor Day Weekend. Marty's pitching gets him into a jam with a full count and two outs. He motions to Wee Bones he will pitch chin music. Instead, the ball travels over the numbers not inside. Jeff leans back thinking he can wallop the high-pitched ball. The better logic pays off for Marty. Jeff's intense swing completely misses the speeding sphere.

"Strike!" declares Umpire Sizemore. "Out!" he announces. The Rascals team wins out over the Wrangler team's attempt to rally.

News about the two games travels fast. Soon, everyone in Skeeter Hill knows which teams have proven to be victorious.

In the early evening, family, friends, children, and other community supporters assemble at the Skeeter Hill Baseball Field for the Memorial Weekend program.

Mayor Polkinghorn addresses the crowd assembled in the bleachers, "In this time of unprecedented success and prosperity throughout our land, I ask that all Skeeter Hill residents come together to recognize how fortunate we are to live in a land where freedom prevails—the land of liberty for all. It is for those who have dared life and limb that we must pause to remember and reflect this weekend more than any other weekend. Their lives and sacrifice have demonstrated that freedom and liberty comes at a great cost. We must hold this near and dear to our hearts."

"Ladies and gentlemen, children of all ages, our program continues with Memorial tributes for members of the community who served in the military, Coast Guard or veterans who have passed on during the previous year. During the time of remembrance, the flood lights over the softball field dim. Darkness closes in around everyone. In the distance, the thud from igniting fireworks can be heard. The sparkling trail of the fireworks twinkles and glistens in the dark of night. From right field to left field the fireworks show entertains everyone in attendance.

With the conclusion of the fireworks, Mayor Polkinghorn approaches the microphone, "Ladies and gentlemen and children of all ages this concludes our Memorial weekend program. Today and every day, let freedom ring." In the distance, the fire truck bell sounds. The Memorial Weekend remembrance and tribute program concludes.

When Willie arrives at the softball field on Monday morning, the grounds keepers have nearly finished with the infield. The base lines for first and third base have been laid. In the distance, his eyes follow the back and forth movements of the mowers. The smell of fresh cut grass fills the air. Final touches on the decorations are being made by the Fire Department Women's Auxiliary.

The game does not begin with the fanfare witnessed on Saturday and Sunday. The umpires take their place on the field. After warm-up pitches, the umpire announces, "Play ball!"

The teams battle back and forth. The Rustlers face Chico's pitching. Chico demonstrates better control pitching as the game progresses. Marty, on the other hand, has difficulty since he did not pitch much of the game the day before. He must limber up his arm. The Rustlers score five runs in the top of the sixth inning to go ahead of the Rascals by two runs. Wee Bones bats first in the bottom of the sixth inning. He gets a base on balls. Tyler trudges back to the dugout after he strikes out. Marty keeps the inning alive with a worm burner toward the pitcher. Wee Bones races to second base. The throw to second base involves too much risk even though Wee Bones is not the fastest runner. His deliberation allows Marty enough time to reach first base and Wee Bones to reach second base. Boos and cheers of disapproval flood the air from the Rustler fans.

Willie knows he will be the winning run. In the swelter heat he plods over to the batter's box from the on-deck circle. Tired, hot, and sweaty from the mid-day sun, he raises the heavy wooden bat. He sees Wee Bones and Marty extend their lead foot like race horses eager to get out of the gate. At this point, it is all or nothing. He keeps his eye on the ball, a spiraling curve ball. Willie focuses on the ball blazing toward him. *Smooth easy swing. Don't try to clobber it,* he tells himself as he draws the bat forward with a steady motion and all of his strength. *Crrrack!* The sound echoes off the maple trees that outline the boundary in outfield. The baseball climbs and climbs left of second base toward outfield. It looks like a pop fly. The center fielder scissor-steps back and over. He looks up in the mid-day sun and loses the ball. The ball lands to the left of the outfielder in the grass out of his reach. It takes on a new life bouncing in the direction of the outfield boundary marked by the chain link fence.

As Wee Bones reaches third base, Coach Sternicki motions for him to run home. The outfielder retrieves the ball as Wee Bones triumphantly steps on home base, pouncing with both feet. At the same time, Marty approaches third base chopping at the bit to run home. He slows up and looks over his shoulder. The outfielder throws toward the shortstop for the relay throw. "Marty, run home. Go! Go! Go!" yells Coach Sternicki frantically waving his hands in the direction of home plate.

After stepping on third base, Marty accelerates and races toward home. The shortstop stands and waits for the ball to arrive from the outfielder. The relay throw is not in time because one run has scored. Marty streaks down the third base line short of breath. Willie casts his eyes on the shortstop who fires the relay throw to the catcher as Willie touches second base. Without hesitation, Coach Sternicki motions with both hands for Willie to continue to third base. Willie turns on the speed and runs as fast as he can. All the while he hopes to reach third before the catcher can make the throw to the third baseman and tag him out. The ball bounces in front of the catcher at the same time Marty touches home plate to tie the score. Instead of trying to throw to third and beat Willie, the catcher eats the ball. Willie holds up at third base. The umpire gives the crossing of the hands for the safe at the plate. He knows all he must do is reach home plate for the Rascals to win. His heart beats faster, and faster. He breathes like a race horse after a grueling training session around the track. Anxious, he stands with his foot pressed against third base waiting for the all-important *crack* for him to bolt for home. His hands sweat. He licks his lips waiting, and waiting. Sweat rolls down his forehead and beads up on his upper lip. He is anxious to score and claim the victory.

The score is tied. Punzak comes to bat. The first pitch is low and outside. He swings at the lazy outside pitch and taps the ball enough. A dribbling ball travels bouncing toward the shortstop. He muffs the catch because the fast bouncing ball is hard to field. Willie stays on third. Punzak races down the first base line and makes it to first. Jimmie Tuttle gets a base on balls. With bases loaded and two outs, Frankie comes to bat. He hits a one-hopper to the second baseman. He backs up to make the catch. Not being squared up, the ball falls to the ground. He snatches up the ball. Not wasting time checking on the force plays at the bases, he fires the ball home. The catcher must turn toward the second baseman for the ball. In other words, to make the catch he must desert his position guarding the plate and stand up to snag the ball on the bounce. Willie slides with his right leg extended. The dust kicks up and swirls around home plate. He cannot see the catcher and has no idea if he has traveled far enough to have reached home plate. His heart races faster and faster hoping he has not missed touching home plate.

All of a sudden, he hears the voice of Umpire Friedan above all the cheering and whistling. "*Safe!*"

The Rascals fans jump up and down and congratulate each other that the Rascals scored to win the game. Weezie cartwheels in the grass in front of the bleachers. Confetti fills the air from the hand held canons. Streamers fly. Mrs. Wince, Mrs. Kushihashi, Mrs. Waldron, and Mrs. Sternicki run out from behind the makeshift food stand at the softball field with their aprons flapping back and forth in the breeze and jump up and down cheering in the infield. The players scramble out of the dugout and swallow up Willie when he reaches the on-deck circle.

The Rascals team wins! Somehow the Rascals team makes the unexpected happen. The pandemonium subsides. Fans, players, and coaches pack up their belongings and equipment and leave. The serenity of nature fills the expanse of the baseball field after everyone disperses. In the reunion pavilion, the Elks Club barbecues half of a chicken and sweet corn for a dollar.

The players scrounge enough money between them for everyone to enjoy a tasty barbequed chicken meal instead of a hamburger or hot dog at the baseball field. In their minds, the win helps add to the flavor of the barbequed chicken meal. After replaying the game over and over, the players become anxious to learn the score and watch the end of the Rebels versus the Sidewinder game. They pack up and walk across Rayner Park to the Little League Baseball Field.

Rayner Park

At the baseball field, the players find a seat and sit together with the Sidewinder fans.

"Hey, I heard you stole one," jokes a fan in the bleachers.

"Yeah, good game guys." Another fan congratulates the players. Other fans applaud.

"Awesome game! You got quite a coach." Another fan extends accolades. Everyone directs their attention to the game with the Rebels against the Sidewinders.

"Out!" yells the umpire signaling with his right hand fist pump.

"Ladies and gentlemen, and baseball fans of all ages, we head into the sixth inning with the Rebels leading by a score of eighteen runs to thirteen runs for the Sidewinders. Don't be shy. Bring your photo moments back to life with photo creations from Snapshot Photos in the Prospector Shopping Center." Mr. Wince provides the score and promotes a fan favorite business.

Coach Hackworth does not let up on his players. He has relief pitchers practicing behind the bleachers with his backup catcher in the sweltering heat. The Rebels players persevere and press on to a win over the Sidewinders.

"Ladies and gentlemen, and fans of all ages, the championship game will be played between the Rebels and the Rascals at five o'clock," announces Mr. Wince. "Your announcer for the game between the Rebels and the Sidewinders has been Mr. Wilfred Wincer of the Wince Insurance Agency on Pioneer Square. Drive safe and we look forward to seeing you for the Skeeter Hill Memorial Weekend Championship game between the Rebels and the Rascals."

The premiere sports event of the spring will be under the lights at the Skeeter Hill Baseball Field. Exhaustion mixed with excitement grips the players arriving to compete for the championship crown. Nearly everyone has grown tired of the festivities and gala events. The game begins without the pageantry.

"Ladies and gentlemen, and baseball fans of all ages, in the visitors team dugout we have Coach Swatkowski and the Skeeter Hill Rascals." He pauses to allow Coach Swatkowski to scale the dugout steps and tip his baseball cap to the crowd. He saunters over to the on-deck circle before he tips his baseball cap. Cheers, whistling, and clapping ushers up from the Rascals bleachers.

"In the home team dugout, Coach Eugene Hackworth and the Skeeter Hill Rebels." Coach Hackworth climbs the steps and travels over to the on-deck circle and tips his hat. Fans in the Rebels bleachers cheer, whistle, and applaud. "Let's play ball," declares Mr. Wince.

Playing at dusk and later under the lights at Skeeter Hill Baseball Field has a distinctive grown-up feeling for players on both teams. The Rascals team congregates around Coach Swat at the on-deck circle. The players extend their arms and place a hand on top of a hand for the team cheer. Coach Ostrander and Coach Sternicki place one of their hands on top of the players' hands. Everyone waits for a moment until Coach Swat places his hand on the very top off the stacked hands for the pre-game salute. "Go Rascals!" Their hands rise up in the air.

Garvin, the starting pitcher for the Rebels, reads the signs from Turk.

The Rascals batters manage to score three runs to lead off the top of the first inning. Since Coach Swat does not have Gooch and KP to help with long ball hitting, he struggles in the top of the first inning. He developed some gadget plays tailored to exploit each team in the tournament designed to exploit their weaknesses. He doesn't have a real playbook because if another coach reads the trick play the coach can make a variation of the play. Instead he know what each player can do except for on the pitcher's mound. Willie has been designated to try pitching in the first inning. Unfamiliar with the duties of a pitcher he cannot get ahead of the batters. Because he pitches more balls than strikes, Chico relieves Willie in the first inning after he loads up the bases with walks. Marty relieves Chico in the third inning. He manages to keep ahead on the count for most batters. Keeping ahead of the count forces the Rebels batters to swing at pitches and not be as selective.

In the top of the sixth inning, the Rascals edge the Rebels by a score of three runs. With a slim lead, the players prepare for the final three outs of the championship. Coach Hackworth implemented a lineup change in the fifth inning anticipating a come-from-behind game. By making the change, he expects the batting lineup will translate into several sluggers coming to bat at the bottom of the sixth. This is his custom-tailored play to exploit the weakness of the Rascals. With a three-two count, Marty cannot throw the deciding pitch and walks the leadoff batter. An infield hit advances the runner to third. With a runner on first and third, the next batter goes down swinging at the low inside pitches. The runner on first base charges for second base as the batter swings at the first pitch. Because the second baseman, Jimmie Tuttle, does not cover the bag, Wee Bones has to eat the throw and return the ball to Marty instead of trying to make a play at second base.

With runners at second and third bases, Huggable approaches the batter's box. Nervous tension mounts because he represents the tying run. Marty checks off the runner at third and goes into his windup. Huggable maneuvers a golf swing to lift the ball into deep left field. Judging the fly ball, Frankie retreats toward the chain link fence by the privet hedge along the boundary of the outfield. He uses both hands and cradles the ball in the pocket of his glove and traps it. The runner from third base tags base and scores standing up. The runner

147

on second approaches third base with a cautionary signal from his third base coach to hold up.

Garvin steps up to the plate representing the winning run. The umpire calls the first two pitches balls. The next pitch, Garvin swings late tapping a ball into shallow right field. Tyler runs up, lowers his glove and tries to scoop up the ball. Garvin races down the first base line and reaches first base. Tyler must back track. He hurries back and plucks the ball out of the taller outfield grass. The fielding delay enables Garvin to set his sights on second base. The third base coach faces home plate watching the runner from second base score. Garvin continues to run the bases forging ahead to second base. Tired and in a hurry, Tyler throws the ball off balance trying the hop technique as he brings his arm forward. The throw sails over Jimmy Tuttle's head into shallow left field. Garvin kicks off second base and runs full steam ahead to third base. Willie runs into shallow left field to retrieve the overthrown ball. Garvin holds up on third base.

"Skeeter Hill baseball fans, we have a tie in the ball game. The Rebels runner on third represents the winning run. After the game, you can hit a home run with Daisy's Car Hop. The right place to go for that 60s malt-shop feeling. Drive on down to Prospector Court and get ready to listen to that 60s sound," announces Mr. Wince. "There is not better sound around to help that shake go down."

Weezie encourages fans, "Go Rascals! Gooo Rascals!" Cheryl jumps up on the first row of seats to escalate the fans emotions and join in the cheers led by Weezie.

Garvin taunts Marty with a comfortable lead off third base knowing Little League rules do not allow leading off. Coach Hackworth has a reputation for stretching the Little League rules. Some of the umpires look the other way. Other umpires strictly enforce the rules, especially when the coach is Mr. Hackworth. Regardless, he toys with Marty's mind and hopes the base umpire is not strict or notice. He knows he will be warned the first time before being called out. Marty goes into his stretch and winds up. The batter tomahawks the ball toward Jiminy Tuttle at second base. He gloves it. Immediately Garvin charges for home racing at top speed. Jimmie Tuttle hurries his throw to Wee Bones. Garvin eclipses the halfway mark on his way to home plate. The ball hops in front of Wee Bones. He changes his position to reach for the catch.

Wee Bones must pedal back toward first base to catch the poorly thrown ball. Where he predicts the ball will land separates Wee Bones from guarding home plate.

Garvin bulldozes Wee Bones

He watches Garvin charge for home and smack his foot down squarely on home plate for the win. He continues running and barges into Wee Bones, trampling him on his way to the home team dugout.

The game comes to an end with the Rebels winning the Memorial Weekend Championship by one run in the bottom of the sixth. The Rebels congratulate each other and immediately migrate to dance around home plate in their celebration.

"Ladies and gentlemen and sports fans, the Skeeter Hill Youth Authority congratulates the Rebels on their win for the Memorial Weekend Championship. Now you can let Curls Salon manage your hair treatments. The beauticians will gladly curl up and dye for you located at the Homesteader Plaza for your convenience. Wilfred Wince, announcing for today's game thanking everyone for turning out and supporting your team this Memorial Weekend. Drive safe on your way home."

Dejected, the Rascals teams salutes the Rebels with the customary handshake and returns to the dugout. Coach Swat stands on the top step of the dugout casting his eyes down the bench inside the dugout. "Gentlemen, a common expression goes something like this, 'Victory comes to those who make the least mistakes.' You played a top-notch championship series. In my heart, you are the winners. The Martial Arts fighter Jim Miller commented, 'The road to success is under construction.' Clearly the top of our game is under construction. We'll get them next time! Go Rascals!"

"Go Rascals," replies the team in unison.

A shuffle of paper can be heard over the open microphone in the scorekeeper's box. "Coach Hackworth speaking. Ladies and gentlemen, can I have your attention. I want to thank Huggable on the Rebels Little League Team for being the most valuable Rebels team player of the championship game by scoring the tying run. I want to congratulate Garvin for the most valuable championship series player for finding a way to keep his team in the game. Individual player recognition will be awarded by the Rebels team coaches. Thank You. I want to thank the Rebels players for clearly being better than the rest of the teams this Memorial weekend."

The Rascals team leaves behind the memory of the lights at the Skeeter Hill Little League baseball field and the experience of a championship game. The burden of their equipment bags and back packs seems heavier on account of the loss. It was not just any loss. It was a loss to the Rebels, Garvin's Rebels. Leaving the dugout the players trudge off in different directions. The championship game slipped from their grasp. For many, the game was an impossible dream. Tonight they walk away with memories for a lifetime, being champions in their own hearts.

Weezie skips up to Willie with her cheerleading charisma and says, "Tough break. You almost beat them."

"We were out played. We needed Izzie, Gooch and KP. With them, we'd have beaten 'em hands down. Coach even said we made mistakes. Get it right! We lost!" replies an irritated Willie as he keeps trudging toward the parking lot and homeward.

Victorian House

A light from and inside a window of the stately Victorian house suddenly flicks on illuminating the dark portion of the visitor's side of the field and shimmers over the landscape. Willie stops in his tracks and directs a curious stare. Troubled by the bitter loss, he resumes his march to the parking lot.

WAKE UP THE BATS

The loss of the Memorial Weekend Championship haunts the Rascals players. After the championship, the team resumes playing the other teams in the league for the second half of the season. They continue their winning ways week after week. The players work on sharpening their skills fielding and batting. Coach Sternicki brought a sawed-off broomstick the length of a bat and a ping-pong ball glued to a piece of heavy chord. The team journeys to the swing sets in the park and practices hitting the ping-pong ball with the stick. The coaches utilize waffle balls to practice throwing techniques. Other ingenious practice techniques are implemented to help improve their skills and make the practices more fun. Prior to playing the Rebels team, Coach Swat decides to make more frequent changes to the roster during the game. After playing another team Coach Swat makes mental notes what he can do to help improve the Rascals. Some changes are implemented during the practices on a trial and error basis. On Father's Day weekend, the two teams face each other again.

Finally, Father's Day arrives. The teams assemble at the baseball field to play against each other for the first time since the Memorial Weekend match up during the championship. Neither team will have the excuse of playing shorthanded. The Rebels have the distinction of being the home team.

Excitement fills the air. Willie's father eyes the baseball field from the scorekeeper's box. For some reason he chooses to be detached from the team and announce the game from a lofty perch. Willie never could understand why his father did not join him on the field once in a while and encourage him. He often observed other parents congratulate other members on the team for an outstanding play or show empathy for an injury. Never once did his father go out of his way to show the slightest interest in anything other than announcing the games. Not even after the games did his father join him on the baseball field or the top step of the porch. Often his mother would join him before or after a game as team mom and always found the time to squat down on the top step and exchange conversation. She took the edge off of some of his concerns going into a rivalry. She especially lent an ear to his worries about the Rebels before the first game. Never did his dad ask one time if there was anything he could do or volunteer for anything connected with the team actives after the season started.

No one imagined that such a rivalry might develop between the two teams. The team play against each other developed into a grudge match. Little did anyone know that the animosity between Garvin and Willie would fuel the rivalry? C.J Heinze argued that such a fueled rivalry is unhealthy for the game of baseball. His ranting fell on deaf ears.

The Rascals developed a strategy for the game against the Rebels. The Rascals lineup starts with players not as skilled at fielding. Coach Swat implements the alternating batters according to height scheme. He has Wee Bones then Gooch. The second pairing is Tyler then Frankie for the taller batter. This batting scheme flusters the pitchers trying to judge a fluctuating batter's strike zone. Beginning in the first inning the Rascals batters switch right-to-left-handed batting after a couple of pitches rattles the pitchers after the batter switches back. The pitching chatter by the Rascal infielders is a shenanigan instituted after the Memorial Championship that bewilders and frustrates the Rebels batters. The antics and good play by the Rascals team catches the Rebels off guard. By the fourth inning stretch, the Rascals team leads by seven runs.

Before playing the fifth inning plate, Umpire Stolz calls the coaches together. "Gentlemen, we have a consideration to take into mind. The Rascals team leads the Rebels by nine runs. The Rascals team bats first meaning the players can easily extend the lead. The mercy rule states that a game is called when there is a ten-run lead at the end of the fourth inning. I suggest we call the game before it gets out of hand."

"I must ask the team. The player's decide," replies Coach Hackworth. "I can't make the call."

"Coach Hackworth, it's not your players' call to make. The game is already out of hand. You won't be saving face by scoring a few more runs. Do you want your players to think Coach Swat wants to run up the score? You must be the one to have your players' interests at heart," reminds Umpire Stolz looking directly into Coach Hackworth's eyes.

"You're talking about the slaughter rule? That's the correct name for it. My team has not begun to fight! You're saying we're not good enough!" proclaims Coach Hackworth as he shovels dirt up against the trousers of Umpire Stolz.

"Running up the score is considered poor sportsmanship. What am I to do? Tell them not to play hard?" Coach Swat expresses his concern taking a glance toward the Rascals dugout.

"I'm telling you we're in this until the bitter end! Those Rascals want a fight? Then they gotta fight!" Coach Hackworth shouts as he scrapes another pile of dirt and kicks it at Umpire Stolz. Before the dust settles, he starts to scrape up another pile of dirt and stones to kick at Coach Swat.

"Game!" announces Umpire Stolz gesturing toward the Rascals team to indicate their victory. He points at Coach Hackworth and signals he is ejected. According to the Skeeter Hill rules and guidelines for coaches, Coach Hackworth faces a suspension for the next game.

The Rascals team wins the game. According to Coach Hackworth, it was not a completed game; instead, it was victory by decision. Skirmishes and harsh words continue between the players during the days to follow. C.J. Heinze argues the point about the question whether Umpire Stolz should invoke the mercy rule with less than a ten-run lead or if the decision to call the game by decision is a victory. The controversy plays out at Chelsea's Drug Store and Aunt Bea's Salon. The rumor mill erupts with another topic going into the Fourth of July championship. Both teams continue on a collision course for the July Championship.

On the Saturday morning of the Fourth of July weekend, players meet at the Methodist Church below the square to participate in the parade. The players are excited to march in the parade showing off their clean uniforms before becoming grass-stained and streaked with dirt. A multitude of activities are scheduled during the Fourth of July weekend but none as important as the baseball tournament to crown the season champion. The Rascals team has been relegated to the softball field for their first game. At the end of the parade, the Sidewinder and Rascals teams are shuttled to the softball field in Skeeter Hill's stretch passenger buses used by the school system for field day transportation.

The game at the softball field begins without any fanfare. Decorations are everywhere. The women have set up the refreshment concession behind the backstop. After the teams have had the opportunity to warm up, the game begins.

The Rascals are the home team. Coach Swat decides with the other coaches to use Chico, Marty, and Izzie as much as possible. Chico is the lead off pitcher against the Sidewinders. The parade may have been a distraction because his timing is off. Nevertheless, he manages to throw strikes about knee-high, which has become his trademark pitch. The ball handling by the Rascals players impresses the fans. After three innings, Izzie assumes the pitching duties.

At the six inning mark, the Rascals team has earned an eight-run lead over of the Sidewinders. Pitching to the third batter, Izzie throws an outside pitch. A bouncing ball hit to Willie enables the Rascals team to turn two. The next batter bunts the ball and jogs toward first base, committing a force out at first with the catch by Gooch when he tags the bag. The team gracefully surrenders the game knowing they cannot close the gap with two outs. All of the Rascals players exit the dugout and flood the infield celebrating the win.

Wearing her customized cheerleader outfit, Weezie bolts out onto the field and weaves her way through the players to meet up with Willie. Spreading out her arms, she wraps Willie in a big hug.

"Gee Weezie. Cut it out! Just because we're best buds you don't need to slobber all over me." He complains pulling away in front of his teammates.

"Willie, we've lived next to each other for years, been chums in school since pre-school. We're on the same team, pal!" Weezie steps back and mingles with the other teammates spreading her cheerleading charisma.

The parents flood the field and congratulate the players on the first win of the tournament.

Quickly, the Rascals pack up equipment and belongings in order to hurry across the park to the watch the Rebels and Rustlers at the Little League baseball field. The game has reached the fifth inning. Willie, Punzak, Izzie, Gooch, Wee Bones, and Weezie find a place to sit in the visitor bleachers with the Rustler fans.

"Hey, Willie!" Izzie speaks up. "Did you know that Buster won't be pitching anymore Rebels games?"

"Caught beaning too many batters like Garvin did to Izzie?

"Naw! His father's moving with Remcore," replies Gooch with a grin.

"Heard the team is getting a super player," explains Punzak. He goes on to elaborate. "Got hurt at the beginning of the season. Had shoulder surgery. Gonna be a junior Leaguer next year."

The Rebels maintain the lead and win over the Rustlers. Since the next game will not be until Sunday afternoon, the group migrates to the carnival on the square. Willie observes the barkers trying to con people into playing a carnival game. He watches the interaction and routines with the carnival workers. Aspects of the routines remind him of baseball with the enticing jargon, ultimately luring batters into playing the kind of game Rascals want to play. The newly instituted infield chanting, which the team plans to use against the Rebels if they play them in the tournament, exhibits certain similarities.

On Sunday, Coach Swat arrives early at the softball field. The players straggle in and situate equipment before starting warm-up practice. Since there is not a brick and mortar concession, the Women's Firemen Auxiliary sets up tables and a canopy tent for cover from the sun or rain. The Gunslingers arrive in several passenger vans and storm the baseball field. Umpire Lindell and Umpire Tobin disembark from a black sports utility vehicle and traipse past the concession and onto the softball field. Their arrival puts him in mind of a dignitary arrival or even the presidents black SUV entourage as seen on TV.

After a few words with the coaches, the game gets underway. The Rascals team has the designation as the home team. Marty takes the mound for the first inning. Willie thinks of the chatter and jargon of the barkers at the carnival. He signals Gooch to start the chatter. At the same time, the fans shout, "Heybattabattabatta! Heybattabattabatta!" The infield chatter begins.

"Curve ball!" yells Gooch from first base.

"Throw slider," screams Willie from shortstop.

"It's a fastball," Punzak yells nervously gyrating at third base.

"Strike!" The infields yell in unison. "Strike!" They repeat the cadence from the beginning over until the pitcher releases the ball trying to get the batter nervous.

Intensity of the chatter swells and becomes confusing causing the batter to be distracted with the banter taking place in the bleachers. Marty finishes his pitching motion and throws the first pitch. The batter swings wildly not knowing what pitch may have been delivered, fastball or curve. Although the cadence succeeded, the coaches decide to use the distraction sparingly. At the end of the Gunslingers' batting inning, only one run scores. Coach Swat congratulates the players as they exit the playing field.

Molly marches up to the batter's box. "Wait for your pitch," shouts Coach Swat. "Don't swing until you see the whites of his eyes." Coach uses the expression to convey to the batters to read the pitch and not swing early. The batters learn quickly to wait for the pitch and not swing just to try to hit the ball unless they get behind on the count.

Molly Mayfield googles the pitcher

By the end of the bottom of the first inning, the Rascals are able to bat six runs across the plate. In the bottom of the fifth inning, the Rascals manage five more runs to extend their lead to nine runs going into the sixth inning. The Gunslingers come to a decision to apply the mercy rule and the game draws to an end. The Rascals win!

Many of the players from the Rascals team return to the carnival after the game, Cheryl and Weezie tag along. Seeing Marty in his Rascals baseball uniform leading the group, a carnie lures him over to the milk bottle toss. Cheryl quickly yells out to him, "Marty, I bet you can knock 'em down and win me that great big panda." Marty's heart begins to race. He feels a sense of fond encouragement. Without much convincing Marty steps up to play the game and throw the softball as hard as he can to knock down all three milk bottles to win the giant panda. He grabs a dollar from his pocket and pays the carnie before Willie or any of the other players have an opportunity to step up. His palms are sweaty as he tosses the ball from hand to hand and studies his target. He is nervous. He hears a voice from the crowd behind him. All eyes are on Marty. "What are you waiting for, Christmas? throw the damn thing!" Marty draws his arm back nearly touching his ear with his thumb. Squeezing the ball firmly in his hand he powers his arm forward with all the strength and determination he can deliver before releasing the sphere in the direction of the pyramid of milk bottles. The ball ricochets off side of one of the two milk bottles on the bottom. The top milk bottle falls down. Simultaneously, Marty drops to his knees and grabs his right arm. He cradles his right arm against his chest, and screams in pain, "Oh my God! Jesus, Mother of…"

"Guys, let's get him to the medical tent, over there on the corner!" screams Willie. Punzak, Gooch, and Izzie step in front to clear the way. Immediately, they usher Marty in the direction of the medial emergency tent.

Marty balks and falls to a knee. Gooch coaxes Marty, "Come on, Marty. It's just over there." Willie slides his arm around his back for support. Punzak does the same from the other side. The boys lock arms grabbing each other's forearm. Next he brings his arms around their shoulders. The two boys practically carry him to the medical tent.

At the medical tent, Mrs. Kushihashi meets the boys and instructs the players to wait outside. "Can I at least have my team captain with me? Ain't got no one else I trust as much."

"Take your shirt off and wait on the exam table."

She exits the tent and retrieves Willie. They enter the examination cubicle. "Hey, Willie! I feel like that guy who broke his arm pitching."

"You'll be all right. Wait and see," responds Willie trying to comfort Marty.

After the brief examination the paramedic sits on a kitchen stool. "I've got some good news, and, I've got some bad news. You're not going to pitch anytime soon. There're many things about the shoulder that can cause an injury, such as the rotator cuff, ligaments, and tendons. Athletes are prime subjects. I suggest no throwing motion for a week. Get plenty of rest. See your family doctor as soon as possible."

"No throwing for a week? He's gotta play—the championship is tomorrow! There's gotta be a way," says Willie. "Got any suggestions?"

The paramedic searches through his portable locker and finds a package. He steps over to Marty and hands it to him. "Here, wear this. It's a shoulder support. I prefer to call it a brace. It will reduce your range of motion and help with the irritation. No pitching. I recommend he sees his family doctor. It's up to his parents whether he can play."

They exit the tent. Izzie points toward the package. "What's that thing in the package?" wonders Izzie "Did he break his arm?"

"It's a sling jig-a-ma-job for my arm," explains Marty taking the package from Willie. "Don't s'pose I can keep this from my parents."

The boys depart and go home for a night of rest. Coach taught the boys to dream the impossible. In the morning, Willie wakes up with the impossible in mind. The Rebels play the Lawmen in the first game of the day on Monday. The bleacher side for the home team side displays decorations fitting a king. American flags, pennant flags, patriotic star garland, streamers, and bunting are on the bleachers and the concession. The Rebels mascot posters are displayed everywhere allowed.

Willie pedals his bicycle to meet up with Izzie and Punzak riding their bicycles to the ball field. "Did ya hear?" Izzie hollers over to Willie.

"Marty's parents won't let him play," Punzak shouts pedaling his bicycle as fast as he can to keep up with the others. "Something about a rotator or something burst then heard it was something, something."

"Who's the snitch? His arm wasn't that bad last night. I was there!" replies Willie somewhat confused with the change of diagnosis.

"I think it must have been Mrs. Kushihashi." Punzak pedals to catch up with the others. "You know how team moms are. Gotta love 'em but can't trust them with a secret," mentions Gooch with a smirk.

"My mom told me that his folks said he can play. Does that make her a snitch?" questions Wee Bones as he dismounts his bike and slips out of the straps of his back pack.

"Naw! Doesn't matter. At least he's all right. We might need him if he can play," responds Izzie.

The game opens with the Skeeter Hill Legion of Honor flag unit raising the flag of the United States. Theda Polkinghorn sings the "Star Spangled Banner." The major ceremony and celebration is reserved for the championship game with fireworks to follow.

Immediately the Rebels deploy onto the baseball field. During the season, the Lawmen team played good enough to lose. Getting into the championship playoff on Monday transpired because of lucky play not skill; *errors* by the opposing team contributed to their wining. The Lawmen score two runs in the first inning. The Rebels demonstrate more power hitting and score five runs. The game moves quickly because of the dominance by the Rebels.

Wearing a new cheerleading outfit, Weezie arrives during the three-inning stretch. She shows off her cheerleading outfit made by her mother and Cheryl. It is stunning. She searches for a place to sit down with a bag bulging with mysterious items. "I gotta surprise for later. What's the score?"

"The Rebels are leading elven to five," Wee Bones tells her while he tries to inspect the bulging shopping bag from the party store. "What the heck is in there?" he asks.

"It's for me to know and you to find out," quips Weezie as she moves the bag between her feet to guard against a sneak peek.

By the top of the sixth inning, the Rebels control the outcome of the game with a comfortable lead. An in-the-park home run gives the Lawmen four points during their last bat. Nevertheless, the game concludes with a score of nineteen for the Rebels and sixteen for the Lawmen. At the moment of the final out, a few streamers and confetti canons shower tiny pieces of paper and poppers accentuating the celebration of the Rebels win.

The Skeeter Hill Baseball Field becomes the stage for the children's program. Toddlers three years of age and younger assemble to parade their decorated tricycles down first baseline across home plate where the judges view the bikes and up the third base line. Everyone, including parents, observe the procession with curiosity and pride. Red, white, and blue streamers attached to handle bar grips and the back fenders fly in the late afternoon breeze. Some tricycles have crepe paper threaded through the spokes. Flags, pennants, balloons, and banners spruce up the bikes. Many of the toddlers proudly ride their decorated tricycles dressed in costumes like a solider, a field nurse, or a medic.

The bicycle judging follows the tricycle parade. The older children present their bicycles for judging. Much like the younger children, they parade the embellished bikes down the first base line across home plate in front of the judges and up third base line.

The individual contest portion of the program starts after the decorated bicycle contest. The races and contests are age appropriate. The younger children compete according to age groups in the apple race carrying an apple on a spoon, then a balloon blowing contest, and several games with water balloons. Ages five and up compete in a three-legged race and a sack race. The edible program events include pie-eating contests, ice cream eating, and watermelon. By early evening, the contests and activities come to an enjoyable end. Pie, Ice cream, and watermelon decorate the shirts and blouses of the children. Family, children, and friends leave with memories and unsettled and perhaps ailing stomachs. With the conclusion of the program before six o'clock, everyone has the opportunity to return home to freshen up and relax before the evening of presentations, awards, entertainment and reflection. The second baseball game between the Renegade and Rascals teams starts afterward.

In the twinkling of an eye, all of the players, coaches, and umpires arrive and go to their designated places and begin the pre-game warm-up drills. The Skeeter Hill Police Cadet Drill Team presents and raises the flag while Mr. Joseph Wexler sings the national anthem.

Quickly the game gets underway. The Rascals are the home team.

Anxiety overwhelms Willie knowing all eyes are on him to throw the first pitch of the game. He exchanges eye contact with the batter. Raising the ball, he goes into his wind-up motion. "Heybattabattabatta! Heybattabattabatta!" comes from the bleachers as fans sing out the familiar chant to distract the batter.

The awkwardly thrown pitch soars downward toward the plate. The batter swings. In a split second, the ball flies over Willie's head toward center field. Unable to control subsequent pitches, he allows six runs to score before the players manage to get the out to end the top half of the inning.

"The Renegades score six runs and the Rascals team has five runs. Those of you who are athletically-minded or want to do some good for your community don't forget the annual Labor Day 5k/10k and half marathon for Cerebral Palsy. Don sit on the sidelines; get into the race for the cerebral palsy community fund. Step up on Labor Day and run. We've reached the halfway point in the game. The Renegades lead with a score of twenty-four runs to twenty-one runs by the Rascals team. Neither team wants to take charge. Speaking of taking charge, don't forget to take charge of your insurance coverage on home and auto and visit the Wilfred Wince Agency on Pioneer Square. And remember, if you're moving across town or across the country, call 911 Long Distance Moving."

The Renegades threaten to widen their lead with bases loaded. Instead, Tommy Akers hits into a double play. In the bottom of the fifth inning, the Rascals team capitalizes on a leadoff walk. All of a sudden, hits by Jimmie Tuttle and Tyler Kushihashi manage to rally the Rascals batters. Frankie Sternicki hits a stand-up double putting the team ahead.

The lead is short-lived with a flurry of hits against Izzie in the top of the sixth inning. Two runs score early. Leading by one run, the Renegades load up the bases with two outs. A pop fly to deep left field allows the runner on third to tag up and score. The Renegades have two runners on base with two outs and lead by three runs. The next batter picks and chooses his pitches. After a talk with Wee Bones, Izzie decides to pitch out of the situation. He throws a fastball. The batter swings. On the subsequent pitch without hesitation, he throws a cookie. Usually a pitcher throws a cookie in an attempt to regain his control after an errant pitch. Izzie throws the slow-lofting pitch to trick the batter.

"Heybattabattabatta! Heybattabattabatta!" recites the Rascals fans.

Thinking the pitch will be another fastball the Renegade batter swings early and strikes out. Izzie and Wee Bones scheme their way out of a jam.

"We have a barn burner here with the Skeeter Hill Renegades leading the Skeeter Hill Rascals by two runs going into the bottom of the sixth inning. Having trouble seeing the forest for the trees? Try Rolling Hills Landscaping. Make your landscape design greener on the other side," announces Mr. Wince.

The Renegade crowd in the bleachers sends out a chorus to distract the batter. "Heybattabattabatta! Heybattabattabatta!"

Molly Mayfield bats first for the Rascals, sending a high foul ball. The first baseman catches the ball behind first base for the first out. Disappointed flipping her pigtails did not distract the pitcher enough to cause him to throw her a more desired pitch she drags her bat behind her on the way back to the dugout.

Molly Mayfield's pigeon toed batter's stance

Punzak stands in the batter's box next. He remains composed while waiting for the pitch of his choice.

"Heybattabattabatta! Heybattabattabatta!" Punzak hears the chanting chorus. He swings at the next pitch. The barrel of the bat travels under the high outside ball, sending it to shallow left field. The shortstop pedals backwards. The left field outfielder runs up on the ball. He sees the shortstop and pulls up. The shortstop glances over while the two Renegade players yield to each other. The ball descends to the ground like a rock between them. Punzak is safe at first base.

Marty saunters over to the batter's box and faces the Renegade pitcher in pain he trembles slightly and muscles quiver because of his sore shoulder. With each pitch, the crowd erupts with the taunting cheer, "Heybattabattabatta! Heybattabattabatta!"

He reaches the full count. Punzak skips sideways to lead off first base toward second base as the pitch is underway. Marty guesses the proximity of the speeding sphere since it will a called strike in his determination he swings. The ball zooms back toward the pitcher. Marty runs down the baseline toward first base. The pitcher dodges the ball allowing to it bounce behind pitcher's mound and roll into outfield. At the same time Marty races for first base for a hit. The fans applaud and cheer.

"We have the tying run on first base. Looks like Willie Wince for the Rascals team will come to bat. Remember your Uncle Jon K. Jenkins has the legal solutions. He will go to bat for you every time. Give a call 517-676-5555 or visit his office on Pioneer Square."

Willie practices his swing and sets up for the pitch. He clubs the ball to center field. The center fielder grabs the ball from the tall grass. Willie rounds first base. The relay throw is on the way. Punzak charges for home. Seeing the throw to the catcher to tag Punzak out, Coach Ostrander yells to Willie, "Take second! Go!" Willie reaches second. Marty holds up at third base. He stands up and massages his shoulder.

"Sports fans, do we have a game! Runners on second and third with one out and a one-run game. Which team will hold their cards close to their vest? Need a tux or formal attire? Stop by CinderFella's Boutique—your place to shop for formal wear and bridal party fashions. Homestead Square is the place. Don't call stop by."

Izzie hits a lazy ground ball to shortstop. Fielding the ball, the shortstop throws Izzie out at first. Wee Bones gets a walk. Bases are full when Gooch steps up to bat. The pitcher goes into his windup.

The fans chirp, "Heybattabattabatta! Heybattabattabatta!"

Garvin and his teammates stand along the chain link fence at the end of the home team bleachers and watch. The pitch is on the way; Marty runs open throttle down the base line toward home. Gooch powers through with a windmill swing. *Crrrack!* He hits a line-drive ball.

The trajectory changes into a slice-in veering from center field to right field. The runners advance around the bases. Marty races down the third base line and scores as he stomps on home place. Willie rounds third and heads home to score. Wee Bones stops halfway between first and second and watches. He sees Willie score and starts jumping up and down to celebrate the win. Coach Swat calls out, "Wee Bones touch second! Don't stop! Run, Wee Bones. Run!" Wee Bones races to second base. Wee Bones steps on second base in celebratory fashion and explodes with excitement and jubilation. The Rascals team did the impossible advancing to the championship against the Rebels.

Garvin looks on and watches the celebration with disgust. Streamers catapult into the sky; confetti showers the fans in the home bleachers. The Rascals team shakes hands with the Renegade players to show their sportsmanship.

While the boys pack up their equipment, Willie comments to Punzak, "You know what hurt us this game and might have caused us to lose the game."

"Not exactly?" replies Punzak. "What ya think it might have been?"

"We didn't have Weezie and her cheerleading. We lost our edge! I hope she is not too embarrassed after what happened to Marty last night. I sure hope she shows up for the next game," Willie wishes under his breath as he grabs his glove before leaving the dugout.

HEY BLUE!!!

Arriving early at the Skeeter Hill Baseball Field, Willie decides to slurp up some cold well water at the drinking fountain before trekking over to the home team dugout. While enjoying the refreshing water from the drinking fountain, he hears someone call his name, "Hey! Willie, how goes it."

He perks up and searches for the familiar voice. A bat slips between his legs. With a twist and an angry push on his shoulder, Willie tumbles to the ground. His arm stretches out to brace his fall. His baseball glove cartwheels a few feet away. At the same time, Garvin stomps on Willie's hand as hard as he can. Relentless, he pivots back and forth grinding his cleats into Willie's hand. "Don't worry, Willie, you won't be needing that glove today."

"Yow! "Oooh yooow," Willie screams as he draws his hand away.

Immediately, Garvin tosses his baseball bat and glove toward the bleachers in the distance. Simultaneously, he races over to the concession booth doorway and yells inside, "Anyone, come quickly. Someone, Willie's hurt! I think he twisted his ankle."

Willie writhes in pain on the ground. Emery Farnsworth runs out of the concession. Casting his eyes on Willie rolling back and forth on the ground he peels off his apron and hustles over to him.

"Oh, God! It hurts." Willie tucks his hand between his legs, tossing and turning on the ground in pain. "Ooooooh, oooow..."

Emery goes down on one knee beside Willie. He spies the bleeding left hand. "Son, what happened? He reaches for Willies mangled hand. "Oh, my God! Hold still, son!"

"I'd da-don't. Oooh!" he gathers up enough strength to speak over the pain and sits up. "My feet tangled up and I tripped and fell. Ooooow. Oh, ooooow. Then Gar..."

Garvin interrupts, "Mr. Farnsworth. I, uh, I saw him fall. I think he must have twisted his ankle or something after getting a drink. Ya know, with all the mud 'round here, walking 'round him in a hurry I accidently stepped on his hand. Honest I didn't mean to..."

"You boys weren't getting into it before the game, now was ya? "Son, get me a bowl of clean water and a clean kitchen cloth," urgently requests Mr. Farnsworth.

"We wasn't fighting or nothing. Honest. Look over there! You can see my baseball glove and bat by the stands." Garvin points to his equipment on the ground by the bottom row of home team bleachers. "Look at my stuff. I wasn't close to him at all. Let's face it, he was in a hurry and slipped in the mud and water."

"Garvin, I…"

"Get me a bowl of water and clean cloth! Son, let me look at your hand." Emery examines the extensive gashes and cuts to the back of Willie's hand.

"Looks pretty nasty. I ain't no doctor but I think it needs medical attention."

Willie holds his hand away from his body in order to limit the amount of blood staining his uniform.

Mrs. Kushihashi exits the concession with a wet towel and a glass of ice water to rinse his hand. "I heard yeah tell the boy." She rushes over to Willie and immediately begins to attend to his injured hand. After the bleeding stops, she wraps his hand with a cloth. Willie flexes his fingers to demonstrate he's all right. At that time, Gooch and Izzie walk around the corner of the concession and discover Willie on the ground. When he tries to stand up, he grimaces from ankle pain.

"Let me get over to the dugout. It's nothing. I just twisted my ankle, that's all," he reiterates. Gooch hands him his baseball bat to use for a cane. Willie walks gingerly with the bat as support. Gradually, he makes his way to the dugout and slowly descends the steps to reach the bench. His ankle does not seem as bad as he first thought.

Izzie arrives skipping down the steps at the opposite end of the dugout. A few minutes later, Kippy and Marty scamper down the steps at the other end of the dugout. Mrs. Kushihashi joins Willie with an ice bag for his ankle and a fresh bowl of ice water to rinse his hand.

In the distance, Coach Swatkowski, Coach Sternicki, and Coach Hackworth engage in a pre-game conversation with Umpire Halstead. The men review and verify any rule changes for the championship game. Mrs. Kushihashi instructs Willie to continue to keep the ice bag on his ankle. She takes the bowl of cold ice water with her.

After she leaves, the players gather around Willie to talk about what happened.

Chico Martinez enters the dugout at the far end and sees a styrofoam cooler next to the team's five-gallon water jug on the bench. He recognizes the water jug but becomes curious about the styrofoam cooler. "Hey, guys! Are there soda pops in here?" he asks. No one responds. "Guys! Are there soda pops in here?" He waits for an answer. Since no one replies, he lifts the top. "Hey, this is pretty light. Must be empty," he exclaims as the top slides off. The bottom of the styrofoam cooler tumbles to the dugout floor. "Are you sure... Yikes! Snakes!" He yells as he scampers up the dugout steps. "Guys, snakes! There's snakes! Snakes in...in..." Before he can finish, the players hustle out of the dugout. Willie hobbles up the steps last.

Coach Sternicki grabs a small can of defense pepper spray from his side pocket and hurries down the first two steps of the dugout. He hesitates while he surveys the situation. Garvin along with several of the Rebels players hustle over to the first base line to watch. They laugh and laugh and laugh.

"Willie, I couldn't find no skunk!" shouts Garvin. The Rebels players run away when the Rascals players start to chase them. Coach Ostrander and Coach Swat hurry over to establish a line of demarcation to prevent any confrontation. Willie sits on the top step of the dugout and watches Coach Sternicki. Coach Swat sends Jimmy Tuttle to find the firemen. Coach Sternicki picks up the cooler and sees a garter snake underneath. With the snake in hand, he extends his arm and watches the snake curl up. "They won't hurt you. Nothing to worry about," Coach Sternicki demonstrates.

The boys shy away as they watch the snake try to coil around his arm. He returns the snake to the cooler. Both coaches engage in a thorough search of the dugout. Coach Ostrander finds a snake hiding in Willie's baseball glove and another in the equipment bag on the floor of the dugout. Two firemen arrive to help with the search. "We got four. We removed all the gloves and equipment, and coats. Boys said there were five. Should be only one more to rustle up, gentlemen."

While the firemen double check for any remaining garter snakes, the players deploy onto the field and begin warms-ups. Coach Sternicki leaves the dugout to play fungo by hitting fly balls for the outfielders to shag. Mrs. Kushihashi arrives with a paramedic to examine Willies injuries. He cleans Willie's hand wound and examines the left ankle.

"I've got good news and bad news," states the paramedic. "Your injuries are not game-threatening. I've got just the thing." He fumbles around in his medical bag. "Here is an elastic glove and wrap. Look no fingers! Should give you enough support. It will be like a brace. Remember, it's a brace for your hand. It will protect your hand while you play. Your ankle, it's not that bad, just a mild sprain. Ice it down. Have your coach put on this elastic wrap for your ankle. You'll run like the wind. Well, maybe not that fast, but you get the idea."

"You saying I can play?" Willie asks.

"You'll be able to play. It'll be a little awkward. Can't tell the extent of your injuries for sure without an X-ray. Keep the ice bag on your ankle until you are ready to play, then limber it up before you run full tilt on it," cautions the paramedic as he packs up his supplies. He holds a brief conference with Coach Swat before leaving the dugout area.

At the conclusion of the pre-game warm-up exercises, the Rascals return to join Coach Swat at the dugout. The players form a semi-circle extending from the far end of the dugout steps to the dugout stairs closest to the on-deck circle. "Gentlemen! Gather in close," directs Coach Swat. "There've been some unexpected injuries recently. I've decided to change the lineup."

"I can play, Coach," exclaims Willie pounding a fist into the pocket of his glove.

"We'll see about that," Coach Swat responds. "This is about strategy and timing. Today we'll reverse the line up and start with the players I had planned to play at the end of the game. Ordinarily we have Chico relegated to right field, but he will pitch today for a game of this importance. Molly Mayfield will be the right fielder instead. Marty Ostrander will play second base, which will not require him to make throws from outfield, so he can protect his aggravated shoulder. Frankie Sternicki replaces Willie at shortstop," declares coach Swat before he checks his clipboard a final time. "I want everyone to get their playing time before we think about winning the championship. By the third inning, I will decide about anyone who has not played, including Willie. I will keep our darling Molly in the middle of the batting lineup until the end of the third inning. She's our secret weapon in pigtails; we'll use her to charm the pitcher. And Izzie will sit down until the fourth inning. All together players—Go *Rascals!*"

They constrict the semi-circle to stack their hands on top of each other. "Go Rascals!"

The Skeeter Hill Police Academy Cadet drill team introduces the colors. While the lines to the flag are being clipped to the state flag the Skeeter Hill, the Daughters of American Revolution sing "America the Beautiful." After the flag raising, the crowd applauds and whistles. "Our national anthem will be sung by Patricia Wainwright with the Skeeter Hill VFW." All of the players stand in front of the dugouts, graciously remove their hats, and place their right hands over their hearts.

"With the conclusion of the national anthem, I want to introduce our umpires for this afternoon. At home plate we have Ian Halstead, our umpire-in-chief. The base umpire will be Edith Carrigan. Make the right call to Miff's Autohaus for all of your truck or auto repairs. Right down your alley on Sage Brush Road off HWY 285."

The Rascals players line up and in single file sprint onto the baseball field one by one to their position in order to start the first inning against the Rebels. The coaches decide to be creative and move Chico to the mound as the starting pitcher. Since the Rebels players are the tallest of the Little League teams, Coach Swat surmises that the shorter pitcher will be an advantage. Perhaps the taller batters will struggle against a shorter pitcher. The newly installed infield cadence cheer might help mask his limited pitching ability. In order to keep Izzie fresh in the latter innings, Coach Swat decides to sit him out until it is time to pitch. He will use deception and misdirection to defeat the Rebels only if necessary. Coach Swat discussed with the other coaches that during the first three innings the Rascals will play heads up without trickery or tailored plays designed to swing the momentum. In spite of the goal of a trick play or a tailored play to make an out or score a run the coaches believe the Rascals are the better team, not losers!

"On the injured list we have Willie Wince. The Rascals shortstop is recovering from pre-game injuries." Garvin begins to clap and whistle. All players from the Rascals team and Rascals fans direct their line of sight toward Garvin in the Rebels on-deck-circle. He shrugs his shoulders. Mr. Wince continues, "Do you have questions about barbeque? See Griller Bill. At Buffalo Pete's on Lower Pioneer Road. And the final members of the Rascals roster are Weezie and her sister Skeeter Hill High School Varsity squad Cheryl the cheerleaders."

With all the players in place, Umpire Halstead ambles over and brushes off the plate. C.J. Heinze walks up to the mound with Mayor Polkinghorn. Holding the game ball, he nods in the direction of the Rascals dugout and says, "I congratulate the Rascals as our home team today." He turns and faces the visitor dugout. "I congratulate the Rebels as our visitors today. I now show the community of Skeeter Hill why I did not pursue a career in baseball." He ceremoniously throws the first pitch that is wide of the home plate and must be chased down by Wee Bones. C.J. Heinze and Mayor Polkinghorn leave the infield to sit in the center of the home team bleachers with other dignitaries.

"Play ball!" declares Umpire Halstead as he crouches down over Wee Bones.

"The first batter for the Rebels will be none other than Huggable Harold Hextall. The Rascals players will be the home team and the Rebels the visitors. Let the game begin. Remember, whether you are home or away, 911 Moving and Storage is one call away at 517-676-5577," broadcasts Mr. Wince from the scorekeeper's box over the PA system.

Huggable steps into the batter's box and grinds his feet into the dirt. After a few practice swings, he stares down Chico. The Rascals team fans engage in the customary cheer with the colorful guidance from Cheryl and Weezie at the helm leading cheers in their matching Rascals cheerleading outfits, "Heybattabattabatta! Heybattabattabatta!"

Without being prompted the infield Rascals players shout out the distraction cadence they devised for this particular game to help Chico with his pitching.

Gooch at first starts shouting, "Curve ball."

Punzak at third yells, "Fastball."

"Slider!" yells Frankie at shortstop.

In unison the players scream, "Strike!"

The first pitch bounces in the dirt in front of home plate. Flustered by the cadence, Huggable delivers a tomahawk chop swing attempting to make contact. The ball whizzes past him.

"Strike!" Umpire Halstead calls out reinforcing the call with his right fist pump. Coach Swat stands in the grassy area beside the on-deck circle and the first base line. "Way to go, Chico. That's it. Throw 'em right in there. Doing good, Chico!" Encourages Coach Swat. Pitching under the pressure of a championship game makes Chico jittery and nervous. He wipes sweat from his forehead and off his top lip from under his nose. Next, he fidgets with the resin bag trying to muster up enough courage to throw the next pitch. Coach Swat continues to cheer him on, "Chico! Read the signs. Plan it in your head." He continues to show reluctance to throw the next pitch. "Throw with power! Chico, you can do it!"

Chico exchanges the stare given by Huggable Harold. He peers into the piercing eyes. He shivers as a cold chill rushes over him. Nervous, he rocks back for his wind up and delivery. Doubt enters his mind. He question himself as he rolls the ball back and forth in his hand and stares at the stitching.

"Heybattabattabatta! Heybattabattabatta!" the fans respond the cheerleading tandem of Cheryl and Weezie the cheerleading duo.

The pitch travels across home plate about knee high. "Ball!" declares Umpire Halstead.

Huggable Harold calls time and steps back to rub his hands together for a better grip on the bat handle. He looks up and takes a moment to exchange eye contact with Chico while he musters up a grin. A chill runs down Chico's back. Huggable returns to the batter's box and resumes his batting pose. Chico nods his head and throws the next pitch in the same manner.

"Strike, two!" exclaims Umpire Halstead. Wee Bones tosses the ball back. Mounting pressure causes him to stand on the mound and hang his head. Trying to relax, he goes through some breathing exercises. After a few moments, he holds up his hand to call time. Coach Swat runs across the diamond to meet Chico. Wee Bones scampers to the pitcher's mound.

"Coach, I don't think I can do this." Chico plucks the ball out of his glove and holds his hand out for Coach Swat to take it from him.

"Chico, outside of Izzie, you're the next best pitcher we've got!" declares Coach Swat staring down at the baseball.

"Coach, outside of Izzie, I'm the only pitcher you got!" Chico quickly qualifies Coach Swat's statement. He withdraws the baseball and holds it by his side still trying to decide if is he will pitch in the game.

"I got a story for you. Ready for a story?"

"I don't know. He's making all these signals I don't have no idea what he wants me to do," Chico explains with a whimper and his chin quivering.

"Chico, there was this great Major League Baseball pitcher by the name of Sandy Koufax. When someone asked how he became a good pitcher, he answered that it happened when he stopped trying to make batters miss the ball and started trying to make them hit the ball."

"That's a good one, Coach. But I can't do neither of them things."

"I'll make it easy for you. When you read the signals, pretend you understand and nod your head yes, a real hard yes. You can shake your head no sometimes, too. Look at the ball in your baseball glove. Talk to it." Chico laughs and cracks a smile. "Throw the only pitch you know how to throw. Throw it over and over again. Make the batter think you have something special in mind for him with each throw. If you think you can throw one outside, tap your glove against your leg. Change things up the way you want to do it. Do what you think you can do like Sandy Koufax."

"I just don't want to let the team down," explains Chico.

Wee Bones speaks up, "If you don't try, you'll let yourself down. That'll be letting your teammates down." He turns away to make the journey back to home plate.

Coach Swat places his hand on Chico's shoulder and bends down to look him in the eye. "We're in this together. Do your part and you'll not have to look back. I promise," says Coach Swat as he gives a soft pat on Chico's shoulder as a gesture of trust and confidence.

Still overwhelmed, Chico sets up. He keeps his eye on the batter thinking he will not be able to pitch around the giant at the plate. His hand nervously shakes as he goes through the delivery and throws a low inside ball. Huggable swings and misses.

"Out!" cries Umpire Halstead with a right fist pump.

Chico achieves his first out in the game. He is elated. The first out serves as a self-confidence builder for him. Listening to Coach Swat's confidence helped him stand his ground and keep the inning from becoming a lopsided score. The Rebels had difficulty at their first bat because of problems judging the pitches thrown by the shortest pitcher of all season, Chico. His short stocky physique and unorthodox delivery did not hurt his cause.

"Rebels step onto the field to protect four runs. Still running around town trying to get all of your errands done in time to pick the kids up from school? Have someone run them for you. Call Annie Oakley Express. Sure-fire way to get your errands done in time, 517-676-8888."

On the way to the dugout, Wee Bones and Chico hook up and talk. The two decide to practice motion and technique together until it's their turn to bat. Mr. Martinez, Chico's father, an assistant coach and trainer for the Skeeter Hill High School baseball team, decides he can help. He puts together a makeshift bullpen for the boys behind the chain link fence in view of first base. The three work together on improving Chico's pitching.

Marty leads off batting for the Rascals team. After a two-two count, a wild, errant pitch speeds toward Marty. The catcher skates to his left and slides his catcher's mitt next to Marty's hip. At the same time Marty scrambles trying get out of the way of the blazing sphere of leather. He arches his back to avoid impact. The catcher partially deflects the baseball. It caroms off the backstop before coming to rest in the grass. Umpire Halstead motions with his right hand, "Take your base, son."

Chico's turn at bat interrupts the impromptu pitching lesson. Luckily he receives a base on balls. The bases are loaded when Wee Bones comes to bat. Garvin gets a two-two count forcing Wee Bones to swing grounding out.

"At the end of the first inning we have the Rascals earning two runs and the blazing Rebels team with four runs. Don't forget Chelsea's Drug for all your first aid needs. It' like having a doctor in the house."

Chico sprints from his first base runner position to the pitcher's mound. On his way to left field, Frankie brings his glove out to him. In the pocket of the glove is a note. He opens the note and reads: *Remember low and inside. You'll get 'em every time, Dad.* He folds up the note and packs it inside his baseball cap. The warm-up pitches give him an opportunity to employ some of the techniques on the field instead of a grassy bullpen. He learns that his throws favor knee-high and inside the strike zone—just like his father's note.

In the second inning, Chico struggles attempting to apply the technique. He pitches into a predicament with runners on second and third base with one out. The batter has a full count: two strikes and three balls. The situation makes Chico feel hopeless because of all the possible runs that can be scored by the Rebels on account of his less-than-stellar pitching. Chico winds up and throws a pitch like Coach Swat told him to throw. When Umpire Halstead calls a ball, Chico feels like he's being punished for not throwing the ball correctly.

"Strike!" shouts Umpire Halstead shaking his right clenched fist.

Wee Bones knows the runners are not likely to try to steal a base since the third base runner would have to run home. The runner on second base must wait for the runner on third to run home before he can advance to third base. He reads the heart break on Chico's face. A trick play he dreamed up comes to mind. He wants the runners to think there is a designed play for the next pitch. He slides out from behind the batter and pounds the ball into his mitt. Wee Bones gives two fingers up signal (little finger and index finger) for everyone to see. Chico mouths the word, "What?" Wee Bones meets him halfway to the pitcher's mound. Curious, Coach Ostrander joins the boys in order to oversee. Using his body, Coach Sternicki shields the discussion from the Rebels dugout and coaches.

"Is this some sort of trick play? I didn't have a chance to practice any trick plays!" says Chico, feeling apprehensive about the prevailing situation and unwelcome surprise.

"Yes," replies Wee Bones. "But it is easy to learn. Listen up! First you have to pitch a strike. He won't hit it. Just pitch a strike. Make sure it's a strike! Anywhere across the plate!" Wee Bones emphasizes holding the catcher's mitt up to block anyone reading their lips during the conversation. "After the pitch, run as fast as you can to the plate. Don't stop. Hear me! Don't stop until you get to the plate. I'm going to flip the ball to you when you get there. Tag the runner out. Think you can do that?"

"Why, uh. Yes, I can do that," he replies with a nervous pitch in his voice. "Remember I'm an outfielder not a pitcher."

"Don't worry about the batter. Just throw a strike. Got it? Tag the runner," reiterates Wee Bones as he slowly lowers the catcher's mitt from shielding the conversation.

"Got it," replies Chico shaking his head in a manner to reflect discernment. Coach Sternicki does not say a word and returns to third base. Resuming the play, Wee Bones crouches down and nods his head. After he describes the made up play to Chico he fears his decision could go horribly wrong. It was a huge roll of the dice to call an unproven play. One run will score. Maybe two runs will score. He raises his glove for the next pitch with apprehension. Chico worries and worries more and more if he can pull off the strike Wee Bones said was a must for the next pitch. He breathes faster, and faster to the point of nearly hyperventilating has he starts his pitching motion. The runners start their lead off base and intently keep their eyes glued on the pitcher.

"Heybattabattabatta! Heybattabattabatta!" comes the refrain from the fans inspired by Cheryl and Weezie dancing back and forth coaxing everyone.

"Hey, Garvin, those pink shoe laces your sister's?" Wee Bones says adjusting his catcher's mitt in the strike zone to suggest the placement for the next pitch.

Curious, Garvin pushes his hands away from his body lifting up the knob of the bat in order to look down at his shoes. At the moment he looks up, the pitch is being delivered. He haphazardly swings. The pitch zooms past him. Woooosh!

"Strike three!" announces Umpire Halstead. "You're out!" He pumps his fist and extends his thumb high in the air.

Wee Bones jumps up and runs in the direction of the backstop chasing the ball. The runner on third base spies Wee Bones in pursuit of an errant pitch. Immediately the coach sends him toward home plate.

"Go! Run!" screams an excited Rebels third base coach.

He charges down the third baseline in the direction of home plate. Knowing the plan, Chico has a head start for home plate after throwing the pitch. Wee Bones waits until Chico almost reaches the plate in order to curtail his pretense of pursuing the ball. He stops, reaches into his catcher's mitt, and grabs the baseball. Very gently, he tosses it underhanded to Chico. Seeing the ball float in the air toward him, Chico's eyes get as large as saucers. As the ball arrives it seems like it has increased in size coming toward him. He catches the ball and turns toward the third bassline. The runner trying to avoid being tagged out tramples Chico and misses touching home plate. The collision results in the baseball falling out of Chico's glove and landing on the ground.

Wee Bones runs over and snatches up the ball. Instinctively he pursues the runner and tags him out before he has the opportunity to return to touch home plate. Dust ushers up from the ground to cloud the play.

All eyes are on Umpire Halstead waiting for him to decide the result of the play. Time seems to stand still while he deliberates. "Out!" he declares moments later.

Uproar in the Rebels stands ensues. The fans shout a collective "boo" and heckle with, "Check your eyes, ump".

Base Umpire Carrigan gestures pointing her thumb up in a pumping motion to indicate the runner has been tagged out. Chico and Wee Bones slap hands as a congratulatory gesture.

"Rebels and Rascals fans, we have a game with the Rebels on top with ten runs and the Rascals team coming to bat with two runs. Looking for some peace and quiet after the championship game? Try the Timber Lake Lodge with horseback riding, hiking, canoeing, and the whisper of the pines for a truly relaxing experience. Call them today! 1-866-my-lake."

Coach Swat takes a moment to visit with Willie in the dugout. "I know your injuries are probably superficial and not that serious."

"I'm not injured, Coach. I've got some scratches on my hand and that's all. Is that what that super-whatever means?" asks Willie confused by the meaning of the word. "The paramedic gave me this glove thingy without no fingers to put on my hand and an elastic thingy to brace my ankle. He said I can play."

In the background, they can hear the roar of the crowd and the crack of the bat "Heybattabattabatta! Heybattabattabatta!" the Rebels fans bark at the Rascals batters.

"I can't examine you. Got a game to coach. I'll put you in with Izzie."

Chico continues to practice with Izzie during the bottom of the second inning. Over the loud speaker system, Willie hears, "That concludes the bottom of the second inning with the Rebels ten and the Rascals team on their heels with six runs for the game. The Cobbler's Affair has shoes for all ages, men and women. Casual, formal, or everyday dress. See them on the Square. Remember if our shoes fit, wear them, walk a mile. Stroll down to Buffalo Run and Prospector Avenue."

The coaching by his father instilled a sense of confidence for Chico as he persists in spite of moments of discouragement. While Coach Swat works with the lineup changes, Chico stands tall and feels like a little giant on the mound into the third inning. The pitches fly across the plate with more zip. Punzak catches a line drive for the third out in the inning.

Mr. Wince updates the fans, "Skeeter Hill fans, at the bottom of the third inning, the Rebels' score is sixteen runs and the Rascals team trails with nine runs. Don't forget our special today: a hot dog and coke for only seventy-five cents at your friendly Youth Authority concession stand."

While Coach Swat concentrates on the changes to the batting lineup, Coach Hackworth approaches him. "Coach, your boys have played one hell of a game. I don't need to tell you the score is sixteen for the good guys and nine for the Rascals bunch. Rebels will widen the lead because we start off the fourth inning. Think about the slaughter rule, Coach! The Rebels score more runs in the fifth and the sixth innings than any other team in Skeeter Hill Little League. Before they get humiliated, anytime you want to call it a game, let me know."

"The score is not even close to a ten-point lead like Father's Day when you lost. It's all about the win to you, isn't it? Do you know that scrapping back to win a game builds more character than you have in your little finger? Buckle up, Coach Hackworth! The Rascals team will take your boys for the ride of their life. I suggest you leave! This is Rascals country!"

"You can't say I didn't give you a fighting chance. Either we run up the score and beat you by runs early in the fourth or invoke the mercy rule later in the fifth. Rebels' humiliation is the name of the game. Name your poison," responds Coach Hackworth hesitating momentarily for an answer. Coach Swat deliberately ignores Coach Hackworth and continues to make notations on his clipboard. Coach Hackworth marches to home plate. He halts and taunts Coach Swat by touching his toe on home plate. He jerks his foot back pretending it's sizzling hot. He dangles his foot like he scorched his toe.

Burning up with anger, Coach Swat descends into the Rascals dugout and stands with his back up against the cement block wall. He hangs his head to hide the hostile fire in his eyes. Attempting to calm his nerves, he breathes heavily. His hand trembles. The dugout is quiet. Players are transfixed by his demeanor. The players silently observe. "You're not having a heart attack or anything like that?" asks Willie as he threads his way through the players to reach Coach Swat.

"I'm fine, thanks, Willie." Having calmed his nerves, he feverishly studies the clipboard. "Gentlemen, I apologize for my tirade.

You boys are putting your heart and soul into this game. You've shown everyone you are the best team on the field. I'm not going to surrender to Coach Hackworth under any terms!"

"Hooray," exclaims several of the team members almost in unison. "Go Rascals!"

"Coach Swat, we got a game to play," urges Umpire Halstead.

"My words precisely, ump." He waves his clipboard to signal he has an important announcement. The players gather around. He rises up onto the first step. "Boys, we got a game to play." He refers to his clipboard. "There will be changes to the batting order. I will post the lineup on the bulletin board right here at the end of the dugout. Willie, Punzak, Izzie, and Gooch, you're inserted into a different order into the batting lineup with Willie as the clean–up batter. Don't try to win this by yourself. It's a team effort. Go Rascals!"

"Go Rascals!" shouts the players in unison.

"Like I said guys, Willie limber up you're in the game! Izzie you're on the mound. It's time! Let's show 'em what we got."

The sound of the air horn from the scorekeeper box signals the Rascals players to take the field for the fourth inning. In the twinkling of an eye, the players run to their positions.

Coach Sternicki blows his whistle. Like a well-oiled machine the players zip the ball around the horn as fast as they can with eye-catching precision. Wee Bones starts the rotation by throwing to Willie at shortstop. He tosses the ball to Gooch at first base. In turn, Gooch throws the ball to Marty at second. Marty catches the ball and throws to Punzak at third. Punzak pivots and drills the ball to Izzie who throws the ball to Wee Bones at home plate. After the first rotation, the players reverse the order in the process. The fans are impressed. It is like a completely different team. All the Rebels players watch in awe. The players do not resemble the Rascals team they observed during the first three innings.

The first batter for the Rebels in the top of the fourth inning hits a pop up fly ball to the Willie at shortstop. He circles underneath it and makes the catch for the first out. He zips the ball around the horn before the next pitch. The next batter hits in the slot between shortstop and the third baseman. Frankie fields the ball in left field and throws to Marty to hold the runner at first. The shortest batter on the Rebels team steps up to bat. Izzie remembers trying to pitch to Wee Bones and the struggles he had finding his strike zone. His difficulty continues because he cannot pitch strikes. The batter gets a base on balls. Coach O calls time and approaches the pitcher's mound.

"Izzie! We need the possibility of a double play."

"I can't walk this batter. Bases will be loaded. They can score more runs! We'll lose." Izzie explains his frustration with the thought of walking the batter.

"Trust me. We'll have the advantage. Put this runner on first with a walk. With bases loaded, you'll have a better chance of turning two to get out of this inning. Pitch low to the next batter after this one. Make him scoop it up and pop up a fly ball."

"Well, if you say so, Coach O. I'll do it. Remember, there's only one out," Izzie emphasizes. Izzie faces Wee Bones and pats his left thigh then extends his glove hand out to his side to communicate the batter will intentionally be walked. Izzie and Wee Bones play pitch and catch. During the third pitch outside, the batter eyeballs the floating ball and thinks he can blast the ball out of the infield. Again, Wee Bones leaves his crouched position behind the plate to catch the slow floating ball. The batter steps forward and plants his foot on the plate in order to whack the ball with his bat. When the bat clubs the ball in into fair territory, Umpire Halstead yells, "Out!"

Coach Hackworth angrily removes his baseball cap and charges toward Umpire Halstead. Clutching onto the bill of the baseball cap he whips it back and forth, slapping his thigh as he rushes up to home plate. Approaching the plate in a rage, he shakes his baseball cap at Umpire Halstead. "It's a strike not an out! He's not out!"

"Out by rule!" declares Umpire Halstead.

"Rule? Rule! You wouldn't know a rule from a myth if it bit you. I tell ya, no out!" yells Coach Hackworth.

Coach Swat ambles over to home plate and stands with his arms folded and observes. Coach Hackworth and Umpire Halstead bicker back and forth. Seemingly, the argument will not reach a conclusion. Casually, Coach Swat withdraws a worn, torn book from his back pocket and flips through it. Nonchalantly he bends back the leaves of the book to the specific section.

"Gentlemen, I have our bible of baseball and I shall read for your enlightenment rule 6.06: a batter is out for illegal action when he hits a ball with one or both feet on the ground entirely outside the batter's box. Once a batter has taken his position in the batter's box, he shall not be permitted to step out of the batter's box in order to use the resin, unless there is a delay in the game action or, in the judgment of the umpires, weather conditions warrant an exception. In my opinion he's out."

"Coach Hackworth, take it up with the Youth Authority. He's out. Rule 6.06. You heard the man. That's final," concludes Umpire Halstead. "Thank you, Coach Swat."

"What's this guy? Mr. Baseball?" Coach Hackworth sarcastically complains while he nervously whips his thigh with his baseball cap.

Izzie remembers coach Ostrander's instruction and fires the low pitch to the next batter. The batter swings at the low pitch and misses. Perhaps Coach Ostrander knew something about this batter. On the second pitch, the batter cocks his bat and swings. The ball soars past him. *Swoosh!* The pocket of the catcher's mitt concludes the pitch with a *thwwaacck!* The next pitch is a cookie to the outside. The slower pitch entices the batter to swing early with a roundhouse swing to blast the ball out of the park. He misses the pitch. "Out!" yells Umpire Halstead with the customary pumping of his right fist.

"Fans, the end is in sight. In the middle of the fourth inning, the Rebels score is sixteen and the Rascals nine. The end of the game is in sight, rubbish." He hesitates. "Rubbish, trash problems? Trash Talk can arrange for weekly pick up and disposal of your unwanted trash. Try Trash Talk to get in the game. Call 1-800- UR- TRASH."

Izzie hollers for Coach Swat to come to the dugout wall and look out at the infield at the mound. The tone of his voice suggests there might be an emergency. His teammates respond to his call and rush up to the dugout wall and gaze out on the field. Coach Swat climbs up a couple steps and directs his attention toward the pitcher's mound. He lays his eyes on Vinny, a wiry, left-handed pitcher with a reputation forged the year before. "During the championship game last summer, he threw four strike-outs in the last three innings of the game. He single-handedly carried the team with his pitching arm," recalls Izzie.

The coaches and players watch as he slings fastballs across the plate. The coaches confer regarding his eligibility. Apparently, the Youth Authority granted him eligibility because of a medical condition and not a self-imposed decision not to play.

"The Rascals team's first batter for the bottom of the fourth inning will be Izzie," Mr. Wince announces to the fans. The Rascals team fans cheer, whistle, and clap. Izzie steps into the batter's box, grips the bat handle firmly, and positions his hands stacked on top of each other under his chin. His feet are separated shoulder width apart. Umpire Halstead squats behind the catcher. The banter begins, "Heybattabattabatta! Heybattabattabatta!"

Weezie leads the Rascals team fans in the Vinny cheer to distract him. "Vinn-ny, Vinn-ny, Vinn-ny." Seeing Weezie alone at the cheerleading duties Molly Mayfield exits the dugout to help her.

He winds up for the delivery. The players in the infield back pedal. Vinny initiates the pitching motion. Izzie draws his bat from his shoulder remembering how Coach Ostrander gave encouragement to the players to place the right hand where the trademark is on the bat and the other hand down on the handle by the knob. Instinctively, he positions his hands on the bat. He swings his body and pivots on the back foot while keeping his hands positioned on the bat with a wide margin of space between his hands. Before Vinny releases the ball, Izzie squares up and lowers his head behind the barrel of the bat to observe the direction of the ball. He employs the bunting mechanics. The Rebels players in the infield are drawn in for the bunt. At the last moment, he pivots back to swing setting his bat angle for the ball to travel toward first base. He hears the clink as the ball strikes the metal bat. The ball sails over the first baseman's head and lands in right field behind first base. He races down first base line. The first baseman is caught in an awkward position because he cannot field the ball. Izzie reaches first base before the outfielder reaches the ball. "Take second! Go Izzie! Go!" yells Coach O waving his arms in the direction of second base.

Izzie turns the corner and continues to run to second base. By the time the ball reaches the infield, he safely reaches second base. Vinny walks the next batter, Tyler Kushihashi. When Punzak steps into the batter's box, the bases are loaded.

Vinny winds up and goes into his pitching motion. He casts his eyes on Cheryl. He does a second take during his follow through straining his neck to gawk at her. She stands at the opening between the chain link fence and the backstop on the visitor's side of the infield. Clothed in a choir robe she flashes him. The ball is thrown wild on account of the interruption of his body mechanics. Izzie charges down the third base line. Garvin chases after him. Garvin sees Cheryl and slows his aggressive pursuit to gawk at her.

Turk pursues the ball rattling around the backstop. Tyler peddles from second to third. Marty advances to second base.

Coach Sternicki breaks out in thunderous laughter. He goes down on his knees laughing. Coach Swat scans the infield for the reason pertaining to such an outpour of laughter. He sprints over to Coach Sternicki and questions the reason for the sudden laughter.

Coach Sternicki tries to choke back the upheaval of laughter, "O-o-over there by the g-gate..."

"Over there by the gate? What?" he questions Coach Sternicki about the hilarious interruption.

"It's Cheryl in a choir robe. She's flashing the pitcher!" explains Coach Sternicki nearly out of breath from laughing.

Beginning to chuckle, coach Swat repeats, "Cheryl flashed the pitcher? She *flashed* him?"

"Yeah, but she has a swimsuit on underneath!" he exclaims laughing. "And it's a bikini!" The two men regale together. The players, umpires, or fans cannot understand the reason for the uproarious laughter. Then the catcher holds up the throw to the pitcher because Vinny is still laughing. Finally, everyone settles down and the game resumes.

The first pitch to Punzak's left-handed batting resulted in a wild throw allowing Izzie to score from third base. The fans resume trying to distract the batter with the chatter, "Heybattabattabatta! Heybattabattabatta!" Vinny tries to catch Punzak napping. He unleashes a fastball low and outside.

He swings and tops the ball unleashing a daisy cutter between Garvin at third base and Huggable at shortstop. The Rascals continue to score on the Rebels before committing the last of three outs. The Rascals team responds with seven runs during the inning.

"Fans of all ages, the Rascals players score seven runs in the bottom of the fourth inning. The Rebels team has sixteen runs and the Rascals team sixteen in today's contest. Remember to stop by Hackworth Meats and pick up a pound of your favorite baloney or deli meat."

"Hey, Hackworth. I think you stocked up on too much baloney. We're turning this around. Better order some humble pie," shouts

Coach Sternicki as he passes by the visitors' dugout on his way to the third base coach's box.

"Skeeter Hill sports fans, we head into the top of the fifth inning with the Rebels score sixteen and the Rascals team sixteen runs. You can score big with the Junk Guy. Clean out that closest, empty the garage; make room for your next project. The Junk Guy can be your man. One man's junk is the Junks Guy's treasure. Visit them on Lower Sage Brush Road or call 1-899- GET JUNK."

Vinny leads off at the plate with a base hit single for the Rebels. Huggable drills a line drive to right field to advance the runners to second and third. The fielders back up to protect against the long ball. Izzie delivers a three-two count before the batter launches a foul ball down the third base line. Punzak maneuvers underneath the ball and makes the catch for an out. A left-handed batter comes up to the plate. Izzie intentionally pitches outside balls since he has trouble pitching to left-handed batters. He hits a one hopper to Marty at second base. After the catch, he throws the ball to first base for the out. Gooch instinctively casts the ball to Wee Bones at home plate. The throw is not in time. The Rebels score another run and advance the runner to third base.

Garvin steps up to bat. On the first pitch, he belts a high pop fly to right field. Jimmy Tuttle rushes up and stands under the descending ball. Garvin streaks down the first base line for the bag. With his glove raised up in front of his face, Jimmy cannot see the baseball very well. Garvin pauses at first to glance into right field. The ball bounces off his glove and falls to the ground. Kippy, racing over from centerfield picks up the ball and fires it. Nearly halfway, Garvin prepares to slide. Marty stands covering the bag. Garvin goes into a slide. Marty swings his glove downward toward the bag. Garvin's foot sandwiches the glove against the second base. Base Umpire Carrigan fights the plume of dust swirling up in the air to set her sights on the glove between the foot and second base. Marty withdraws his glove and pokes Garvin in the stomach with it while holding the ball in his glove. Garvin's foot still remains inches away from the bag because he is coughing from the dust in the air.

"Out!" declares Umpire Carrigan motioning with the familiar thumb in the air.

"The Rebels score five runs making twenty-one the total runs. The Rebels take the outfield and the Rascals team comes to bat with sixteen runs. Do you have trouble waking up in the morning? Do you feel run down in the morning? Need a pick me up? Visit the Donut Hole and Coffee Hut at the Miner's plaza where you get a refreshing coffee and fresh baked donut special every day of the week. It's the boost you need to the start off the day."

Tyler Kushihashi steps into the batter's box to lead off the fifth inning. Immediately he strikes his batting pose. The Rebels fans start the common banter, Weezie leads the Rascals fans in a cheer, "Heybattabattabatta! Heybattabattabatta!"

"Vinn-ny, Vinn-ny, Vinn-ny." The Rascals fans chant over and over. Vinny nods and removes his hand from his baseball glove to start his pitching motion. Before he has the opportunity to release the ball, Tyler swings back and raises his bat mimicking a swing for the Baltimore chop. The change up batting stance distracts Vinny's rhythm. His pitching mechanics are interrupted. He tries to check his delivery. Instead, he delivers a wild pitch. The errant ball hits Tyler in the shoulder, bounces up, and strikes his helmet. An eerie silence settles over the Skeeter Hill Baseball Field. Clearly this was an errant pitch and not intentional.

The banter by the Rebels' fans abruptly stops. The cheers to hassle Vinny immediately halt. The only sound is the baseball clanging around the backstop chain link fence as Tyler's helmet spins off his head. Immediately he drops his bat and cradles his head with both hands. He stands still with both hands pressed against the side of his head. Umpire Halstead rips off his cage and discards his chest protector in order to check on Tyler.

Coach Swat hustles over to Tyler from his on-deck perch. The Rascals players exit the dugout and charge toward the on-deck circle. Coach Sternicki and Coach O migrate over toward the pitcher's mound in case the players decide to retaliate.

The Rebels players exit the dugout and abandon their positions on the field. Simultaneously, the players race to the pitcher's mound to protect Vinny. Officer Higby jumps down from his bar stool perch behind the chain link fence and sprints through the home team gate opening and waits below the pitcher's mound making his presence known.

Standing next to pitcher's mound, Garvin shouts at Willie by the on-deck circle, "Admit it. You've lost the game. You're nothing but skunks!"

Huggable says, "Yeah, you'll never catch up. Face it, you're skunks!"

Willie hurries toward the pitcher mound to retaliate. Traveling from the on-deck circle he is intercepted by Officer Higby before he reaches the pitcher's mound. "We're not skunks. A skunk smells its own hole first," Willie yells at the top of his voice while being restrained by Officer Higby. The Rascals congregate on the infield by the first base line ready to support Willie while keeping a close eye on Tyler.

Huggable Harold yells, "You skunks can't count. We're ahead."

"Go figure." Garvin adds an additional sarcastic remark. "Do the math!"

"Everyone! Back to the on-deck circle. Rascals, one and all!" shouts Coach Sternicki approaches the player and gives hand gestures for the players to step back toward the on-deck-circle.

Rascal players retreat to watch Tyler from the on-deck circle. Everyone watches with concern and interest. The ball did not hit him as hard as the ball hit Izzie during the game earlier in the season. Without a doubt the ball was not thrown with an intention to hurt Tyler.

Tyler wobbles as the paramedic escorts him off the field. His father rushes through the gate in the chain link fence next to the backstop and meets him. The three walk off the field.

Coach Swat calls the Rascals together at the on-deck circle. The players crowd around him. "Gentlemen, we've had a lot of unexpected injuries. A team's chemistry doesn't become evident until players face adversity. When you go out on that field don't expect the impossible, achieve the impossible!" He pumps both hands in the air Rocky Balboa fashion and shouts. "Go Rascals!"

"Go Rascals!" yells the team as the players prepare to resume play.

"Gooch, grab your lid. You're on base." Coach Swat selects Gooch as the pinch runner. "You're running the bags for Tyler. He'll be okay. Got tapped on the shoulder and noggin."

The Rebels players slowly return to their positions on the field and others return to the dugout.

Vinny walks the second batter of the inning. Next, Marty Ostrander approaches the batter's box. He sets his feet and rehearses with a few practice swings. During the follow-through of his next pitch, he releases the ball early. The ball sails over Marty's head in the batter's box. While the catcher chases down the baseball, Gooch advances to second base. When Punzak comes to bat, the bases are loaded. He hits a double.

"Ladies and gentlemen, this is your neighborhood insurance agency, the Wilfred Wince Agency, in beautiful downtown Skeeter Hill on the Square giving you an up-to-the-minute recap of the season championship game. At the end of five innings, the Rebels have twenty-one runs and the Rascals team has twenty runs cross the plate. The Boiler Plate Man can fix your furnace and cooling needs. Pay him a visit on Haystack Road by Gun Club Road," informs Mr. Wince over the PA system.

ROUNDING THIRD...

"At the top of the sixth inning, the Rebels have twenty-one runs and the Rascals team has twenty. Remember the Pet Me pet store for your cuddly friend's needs. We're your neighborhood pet supply store at the Hitching Post Shopping Center. The first batter in the top of the sixth inning for the Rebels will be Huggable."

After he selects his bat, Huggable traipses over to the batter's box. Judging Izzie's release, he swings and connects, driving the ball into deep center field for a double to start off the inning. Vinny steps into the batter's box and exchanges eye contact with Izzie before he taps on the plate and practice swings to suggest where he wants the ball pitched. He positions himself with a sense of arrogance challenging Izzie to pitch the ball where he is setting up. He carries himself with an aura of I've been here before I'm much more of a baseball player than you. He plants his feet and takes a few more practice swings. Weezie and Cheryl start their routine for the Rascals fans to recite the familiar chorus, "Heybattabattabatta! Heybattabattabatta!"

Izzie goes into the stretch and delivers the pitch. The outfielders back up into the shadows of the towering privet hedge. On the first pitch, he taps the ball down the left field foul line in fair territory. Much like the coffin corner in right field, without the strange bounce the ball continues to roll to the privet hedge boundary. Huggable scores after rounding third base. Vinny trots around the bases reaching third base after the throw from Frankie Sternicki in deep left field reaches Punzak at third base.

Ricky Rodriguez comes to bat. Before every pitch, Wee Bones gestures by shaking his mitt in the direction of third base that he wants to throw to Punzak trying to get Vinny to stand closer to the base, where he is less prone to bolt toward home. Ricky reaches full count. Willie's leg bothers him as he squares up to field the one hop ball on the way to shortstop. Ricky cruises down first base line and reaches the bag with ease. Vinny holds up at third.

Garvin steps up to bat. Shaking his bat, known as the black bomber, he hopes to score a few runs with his trusted long ball bat. The Rascals players back up knowing the reputation of the weapon of choice. The shiny black bat has been his favorite during clutch situations in years previous. He practices a few swings and cocks his right elbow back and exchanges eye contact with Izzie.

"Heybattabattabatta! Heybattabattabatta!" The girls become frantic in their cheerleading as the chorus swells up from the Rascals fans. The cadence begins from the infield. He flexes at the knees and prepares for the next pitch "Heybattabattabatta! Heybattabattabatta!" comes from the players and fans louder than before.

The ball speeds toward the strike zone knee high on the inside. He initiates his swing. *Crrrack!*

The ball accelerates elevating from head high seemingly traveling faster than the speed of light toward second base. Willie side steps from shortstop and lifts his glove. Jumping as high as he can, he extends his arm hoping to stretch his glove into the path of the line drive. The ball zooms in his direction. *Thwwwaaack!* The ball lands in the pocket of his glove.

Willie's fantastic catch

When he comes down to the ground, his right leg buckles underneath him. He tumbles to the ground with his baseball glove raised for all to see.

"Home, Willie! Throw home!" screams Punzak at third base.

"Willie throw home! Now, throw home!" Izzie yells. "Hurry! Throw it!"

Vinny tags up and immediately charges toward home plate. Wee Bones covers home plate in anticipation of the throw. Willie rolls up onto his knees. He throws from one knee like they learned in practice. He sees Vinny approaching the halfway mark down third base as he releases the ball. The ball and Vinny continue on a collision course. Wee Bones places his mitt to trap the low throw. Vinny goes down into a slide. The ball arrives low and on the baseline side. Immediately, he cradles the ball in the pocket of the baseball mitt. He covers the ball with his right hand to protect it like a raw egg and instinctively swings his mitt across the base line. Vinny approaches home plate at breakneck speed. Izzie races to help Wee Bones cover home plate in case Vinny does not touch home. The mitt slams against Vinny's knee.

Umpire Halstead sets his eye on Vinny's heel dig in but remains more than six inches away from the plate. Vinny's momentum carries him closer and closer to home plate. His knee clips Wee Bones as he ploughs into him. Dirt and dust rise up from the ground. Wee Bones flips in the air and tumbles over the top of Vinny. His hand firmly presses against the baseball in his mitt while his body makes a few revolutions before coming to rest. Tipping his glove over like a serving tray, he lifts up his mitt to show Umpire Halstead.

"Safe!" he announces with his arms flying in the scissor-motion to gesture Wee Bones unsuccessfully tagged Vinny out. The frantic conclusion to the play ushers up cheers and whistles of celebration from the Rebels fans.

In contrast, the Rascals fans usher up a chorus of 'Booboo." While the dust settles, Garvin decides to advance to second. While Wee Bones tries to argue the call with Umpire Halstead, Garvin races toward the halfway mark in his journey to second base. "Wee Bones. Throw! He's coming. Throw the ball! Second base!" yells Punzak. Willie joins the chorus to attract Wee Bones's attention, "Hey, Wee Bones! Throw the ball! Throw it now!" Base Umpire Carrigan ruled

Willie touched the ground with the ball and flubbed the catch. Garvin keeps running past first base with a head of steam for second base.

Izzie rushes up to him and plucks the ball from Wee Bones's gesturing hand. Winding up, Izzie slings the ball to Marty at second base. In the commotion, he did not see Ricky Rodrigues at third. The ball soars toward second base. Punzak rapidly extends his glove hand to get Marty to throw the ball to get Ricky in a hot box between third base and home plate. The ball travels into the pocket of Marty's glove. *Thaaawwwwp.* He swings his arm across the second base line side of the bag. Thinking he will sneak into second base because all of the action is at home plate, Garvin does not slide. His fatal mistake! Marty tags him out before his foot touches the second base bag. "Out!" shouts Umpire Carrigan raising her fist and customary protruding thumb. In the meantime, Ricky Rodrigues scores reaching home from third base.

"Hey Garvin. Your black what-cha-ma-call-it ain't nothing but a wet noodle!" heckles Willie while he polishes the pocket of his glove with spit.

The next batter for the Rebels fouls out for the end of the inning. Marty tucks his injured arm suggesting he may have caused additional injury the tag. On his way to the dugout he gently massages his arm trying to avoid any of the coaches observing his concern and taking him out of the game. Punzak races over to him to scold him for not throwing the baseball to third to catch Ricky in a hot box. Coach Sternicki interrupts any verbal altercation from ensuing and quell the team's momentum.

"What an out, baseball fans! The Rascals team held the Rebels to three runs in the top half of the sixth inning. The Rebels have twenty-four runs and the Rascals have twenty runs. Pancakes are not just for breakfast anymore. The House of Stacks serves breakfast from 6:00 am to 10:00 pm. It's not just a sticky delight. It's always breakfast time on Old Wagon Trail by the Year 'Round Farmer's Market.

"The leadoff batter for the bottom of the sixth inning for Rascals team will be Wilbur Bonnefield, known by his teammates as Wee Bones. The Royal Knife and Fork home-style family restaurant has a dinner plate ready to serve at your request to serve up a feast. Stop by at Homesteader Shopping Plaza and bring your appetite," announces Mr. Wince.

The fans clap, cheer, and stand up as Wee Bones walks from the on-deck circle and migrates to the batter's box. He enters the batter's box and points to left field like Babe Ruth did to indicate his intentions to hit what became a historic home run. Fans clap and whistle at his sense of humor. He taps home plate with the bat—his good luck superstition. With one hand he twists and pats down on the unforgiving batter's helmet to force a better fit. He raises his bat and meets the pitcher's eyes. The first pitch is a ball. He takes the next pitch, a strike. He asks for time, steps out of the batter's box, walks around behind Umpire Halstead, and steps into the left hand side batter's box to bat left-handed.

Pitching to a short left-handed batter becomes a more problematic challenge. Vinny manages to pitch a full count with three balls and two strikes. Wee Bones calls time. Again, he walks around behind Umpire Halstead and steps into the batter's box for right-handed batters. Without a word, Wee Bones takes a few practice swings and cocks the pat for the next pitch. Umpire Halstead motions for Vinny to throw the next pitch.

"Heybattabattabatta! Heybattabattabatta!" ushers up from the Rebels fans.

The ball floats high and out of the strike zone. Wee Bones's shenanigans enable him to get on base. The next batter is Kippy Waldron. He is like a Norman Rockwell picture with pants bulging, an oversized jersey, and an ill-fitting batting hat. He casts his weary eyes on Vinny. "Heybattabattabatta! Heybattabattabatta!" He checks his swing on the first pitch.

"Ball!" calls Umpire Halstead.

Kippy calls time. Stepping out of the batter's box, he cinches up his belt. Returning to the batter's box, he makes ready for the pitch.

"Heybattabattabatta! Heybattabattabatta!" The next pitch is a ball. He calls time and steps out of the batter's box. He ties his shoe and returns to the batter's box.

"Heybattabattabatta! Heybattabattabatta!" Vinny throws a ball. Kippy calls time and walks around to bat left-handed.

"Heybattabattabatta! Heybattabattabatta!"

The ball is outside. "Ball four." announces Umpire Halstead.

Coach Hackworth stomps out to the plate. "What is this? They can't win fair and square? They have to cheat?"

"I beg to differ. The boy's shoe definitely was untied. His pants are sagging, and he did need to cinch up his belt. And he has the right to change from right to left, usually only once during the time at bat."

"You...you... He can't do that," objects Coach Hackworth.

"I think he just did," calmly admits Umpire Halstead. Coach Ostrander waves him to take first base. The base on balls moves Wee Bones to second base. Kippy reaches first base avoiding the force out. Vinny strolls over to talk to Huggable at first base. He gestures in the direction of Wee Bones on second base. Next, he points at Gooch at the on-deck circle on his way to home plate. They both nod standing close to each other. Walking back to first base, Huggable drops his arms to his side. Vinny holds his glove in front with his right hand inserted in the pocket. Bringing his glove up for the stretch, he abandons his stretch motion, jumps off the rubber and glances at Kippy's lead off first anticipating the pitch. Vinny withdraws his hand from his glove and pretends to toss an over-handed throw to Huggable. Immediately, Kippy takes two steps back and lunges for first. Huggable withdraws the baseball from his glove and tags him out.

"Out!" yells base Umpire Carrigan. Wee Bones remains safe on second.

Umpire signals out!

Huggable returns the ball to Vinny. He shows him a fist pump as an okay sign.

Gooch enters the batter's box and assumes an unusual stance. Most batters do not exaggerate flexing at their hips.

James O. Jenkins

Gooch dances in batter's box

Flexing at the hips resembles a dancer in the sixties twisting his lead foot then rocking back on the other foot similar to a dance called the twist. His batting and dancing receives a chuckle from the fans and reduces the banter by the Rebels fans because of the distraction, "Heybattabattabatta! Heybattabattabatta!"

Vinny eyeballs Gooch's stance and grip on the bat. Gooch sways back and leans into the throw as he dips his back shoulder and drives the ball like a blazing comet toward left field. With his baseball glove outstretched, the left fielder anticipates the baseball being trapped by the webbing of his fielder's glove. Instead, he misjudges. The baseball sails into the corner of the left field, the coffin corner. It hits the fence by the foul pole, settling into deep left field for the left fielder.

Wee Bones bolts for third base. His sagging pants trip him up while churning his legs. He stands up and resumes his journey to third base.

"Rascals fans, Wee Bones stands on third. Gooch gets a stand-up double. The Rascals have one out in the inning. Feeling, flat, worn out, deflated lately? Visit the Tire Genie in the Conestoga Plaza for all of your car or truck tire needs. Wheel away in the comfort of a softer gentler ride. It's like riding on air."

Frankie treks over to the batter's box. Stalling, he practices a few swings. With his bat poised for the pitch Vinny goes into the stretch.

"Heybattabattabatta! Heybattabattabatta!" In a split second, Vinny delivers the pitch. He swings slamming the bat into the ball. *Clinnnk!*

The ball flies in the direction of first base. Huggable scissor-steps to his right. Huggable scissor-steps left. The right fielder charges toward first base with his glove poised to make the catch. Huggable stops and lifts his glove. He misjudges and dances to the right bumping into the right fielder. The ball drops in fair territory.

"Fair ball" announce base Umpire Carrigan. Vinny fails to run over to cover first in the absence of the first baseman. Frankie races down to the uncovered first base for a hit. Wee Bones runs for home to narrow the lead. Gooch advances to third.

"Game fans the Rebels have twenty-four runs and the Rascals twenty-one runs. The Rascals team is cutting the lead close. Remember Jed's Close Shave for your hair cutting and styling needs. He's a cut above the rest. Stop by the barber pole entrance on the square." Mr. Wince fills in with a blurb to take up time.

Punzak approaches the plate and he tries to interject some humor on the way to the left-hand batter's box, "Hey, ump! Couldn't find my left-handed bat. Not anywhere. Got me a cork-filled one, instead." He laughs at his joke. The cork-filled bat is a specially modified bat. In professional baseball, modifying a bat with a foreign substance is illegal and has been the subject of one of C.J. Heinze's rants at the Chelsea Drug store smoker's forum in the tobacco corner. A specially-modified bat with sawdust, cork, or anything like a bouncy substance will constitute a violation of the United Federation of

Baseball League rules and can result in the ejection of a player from the game. Generally, only wooden bats are corked. Punzak holds up a metal bat that would dispel any thought of a modified bat and puts the umpire's mind at ease.

"Heybattabattabatta! Heybattabattabatta!" The pitch is down and away. Punzak observes the sign from Coach Sternicki for him to swing away. He takes a few practice swings. Vinny sets and goes in motion to throw the next pitch.

"Heybattabattabatta! Heybattabattabatta!" Punzak swings at the inside ball not intending to hit the ball according to the sign given by Coach Sternicki. Instead, the poorly thrown pitch tails off, resulting in the ball skipping off the end of his bat during the course of his check swing. The squibber down third base line holds Gooch on base. Frankie reaches second. Punzak gets a base hit. The left fielder relays the throw to the catcher. The catcher eats the ball and throws back to the pitcher. Punzak reaches first base.

Marty steps up to the plate to bat next. His shoulder pain has gotten worse limiting his range of motion. He worries about getting the second out. He chokes up on the bat for control. He worries he cannot deliver a full power-swing because of the increased shoulder pain. He thinks to himself, "For the team, for the team." He manages to tap the ball between shortstop and second base. Vinny swats at the rising ball with his glove driving it to the ground and directing the bouncing ball beyond second base. It comes to rest behind second base. Marty cradles his arm and runs down first baseline. His shoulder broadcasts pain to every part of his upper body with every step he takes. He contemplates telling Coach O to have someone run the bases but the exhilarating experience overrules common sense. Furthermore he cannot tell his father to take him out of the game. Punzak safely makes the journey to second base. Gooch scores from third base. Frankie advances to third base.

Wanting to strike Willie out more than anything, Vinny winds up and throws a low inside fastball. The ball curves on the way to the plate. Willie steps back and summons all of his strength for the swing. He connects. *Cccrrack!* A shoulder-high speeding ball passes Vinny on the mound. Because he had to step back, the direction of the ball is different than he anticipates.

Curious about the trajectory of the ball because he changes his stance, Willie hesitates at home plate to watch the flight of the ball as it rises into the sky.

"Willie, Run! Run, Willie!" the Rascals yell and scream anxious because he has not started his pursuit of first base. Willie inches toward first base taking slow gliding side steps down the first base line. Players jump up and down. Unable to contain themselves, they pound on each other with their fists. Nervous fans scream practically in unison. "Run! Run! Willie! Go! Willie! Go! Run!" Cheryl and Weezie become frantic screaming at the top of their lungs.

Coach O travels outside the coach's box at first base and sprints a few steps down the grass in foul territory along the first base line, "Willie, Wake up! Run, boy! Run!"

Willie snaps out of his daze watching the ball and starts running toward first base. The ball drops in left-center field for a base hit. Frankie races home to score. Punzak hurries to third base. Marty experiences trouble swinging his arm for balance as he runs. Cradling his arm makes attaining speed difficult. In the excitement at bat, he must have swung at the ball harder than he expected and strained his arm even more. Maybe he strained the arm muscle more than he realized?

"Marty, pick it up. Run, boy," shouts Coach O returning to the first base coach's box and gyrating with every word.

He hears his father's coaching but cannot move his arm back and forth freely in order to get into a rhythm running. He tells himself to keep his eyes fixed on second base and run as fast as he can. Every step closer is an accomplishment because he is not out.

"Hurry. Marty! Run! Run! Run!" screams Coach Swat from the first base sideline.

The left fielder hurls the ball to second base. The ball soars like a bolt of lightning to the second baseman. Reluctant to slide into base because of his shoulder pain, and inability to do so correctly, Marty wraps up and spins around to land on the base on his side instead. The second baseman grabs the ball and swings around. Marty and the second baseman tumble over second base. The second baseman maneuvers the glove underneath Marty as the two fall to the ground. Marty misses second base. The tag is successful.

Frustrated, Coach Swat throws his clipboard on the ground and stomps on it. Afterward he exchanges eye contact with Chico. A sense of guilt wells up inside him. He sees Chico wide eyed, watching with his jaw wide open and speechless at Coach's behavior. "Sorry, son. I should've had you in the game to pinch run for Marty. My fault. Coaches shouldn't behave like that. We're people, but not like that."

"Sports fans, we have runners at the corners with two out. Rebels have twenty-four and the Rascals have twenty-three with the tying runner, Punzak, on third. It's time for a little magic. You'll see it once and play it in your mind over and over again. Call Déjà Vu Magic at 517-676-5551 for anything from children's parties to adult parlor entertainment."

"Play ball!" Umpire Halstead declares as he crouches down behind the catcher. Vinny checks off the signs. Deliberating about the pitch, he removes the baseball from his glove and starts his wind-up going into the kick. "Heybattabattabatta! Heybattabattabatta!" comes the cheer from the Rascals fans loud and clear.

KP digs into the batter's box. He watches the release and swings. The ball pops up high toward shallow center field. "Run! Run, Punzak! Go home! Go! GO! Go!" yells Coach Sternicki side stepping down third base to lead him.

"Come on home! Hurry! Hurry! Hurry!" yells Coach Swat from across the diamond.

Punzak churns his legs to sprint down the third base line toward home plate. Willie sees Punzak running down third base line. He hesitates thinking he must tag up.

"Willie, run! Run, Willie!" shouts Coach O at first base as he waves his arms like a windmill. The center fielder has trouble with the flood light illuminating the outfield at night and misjudges the descent of the ball. Consequently, he decides to take a step back and catch the ball on the bounce.

"He dropped it! He dropped it! Now, home, Punzak! Punzak, now! Touch home plate! Now!" directs Coach Swat jumping up and down ecstatic. Right away the center fielder retrieves the ball on the bounce and throws the ball to the shortstop to relay to home plate. Punzak starts down third baseline toward home. Turk stands ready for the relay. The shortstop throws up his hands up causing Turk to lose sight of the ball. Punzak goes into a slide nearly bowling down Turk before he steps away. At the same time, the ball overthrown ball misses the shortstop and bonces several times traveling toward home plate. Thinking the shortstop caught the ball after waving his arms

200

Turks returns his attention to the runner. Not knowing where the ball has disappeared to in the infield. Turk steps away from the plate relieved he is not involved in a collision with Punzak, instantly he wipes the sweat away from his forehead to avoid sweat from dripping into his eye to blur his vision and to make ready for the next play. At that precise moment the ball wizzes past him and rattles around the backstop.

Turk's split second mistake

"Safe" announces Umpire Halstead stepping out of the way to make the call.

Coach Sternicki catches sight of the error and calls out to Willie. "Third! Willie, run! Go! Go! Willie, third!" yells Coach Sternicki. Willie rounds second and hobbles toward third base. The pain from his ribs restricts his movement and ability to run faster causing him to snort and puff instead of breathe normal. Garvin guards the bag by blocking the baseline, his eyes showing pure hatred. Vinny chases after the runaway baseball. Garvin stands at the ready shaking his out-stretched glove anticipating the moment of truth.

"Who rules?" Garvin shouts in preparation to catch the ball. Tension mounts knowing that Willie represents the winning run. The ball screams toward third base and the waiting glove to tag Willie out. The defining moment is at hand.

In a spilt second, Willie recalls Ty Cobb utilizing his cleats as weapons. As he goes down in a slide, he points his toe toward the bag without any consideration for Garvin's leg that guards third base. Every time he slides, he tries to portray his favorite baseball player without intent to use his cleats as weapons. This time is for real—no more practice. During the course of the slide, Willie's lead foot smashes into Garvin's ankle. Undoubtedly, Ty Cobb must have led with his cleats in the same fashion.

Unfortunately this time Willie snags a rubber cleat on the cloth bag and turns his ankle. It buckles up in the process turning him on his side. Something does not feel right. His ankle tingles. His shoe seems to be getting tight and his foot is throbbing. He steadies his eyes on Umpire Carrigan.

"Safe!" declares base umpire Carrigan. Dust billows up covering third base. He coughs and gags from the dry dirty dust.

Willie asks for time. Base Umpire Carrigan grants his request to recover from the nasty slide into third base. During the simple process of standing up, his right ankle gives him more pain than when he fell by the drinking fountain before the start of the game. His knee buckles, causing him to almost fall down. He steadies his weight with his toe until he can place more weight on his foot. Coach Hackworth rushes over from the dugout to check on Garvin. Gradually Willie applies more weight to his foot as he rocks it back and forth preparing for the final burst toward home. As he starts to wipe off the dirt from his cleats he catches sight of how badly Garvin's pants and socks are torn up from the rubber cleats. Garvin tries to stand up.

Copyright Registered

Garvin's Ty Cobb injury

"My leg! Oooow my leg!" screams Garvin as he twists and turns on the ground bringing everyone's attention to his lower leg. Willie observes the cuts and deep lacerations to the skin around his ankle and the shredding of the uniform sox. When he thought he caught his cleat on the cotton bag it must have been Garvin's sox instead. The wrenching of his ankle seems bad enough he wonders how much Garvin may have injured his ankle. Maybe he broke his lower leg? Coach Hackworth arrives and immediately attends to Garvin. He examines his ankle and immediately removes the stoking from the abrasions.

"This does not happen with ordinary cleats. I'd have those cleats checked, ump!" Coach Hackworth suggests with an unwavering suspicion as he stomps away toward the dugout.

In the meantime, Coach Sternicki attends to Willie. He leans over and whispers, "Son, what I want you to do is called 'the suicide squeeze.' The moment Vinny's arm goes into forward motion to release the pitch, you charge for home. Run as fast as your two legs can carry you. Got it?" It is a rhetorical question since he does not wait for an answer and pats Willie on the back.

Willie watches Garvin, and his thoughts drift to another incident with Ty Cobb. Apparently he was the victim of an attempted robbery that caused him to sustain a slashing with a knife down his back. According to the legend, he played baseball the next day. During the game, his teammates saw blood leaching through his uniform. The only complaint was the soreness in his back limited his ability to throw or catch the ball because he could not extend his arms. The thought of Ty Cobb helps Willie to try to dismiss the pain he feels in his ankle.

As he tests his weight on his right foot Garvin receives medical treatment. Coach Blanchard gives him some medicated gauze pads to place on the cuts from the rubber cleats. Leaning back and forth applying weight periodically, Willie tries to adjust to the level of pain before he must endure the charge toward home plate. Everyone resumes their positions on the baseball field. Willie places his right foot against the third base bag, postured to make a run for home plate. He stares straight ahead and sees home plate shimmering in the floodlights. In his mind, Willie tells himself, *When Vinny pitches...suicide squeeze!*

"Play ball!" announces Umpire Carrigan.

When he races for home, it will be the first time he will place full weight on his right foot since sliding into third base. Pain shoots up his right ankle with any movement against the third base bag. Garvin begins to crowd him to back up toward the bag.

"Play ball!" announces Umpire Halstead.

"Sports fans, we have two out with runners at second and third. The Rascals have tied the Rebels with a score of twenty-four runs. We have the winning run on third base." He pauses. "Don't go home empty-handed after the game. Pick up a pizza at Guido's New York Pizza & Deli at Wagon Wheel Street and Ames Court. The right spot around town for Italian pizza. Guido says score with his pizza tonight. Run for it."

Knowing he represents the winning run, Willie bides his timing with the pitch for the suicide squeeze. Izzie struts up to the plate. In the back of his mind, he thinks an out will mean they go to the seventh. Knowing it will be an advantage that the older and more experienced players on the Rebels team who are able to play easily into the night, he determines he must avoid a tie. At all costs, he must avoid going into the seventh inning. Izzie exchanges eye contact with Willie and tips his batting helmet meaning he intends to swing on the first pitch. He squares up and takes a couple practice swings before he stares down Vinny. Both players know it will be a suicide play—not sandlot, but like Coach Swat taught them. The first pitch will decide the outcome of the game.

Vinny goes into the pitching motion. First he goes into the stretch. He draws back and goes into motion.

"Heybattabattabatta! Heybattabattabatta!" erupts from the Rebels bleachers.

"Hey, Vinn-ny" come Weezie voice from the sidelines. "Hey Vinn-ny."

On the sidelines in the home team gate opening between the dugout and the backstop, Weezie performs her can-can dance as a distraction in a show hall dress made for the occasion. Vinny turns his head to catch a glance of Weezie flashing her dress. His arm comes down with a sloppy fastball and releases off stride. Turk tries to cover home plate anticipating the ball arriving below knee high.

Willie makes his move the instant he sees Vinny's downward hand motion, the one clutching the baseball, raise above his head. Standing in front of third base, Garvin straddles the baseline pretending he is waiting for a throw to tag the baserunner or set up in the hotbox. Garvin holds his ground with both arms outstretched, forcing Willie to step outside the baseline into foul territory. Stepping outside the baseline will result in an automatic out and thus the end of the inning. Instead, Willie makes a coy move and slips his right foot inside the front of Garvin's left leg and hooks him. Subtlety but gently, he gives him a little push on the back. In a split second as Vinny's arm lowers with the ball to release the sloppy pitch, Garvin leaves his feet and plummets to the ground. The maneuver successfully and nonchalantly trips Garvin and goes undetected by Umpire Carrigan. He remembers that move from Cub Scouts taught by Officer Dillard. Izzie connects with the pitch. The *cccrrrack* of the bat sounds like a starter's pistol for him to run. Izzie's heart beats in rapid succession, *thump, thump, thump.* The ground ball skips by the shortstop on the third base side. The shortstop lunges for the ground ball. It is too close to third base. Unfortunately, he can see the streaking ball will be too far out of his reach. Unable to stop its acceleration, the ball speeds into left field almost simultaneously to the moment Willie wins the shoving match. Out of the corner of his eye, Willie captures sight of the ball streaking by at the same moment. Garvin has not opportunity to make a play on the ball. Able to stay inside the baseline, he struggles to gain his balance. With the sound of the crack of the bat keeps ringing in his head, he stands upright. Quickly he plants his right foot and grimaces with pain. His hair stands on end as the torturous distress grips his entire being. Debating, he looks up and sees Izzie racing toward first base. Coach O stands at the first base coach's box poised to cheer Izzie onward to avoid an out. He casts his eyes on his teammates scrambling out of the home team dugout and racing up to the first baseline. Their speedy exit encourages him because all eyes are on him—they depend on him. In his mind he thinks to himself, *For my pals, I can do this. For my pals, I must do this! I've got to make it!*

Willie fixes his eyes on home plate. Perhaps he sprained his ankle sliding into third trying to be like Ty Cobb. Maybe the little tripping stunt with Garvin aggravated his ankle even more. Regardless, he must run home in spite of how much pain he must endure. It is for the win! Immediately, he resumes the journey to home plate. He steps down with renewed determination. His knee buckles and he pulls up. "Oooow. Oh, Oooow."

Across the diamond his teammates anxiously assemble around the on-deck circle to watch with eager eyes. He cannot go on. Reaching down, he grabs his knee with both hands and looks in the direction of Coach Swat for an answer. Instead, he sees Punzak, Gooch, and Wee Bones cheering him on from the on deck circle across the diamond next to the first base line within feet of home plate.

"Go, run, run, Willie," he can hear Wee Bones homespun accent shouting over the noise of the fans.

In spite of the anguish, he must go on—there's no turning back. He tries going into a hop, skip, and a jump in order to hurry down the baseline.

Ahead he sees Turk facing the direction of relay throw from Garvin. Turk's eyes seem to look through him with an evil stare. Willie is nothing but dill weed to him. He pulls up and slows down, again writhing in pain.

"Don't stop, go Willie, go," yells Gooch waving his hands as he intermittently shakes both hands in the direction of home plate. Seeing Gooch helps wash away the pain. He does not accept any excuse for failure.

Seeing home plate in his sight line, Willie tries to summon as much strength as he can to finish the journey. He starts huffing harder and harder to make the pain go away in his pursuit. With every breath, he snorts and huffs and huffs because of the pain and anguish.

Anything to help the torment with each step go away he thinks to himself.

"Run, baby, run!" yells Coach Sternicki offering encouragement from the third base coach's box. His booming voice serves as a prod from behind.

"Willie, don't stop! Run, Willie, Run!" shouts Weezie jumping up and down next to the chain link fence. Her cheerleading voice has become welcome throughout the season, especially with the addition of her sister. In a flash, he remembers the first day of practice when she sat alone in the bleachers and watched. Coach reminded them that playing the game of baseball would be a team effort. He thinks, *I can't let the team down. I've got to make it!*

He casts his eyes on home plate and takes a few deep breaths and puffs a couple more times to blow away the pain. Next, he chews up more real estate with a hop, skip, and a jump. He stops and puffs and puffs as though he is out of breath. He hears the cheers from his teammates over and over again. The distance is not enough—he has too far to go. Surely he will be tagged out.

He hears Izzie call out, "Hurry! He's going to throw the ball!" Willie performs another hop, skip, and a jump and another hop, skip and a jump a little faster. He must stop! While he takes a few deep breaths, he uses the time to turn and glance over his shoulder to see if Garvin is the one who will be throwing the ball or if it will be the outfielder. Anxiously, he sets his sights on Garvin and observes him catching the ball from the outfielder. It will be a long throw for Garvin to hurl the ball with all of his strength from behind third base to Turk at home plate. Garvin has not tested his injured ankle. Maybe his injury will fail him? In preparation to hasten the trip toward home plate, he takes a few more snorts like a bull in the bullring before making a charge at the matador. He tells himself, *I must not let my friends down. They are depending on me...*

All of the Rascals players stand in the grassy area in front of the dugout assembled in a group by the on deck area as they yell, "Run, Willie. Don't stop!" Run! Run! Run, Willie, run!"

Coach Swat shakes his fists and yells at the top of his voice, "Run! Willie! Don't stop! Run, boy, run!" The anticipation, excitement, and thrill of the game can be read in his eyes. A man who walks half bent over and takes half a step with each stride, stands screaming and yelling with a vibrant jump in his step.

Willie can hear the Rascals fans cheering and yelling for him to touch home. Ordinarily he would not be able to go any further because his leg is cramping up. He swallows hard and tilts his head backward. His bruised ribs scream back at him. His gaze back at third tells him he has reached the half way mark. How much more must he tolerate? He wants nothing more than to quit. There's always next year. He'll be a little older, a little wiser, and a...

He can't quit. "Baseball is not a game for quitters." At that moment, he happens to glance at the announcer's window. In a fraction of a second, Willie sees his father's wisdom, principles, and philosophical ways looking down with his scolding and often tender loving eyes that can say more than an encyclopedia in one glance. Most assuredly there will not be a next year. His father always said, "Maybe next year." The somber statement of his father echoed in his mind as an excuse for not fulfilling his promise. His teammates, the fans, or his family will not be disappointed, not this year! Driven by the cheers on the sideline, encouragement ringing in his head, Willie knows a hop, skip, and a jump will not win the game. With an invigorated affirmation, he charges with a spirited self-will to resume the journey to home plate. He must dig in and tough it out the rest of the way home.

Turk, the Rebels catcher, straddles as much of home plate possible, making scoring a chore for any runner. Coach Hackworth taught his catchers to be positioned facing third base to avoid injury from a runner.

Copyright Registered

Turk waits for ball from Garvin

Facing third, he waits for the relay throw from Garvin while aggressively guarding home. He has every intention of disappointing Willie's determination by tagging him out at home plate. An out will give the Rebels' an opportunity to defeat the Rascals attempt at being victorious.

Willie remembers Coach Swat telling the team that a player is out if a player is standing up and runs into a fielder or catcher who may be holding the baseball. At that moment Willie casts his eyes on an opening between the catcher's legs and spies the white of home plate: the Promised Land! Without question he confirms he must slide. Undoubtedly, there will be a collision accompanied by more intolerable pain and anguish.

"Go! Go! Go! Willie, Go!" screams Punzak jumping up and down next to Coach Swat on the edge of the on-deck circle frantically waving his baseball cap.

In his field of vision, Coach O runs down the first base line from the coach's box yelling every step of the way. "Slide! Slide,

Willie! Slide!" Since Coach O has exited the coach's box, he knows Izzie has safely stepped on first base. Turk casts both eyes on the baseball as Garvin fires the ball toward home plate. With all of his strength he launches a blistering throw on target for home plate and the waiting catcher's mitt. Willie convinces himself all he needs is a burst of speed to complete the journey to home plate.

"Now, Willie, slide. Slide, my boy, slide!" yells Coach Swat from the on-deck circle jumping up and down and waving his hands toward home plate. Willie hears the familiar voice above all the noise and commotion. A voice of conviction and the voice of a coach's direction swells above the crowd and reaches Willie's ears. He knows it is time. Motivated by the encouragement of his teammates and support of his coaches Willie forges on toward home plate with the doggedness he vows in an instant he will do everything in his power to reach home plate. His bruised ribs cry out with an increased degree of pain in his spirited journey nearly thwarting his mission.

About five feet from home plate he throws his arms up into the air. His bruised ribs scream pain. Turk leans toward third for the speeding ball thrown from Garvin. The arrival of the ball will be an instant away. As he goes down into the sliding position, he tucks his left leg underneath with the left foot under the knee of the right leg. Willie thrusts his right leg forward extending his foot as far forward as possible in spite of the pain in his ankle and knee. Keeping his arms and hands in the air he makes sure not to drag them on the ground to slow him down. His ribs transmit an unbearable amount of pain. In a fraction of a second he will know if his mission has been accomplished.

Simultaneously, Willie's heel digs into the dirt a few feet from home plate at the precise moment the baseball arrives in the vicinity of home plate. It bounces in the dirt above Willies head and soars toward Turk's catcher's mitt.

Ball arrives in front of Turk's mitt

He makes the catch and swings his mitt across third base line for the tag and the out. Dust ushers up in heavy plumes covering the area around home plate. Visibility is obscured because of the intense dust caused by Willie sliding into home plate.

Intuitively, Turk knows not to stretch his arms out further to make a tag. Immediately he twists his body rotating his left knee in the direction of the base path to avoid injury and to allow Willie to pass by avoiding a tumultuous collision.

"Safe!" yells Umpire Halstead as he reinforces the call by displaying the sign with his arms crossed and thrusting them outward in dramatic fashion.

Umpire signals safe!!!

Turk jumps up withdrawing the baseball from the catcher's mitt to show Umpire Halstead.

Turk produces ball for umpire

"Safe!" declares Umpire Hallstead "The ball hit the dirt a moment before his heal slid across the plate. Safe!" He makes the familiar sign crossing his arms in a sweeping motion and extending them out to his side. The mark across the plate made by the heel of Willie's shoe can plainly be seen as he remains on the ground in his sliding position. The heel of his shoe rests on the opposite side of the plate. Exhausted and disappointed Turk falls to the ground releasing the ball from his hand. The ball lands beside him. After a few moments he grabs the ball and comes to his feet.

Turk falls to ground drop ball exhausted

Simultaneously Willie slaps his hand downward on home plate claiming victory for the Rascals. Immediately he grabs his leg and rolls back and forth working out the cramp. Willie massages his calf muscle and shows signs of pain and exhaustion. Next he jumps up and hobbles over to the backstop with a hop, skip, and a jump. In a matter of moments, he catches his breath and the pain subsides. No longer does he need to huff, puff, or snort on his appointed journey. Maybe his ankle sprain inhibited him from running as fast as usual. But the onset of the leg cramp slowed him down coupled with the injuries made rounding third the most difficult trip of running the bases, genuine test of fortitude and team spirit. Gingerly, he limps back to home plate favoring his leg. Along the way he glances down the third base line to cast his eyes on a dejected Garvin dragging his leg as he toddles down third base line. "Hey, Garvin! Who are the skunks now? Do the math!"

Returning to home plate, Willie goes down on his knees inhaling the deep breaths of exhaustion and with a mixture of pain and fortitude he kisses the five-sided piece of rubber so treasured in baseball. Willie stands up and shakes a double fist pump in the air in triumph a la Rocky Balboa fame. Turk stands beside him holding the baseball knowing the game has come to an end.

"Hey, Willie. I think this belongs to you. Good game, pal."

"Thanks, Turk, but..." replies Willie gazing down at the ball. "Good game?"

"By the way, I never touched you. You're safe in my book."

His teammates swallow Willie up. Immediately the celebration begins as they swarm around him. All of the players jump up and down, pat each other on the back, give each other high-fives, and surround home plate to do the 'Go Rascals cheer. The Rascals have been victorious when it matters the most, the season championship. All of the Rascals fans erupt celebrating the unexpected. Parents flood the field and congratulate their victorious Rascals players. Confetti poppers explode. Streamers fly in the air. Horns blare. The celebration is enormous. Firecracker explosions on the infield punctuate the moment. An official Rascals Little League unit stretches the banner in front of the pitcher's mound. It reads: "Our Rascals Team, Little League Champions." A group of volunteer firemen stand in back of the banner.

Mayor Polkinghorn broadcasts from the scorekeeper's box, "Skeeter Hill Little League fans! Rascals Team!" Mayor Polkinghorn salutes the team with reservations. "The Youth Sports Authority and Office of the Mayor congratulates you! You took us on a ride until the last run scored. Congratulations, Rascals coaches. Coach Swat, congratulations for volunteering to take this group of boys and giving them the opportunity to learn to dream and succeed as a team! I personally congratulate all of you!"

The Rascals coaches corral the players and have them line up for the customary handshake after the game. The Rebels reluctantly venture out on the filed from seclusion in the dugout picking up belongings and equipment. Jubilant and thrilled, the boys shake the hands of the Rebels players with joy written on their faces. When Willie reaches out to shake Garvin's hand, Garvin pulls back and says, "I don't shake the hand of a skunk. This ain't over." He walks away and sprints to the dugout without looking back. Coach Hackworth stands beside the dugout steps with his arms folded across his chest and an expression of disgust on his face. The Rebels are stunned. The team without a name that was built from cast-off players and a lackluster coaching staff outplayed the Rebels and their conniving tactics and experience. The misfit team had demonstrated courage, chemistry and team spirit through their struggles and shortcomings to achieve the unexpected and to achieve the impossible by defeating not only the other teams in the tournament but finally the Rebels to win the championship. It was fun. In the words of Garvin, "It ain't over." Defeating the Rebels does not settle the score between Willie and Garvin. It ain't over.

During the team handshake, Mayor Polkinghorn, Mr. Lindeman, and Mr. Wisenhut with the Youth Sports Authority travel onto the baseball field with several boxes and summon the players. One by one they hand out a ten-inch trophy to each player and shake their hand to formally congratulate them. Coach Ostrander and Coach Sternicki accept the team trophy.

Wee Bones cannot take his eyes off the trophy in his hands as he meanders in the direction of the dugout. During his travel, he nearly bumps into Officer Higby. "Sorry, sir." He steps around him and pauses for a moment and says, "Remember last year when you complained to Willie and the rest of us when there was a fight on the pitcher's mound? You told us to make something of ourselves. I think that just happened; we're the champions!" Wee Bones smirks and chuckles a little as he says goodbye to Officer Higby and resumes his journey to the dugout. In his field of vision he captures the Victorian house in the distance. At the same time the light in the window chases away the dark of night outside and can be seen from the baseball field. Wee Bones and his pals still wonder about the stately mansion that overlooks the baseball field. Who lives in the enchanting house?

Willie's father intercepts him on the baseball field after he receives his trophy.

"Dad!" Willie says surprised as the two stroll away from the frenzy of the crowd.

"Son, you taught me a lesson this season and took me back to school today. Two teams played here today. One team had a lot of heart and one simply was all about business and wanted to try to outplay the other. On your charge to home plate, as banged up as you were, you showed to everyone the will to win, and it wasn't for Willie Wince; it was for the Skeeter Hill Rascals."

"But Dad..."

"Listen, son, I embarrassed you in front of your teammates by not taking the time to share in your wonderful baseball life. It was a drudgery for me to involve myself with your team. Instead I preferred the lofty perch of the announcer's box where I lived in my own little detached world. Look at Coach Sternicki and Coach Ostrander—they took time out for their boys, but I didn't do it for one game…not one! Even Chico Martinez's father helped his struggling son today. I chose the stellar life in the press box away from you and your teammates."

"But Dad…"

"Not once did I congratulate you on a job well done or for an out you made or when you tried to hit the ball to the fences. I saw those special times. That's going to be different now. We're going to take a page from that game day program of yours—mark my words. I'm going to be by your side every step of the way from here on out. Congratulations, son! I don't need to do the math; you simply pulled on one too many heart strings." He gives him a handshake and a gentleman's hug. "I love you, son!"

"Hey, Mom! I was looking for you."

"Congratulations, son!" Willies mom says and gives him a huge hug and a kiss as a just reward for a successful season. He rubs off the wet kiss with the palm of his hand.

Weezie and Cheryl arrive to give their accolades. Willie gets a kiss from Cheryl that leaves her trademark cherry-flavored lip gloss imprint on his cheek. He fans his hand close to his cheek to smell the cheery-flavored lip gloss.

"Oh Willie, I think I should wipe that lip gloss off," his mother comments as she searches her purse for a tissue.

"Naw, mom. Let's leave it there 'til we get home. I want to see what it looks like," Willie comments blushing and tilting his head from side to side basking in the flood lights of the Skeeter Hill Baseball Field. "I can smell the cherry. I bet it must taste good too."

"I can hardly wait until I get to wear lip gloss," Weezie says for Willie's benefit, but it goes unnoticed.

At that moment Mr. Wisenhut retrieves a portable amplifying system and addresses the fans from home plate. "With the conclusion of the Skeeter Hill Championship game, I'd like everyone to turn your thoughts to the Fourth of July and what it means to all of us. As we celebrate our nation's freedom this Independence Day, we honor the courageous men and women dedicated to preserving it. Remember, freedom is not free, so thank a veteran for their sacrifices! I turn the announcement of the Fourth of July Program over to our Mayor."

Mayor Polkinghorn takes charge of the microphone and continues the announcement of the proceedings, "The City of Skeeter Hill, with the cooperation of the Business Association and Chamber of

Commerce, invite you to return this evening at 8:00 pm for the fireworks and pyrotechnic show put together by our illustrious firemen. I promise it will be a much different fireworks show than the Rascals team brought us. Nevertheless, we will still see fireworks, rockets, showers, pop bang, and streamers in the night sky. Bring your blankets to spread out on the infield. Sit with family, friends, neighbors, teammates, or anyone willing to share a blanket. Everyone is invited. The concession will have free popcorn. No drinks. This holiday is a solemn, glorious holiday. It is an occasion memorializing our military conflicts and the cost of life mixed with celebration of our liberties and freedoms that their lives defended for us to have a way of life with freedom of speech and to live without fears, threats, or retaliation. Our forefathers established justice where we can live fairly with others and be judged in a court of law by one's own peers. Most importantly, it's a holiday to commemorate our heritage, ever mindful that we are one nation not only born from new ideas and faith in fellow man but under God, indivisible, with liberty and justice for all. Let that be our pledge for years to come."